Shot By Shot

film directing
shot by shot
visualizing from concept to screen

by steven d. katz

Published by Michael Wiese Productions, 11288 Ventura Blvd,
Suite 821, Studio City, CA 91604, (818) 379-8799, in conjunction with
Focal Press, a division of Butterworth Publishers, 80 Montvale Avenue,
Stoneham, MA 01801, (617) 438-8464.

Cover design by Barry Grimes
Cover photograph by Geraldine Overton
Interior design and layout by Douglas R. Kelly and David A. Shugarts
Illustrations by Frank Bolle and Steven D. Katz

Printed by Braun-Brumfield, Ann Arbor, Michigan
Manufactured in the United States of America

Copyright 1991 by Michael Wiese Productions
First printing, June 1991

ISBN 0-941188-10-8

Library of Congress Cataloging-in-Publication Data

Katz, Steven D. (Steven Douglas), 1950–
    Film directing shot by shot : visualizing from concept to screen/
by Steven D. Katz.
        p.   cm.
    "Published . . . in conjunction with Focal Press"—T.p. verso.
    Includes bibliographical references.
    ISBN 0–941188–10–8 : $24.95
    1. Motion pictures—Production and direction—Handbooks,
manuals, etc. 2. Video recordings—Production and
direction—Handbooks, manuals, etc.   I. Title.
PN1995.9.P7K38   1991
791.43 ' 0233—dc20   90–70213
                                                   CIP

ACKNOWLEDGEMENTS

I would like to express my thanks to the people who gave me valuable assistance in the preparation of this book. Assistance is an inadequate term for all the patience, time and knowledge that colleagues and friends generously provided. First is my friend Michael Wiese, who as a filmmaker and publisher thought that a book on the subject of visualization would be of interest to other filmmakers. Michael supported all the decisions that in the end cost additional time and money but that resulted in a better book. For this I will always be grateful.

Both Joe Musso, president of the Production Illustrators and Matte Painters Union, and Gene Allen, executive director of the Society of Motion Picture and Television Art Directors, were not only highly informative about their respective crafts, but saved me months of research by helping to arrange the many interviews with their members whose illustration and design work appear in these pages.

Two production illustrators in particular, Camille Abbott and Harold Michelson, gave generously of their time and expertise in helping me prepare the text and diagrams explaining the Michelson method for camera angle projection. In addition, they offered valuable insights into the craft of continuity illustration and encouragement by way of their enthusiasm for the movies.

Special thanks to Steven Spielberg, who was especially generous in providing me with the lengthy storyboard sequence from *Empire of the Sun*, a portion of which appears in the book; to Robert C. Carringer of Illinois University, who was consistently able to direct me to useful sources of information on production design on the rare occasions he was unable to answer questions personally; to Mary Corliss of the Film Stills Archives in the Museum of Modern Art, who provided the storyboards from *The Birds* and valuable suggestions for researching production design.

The artwork from *Beverly Hills Cop II* and *Flashdance* was provided by Paramount Pictures; artwork from *La Bamba* is courtesy of Columbia Pictures; and *Blade Runner* artwork is courtesy of Warner Bros. Pictures. The *Citizen Kane* art from which the reproductions were taken is in the Rare Books and Special Collections Library of the University of Illinois. (© 1941 RKO Pictures, Inc., Ren. 1968 RKO GENERAL, INC.)

On a more personal level, Doug Sheffer, Jim Coon, Scott Deaver, and my longtime producer and comrade Carl Shea all lent the kind of support only friends can provide.

Warmest gratitude goes to my sister, Barbara, and parents, Betty and Stanley Katz for understanding (most of the time) that the basement could be a studio, and for the continuing belief that I would someday graduate to the real thing.

Above all my thanks go to my wife and best friend Jane for more love and understanding than anyone could unreasonably expect.

For Jane

TABLE OF CONTENTS

INTRODUCTION

I t's something of a parodox that film, the art that most resembles our daydreams, is the one most difficult to bring into existence. After all, we need only close our eyes and we are in a darkened theater of our own making, screening the movies we'd like to see for an appreciative audience—ourselves. Because we suppose our imaginations are naturally cinematic it is particularly frustrating that we cannot easily commit what seem like fully formed works of art directly to film. If only we could express our daydreams as easily as the musician improvises a melody or as the painter controls color and form on the canvas. Of course it's only an illusion that we dream in sequences ready for national release. What matters is that while most artists can easily create works in their respective mediums, accumulating experience day after day, a filmmaker has difficulty practicing his craft unless he can afford the considerable expense of film production.

Unfortunately, this is simply beyond the means of most artists. Even in film schools, most students are lucky to complete two or three 16mm short films in a period of four years, which means that only a small portion of their time is spent making films. In the world of mainstream features, screenwriters and actors who have managed to use their success to leverage a directorial opportunity would be hard pressed to find another way to gain experience before taking the reins of a full-scale multi-million dollar movie. This gives new meaning to the notion of on-the-job training.

In film schools the primary method of teaching is the study of the film technique of classic films and the styles of famous directors. There are editing and cinematography courses, but these are largely devoted to technical processes and procedures. Necessary as these skills are, true hands-on work and discovery is limited.

This lack of direct experience is perpetuated in mainstream film production where the primary creative positions—screenwriter, director, cinematographer and editor—divide the individual artist's vision into component parts. There are unavoidable practical reasons for this division of labor, but the fact that this type of organization exists doesn't mean that the filmmaker should take management courses instead of learning the subtleties of his craft. The compartmentalization of image, sound, language and continuity fulfills the needs of efficiency, but it is a hierarchy that is fundamentally different from the way in which we visualize. The question is whether the expression of this organic, unified experience is a single craft or a combination of individual skills. My answer, and it is a personal view, is that the visualization of shots and sequences is very much a single craft called shot flow.

Shot by Shot is about shot flow, principally in narrative film, with the goal of exploring the practical relationship between the three-dimensional reality of the space in front of the camera and the two-dimensional representation on film and on the screen. These are the two mediums in which the filmmaker must work: the set or location, which is a medium in the sense that it is a consciously manipulated space, and the exposed film, which resembles traditional materials in the graphic arts.

The basic method used in this book is the side-by-side comparison of cinematic techniques using illustrated and photographic storyboards. Unlike the screenplay, which has been studied in depth, the storyboard is one of the least understood or documented aspects of film production. It is used not only as an instructional tool in this book but also as a useful technique for filmmakers who can describe in pictures what the screenplay describes in words. What you can expect to find in *Shot by Shot* is the working out of narrative and visual problems on paper and the basic vocabulary of techniques from which solutions can be fashioned.

If you have leafed through the book you will have seen the many photo sequences that seem to present an encyclopedia of staging and narrative strategies. While I hope these sections are thorough, it would be incorrect to think of them as compendiums of stock solutions. The reasoning behind demonstrating so many versions of such familiar strategies as the over-the-shoulder shot is to accumulate the type of experience that would come from lining up hundreds of shots and editing dozens of sequences. While there is no substitute for actual filming, there is also no substitute for working out your own storyboard, each mode of expression posing a unique and rewarding challenge to the imagination. In all cases I have critiqued the examples in the first person, expressing my own opinions rather than stating indisputable facts. The point of all the examples in the book is to encourage your critical sense, so that when you step out onto the set and face a complex staging situation you will have the foundation from which to devise your own solutions.

There are many ways to visualize a film besides storyboarding. Video and computers are useful alternatives, but the process of putting images together and working out an idea in successive versions is the best way to develop a critical eye and cinematic sense. Storyboards do not, as is often supposed, interfere with improvisation or documentary techniques if you choose to use them. My own experience is that artists who are driven to rewrite the rules are never stifled by first learning traditional techniques.

Not every film and sequence should be storyboarded or even scripted in detail, but film, which is the most protean of arts, is flexible enough to include the preferences of any filmmaker. The classic opposition between expressionist and realistic film styles remains unresolved, left, as always, to the specific experience of the individual filmmaker. For me, the design of a sequence, like writing, is one of the great pleasures of narrative filmmaking. While the search for the perfect sequence may involve a great deal of hair pulling (my own) and dozens of takes, a few graceful shots in the finished film make the effort worthwhile.

About the Photographs and Storyboards Used in this Book

The photoboards used in this book were shot with a Nikon F3 and an Olympus OM2n using a variety of fixed focal length and zoom lenses on Kodak Panatomic x and Plus x films. As often as possible I have tried to approximate the compositional qualities of the most widely used motion picture formats, but for a variety of technical reasons (discrepancies in the measurement of focal lengths by lens manufacturers and the difficulty in determining exact focal lengths of zoom lenses at discrete positions throughout their range, for example), differences are inevitable.

35mm SLR cameras use an aspect ratio of approximately 1.5:1, which is somewhere between the full Academy aspect ratio of 1.33:1 and the 1.65:1 ratio popular in Europe. Therefore, cropping was necessary during the printing stage to widen the frame to the various wide-screen aspect ratios in common use for theatrically released motion pictures. There are three aspect ratios demonstrated in the book: 1.5:1, 1.85:1 normal wide screen and the extreme wide screen proportions of CinemaScope and Panavision 70mm 2.35:1.

For all these reasons, the focal lengths and apertures accompanying many of the storyboard photographs should be considered estimates. Duplicating the same perspective, depth of field, focal length and composition with a motion picture camera and lens will necessarily yield a different focal length.

Sadly, production art is rarely preserved with any consistency by the movie industry. The production illustrations in this book are frequently reproductions of photocopies of original art, the originals having long since disappeared, even in the case of recent films. The result is that much of the shading and tonal quality of the work is lost. Even in the case of the most deteriorated reproductions, however, the work has been reproduced in the more costly half-tone process to preserve as much of the tonal range as possible.

Because storyboards and production art vary considerably in size, reflecting the particular use, style of the illustrator and preferences of the director, most of the artwork has been reduced to fit the format of the book. Some of the illustrations were reduced as much as 50%, but in all cases the individual artists were consulted in order that the best presentation be made consistent with the space available.

Part I

Visualization:
The Process

"Vision is the art of seeing things invisible."

Jonathan Swift

1 VISUALIZATION

I f you've ever seen a boy lying in the grass, eye-level with his toy soldiers, then you've seen the impulse that is the visual basis of the Hollywood movie. The boy is framing the action as a filmmaker might, eye-level with his miniature figures so that charge and retreat are all around him. Up close, the toys are no longer painted miniatures, but life-size warriors moving in a world that is not to be observed but experienced.

In his landmark book *Qu'est-ce que le Cinéma?* French film critic André Bazin used the term *presence* to describe the moviegoer's sense that he is within the same spatial/temporal continuum as the picture on the screen. He regarded this illusion as the fulfillment of a tradition of verisimilitude in western painting that began with the discovery of linear perspective during the Renaissance. This geometrical way of depicting space enabled painters to create pictures that were a reasonably accurate representation of three-dimensional reality on a two-dimensional surface. Photography is able to achieve the same effect automatically, and the viewer sees a result that shares the optical qualities of human vision.

But motion pictures takes the illusion one step further and convey the experience of *seeing* things as they happen or, as Bazin referred to it, presence—something that both painting and photography fail to convey completely. This is because when we view a painting or photograph we are always aware of the surface of the picture. Something very different happens when we are viewing a film. Instead of seeing the picture surface we are included in the pictorial space projected on the screen as if it were real three-dimensional space.

The Continuity Style

The nearly perfect illusion of depth was what set motion pictures apart from all other methods of reproduction in the graphic arts at the turn of the century. The editorial and photographic strategies of Griffith, Porter and the other pioneer filmmakers built on this basic tendency of the motion picture viewing experience, avoiding any sort of technique that drew attention to the illusion itself. This was in keeping with their immediate artistic heritage, largely nineteenth century theater, literature, magazine and book illustration and photography. As it turns out, many of the basic strategies of the movies that we have come to call cinematic, or at least the conventions of what is known as the "continuity style," were developed or suggested in the popular art of the nineteenth century.

Today, the style has broadened to include some of the conventions of cinéma vérité, experimental and avant-garde film, but is largely faithful to the original storytelling strategies of the Hollywood movie, which by now is an international style. The ideas in this book are taken from this basic vocabulary of techniques, but filmmakers will find that learning this style should not inhibit experimentation. In fact, in the 1980s two other popular visual forms, the television commercial and the music video, borrowed a variety of techniques from avant-garde and experimental films and introduced them to a mass audience. In the future, this will probably permit filmmakers to further extend the range of the continuity style.

My expectation is that a filmmaker who learns the various framing and staging ideas of the continuity style will gain a heightened awareness of composition, editing patterns and three-dimensional design. Even if he chooses to reject every specific strategy that is outlined in this book, he will be better prepared to strike out on his own.

Visualization

It's a conjurer's word really. How else would you describe something that turns dreams into reality or makes the imaginary visible? Magical as it sounds, visualization was just another description of the creative process until the human potential movement discovered that it could be put to work.

The promise is that we all have the power to decide our destiny, one image at a time, if we learn to channel our creative energies. Sports psychologists were the first to use visualization this way, instructing athletes to envision themselves executing an event perfectly—what amounts to visual chanting. This latest version of positive thinking is probably beneficial if there is a specific goal to picture, but how does the artist use visualization? What goal does he imagine?

The answer is that the artist rarely has a specific goal in mind when he begins work, so that the process of visualization is actually the search for a goal rather than the attainment of one. This is quite different from seeing an image in the mind's eye and trying to duplicate it in some medium, which is essentially what the athlete does when he pictures an exercise he has done thousands of times in practice. While the ability to create a work precisely in the imagination might seem like a great advantage to an artist, I don't think that has very much to do with the creative process, nor does it sound like much fun.

This more or less brings me to my own view, that visualization isn't a strictly cerebral process, but rather the merging of the physical act of making or doing with several different mental processes that together we call imagination. It isn't until our visions emerge in a raw state while we are at work drawing, writing or editing a film sequence that our creative energy is fully engaged in the process of visualization.

The handiest real-life description of the visualization process I can offer is my experience writing even this brief chapter. This is draft number three of Chapter I, parts of which are new, based on selected ideas from two other chapters that were cut. But a little more than a year ago, before I began writing, I imagined that the content and the language for this chapter was right at hand, and that inner voice that speaks to writers in seemingly finished prose was whispering as deceptively as ever.

For me, the actual work of visualization was in all the drafts and revisions. As I understand it, the imagination does not guide the hand, but is led by the hand when we have forgotten ourselves in the application of some craft. Once each stage of invention is committed to some substantial form, it is like a mirror revealing the imagination to itself. Suddenly, things we did not see before become clear, or new possibilities emerge, and there is new material to work with. This twofold experience of imagining through craft, and the revelation at what has been created, is my understanding of visualization.

All this is pertinent to the filmmaker's craft since the two most important aspects of visualization, the physical connection with the medium and the opportunity to review and refine work as it is created, are hard to implement because of the complexity of film production. The problem is greatest for the narrative filmmaker whose work must be financed by a company or institution and who has to work within the high-pressure environment of a production schedule. Under these circumstances, hands-on visualization is restricted to the screenplay, which, unfortunately, is not a graphically specific form.

In practical terms, visualization is the interaction of two types of activities: immediacy and reflection. In film, immediacy means devising the content of the shots and their order in a sequence in a single, uninterrupted process. The goal is to evaluate the materials moment to moment as they are shaped, trying many combinations of ideas and comparing them instantly.

Reflection is really nothing more than a good night's sleep between drafts of a screenplay, versions of a storyboard or rehearsals with the cast. Reflection is the process that restores balance to the intense and myopic relationship to the materials that immediacy produces. Visualization must include hands-on picture making in some tangible medium. Making ideas visible before they are put in front of the camera is a necessity.

The filmmaker who fills the blank page of a screenplay with a tightly composed scene may still be very far from knowing what shots will ultimately tell the story he is writing. But what happens if he is presented with an empty frame representing the first shot of the same scene?

Now the filmmaker is confronted with a variety of visual decisions that the screenplay does not address. The blank square may at first seem daunting, but filling it in is not a final statement, only the beginning of visualization. Each stage of the process, which requires dedication and a sense of fun, is most active when we are open to new ideas. Most often these appear as fragmentary, illusory images or incomplete thoughts that must be discovered. And discovery comes as one stage in the working process.

It begins with an alertness to visual possibilities. Artists and photographers generally agree that their visual memory improves when practicing their crafts. This ability to remember the past is an aid to envisioning in the present. After alertness comes exploration. The first line in the panel of a storyboard should be made with a sense of freedom. There is no such thing as a mistake in visualization, only alternative ideas. And exploration ultimately leads to discovery.

These are all stages of thought, each one leading to the next. The process is only completed when the filmmaker has created something he can use. Knowing when to stop working on an idea is as much a part of visualization as devising dozens of shots for a sequence.

Visualization is only one step in the filmmaking process. A film cannot be designed solely on paper, whether this is the script or a storyboard. Storyboards or any other visualization tool will change when the shooting begins. The goal, however, is not to visualize to eliminate decisions on the set or to streamline the production process (though this is often beneficial). Visualization is a way of coming up with new visual and narrative ideas before shooting begins. This may be merely a single arresting image in a scene or the decision to stage action for a long sequence shot rather than fast cutting. It may help you find the dramatic center of the scene, or it may reveal a dishonest line of dialogue. Surprisingly, the individual compositions in a storyboard are not necessarily the main benefit of visualization. If the staging of a scene is previewed on paper and subsequently improved, then the storyboard has helped focus the vision in the final film.

Underlying this approach to filmmaking is the drive to create great sequences. From the moment a script exists and work commences, the director should strive to make every shot and every sequence count. Relinquishing this task to others is not what is meant by collaboration. Cinematographers and editors do their best work when the director is contributing and setting high standards for design.

2 PRODUCTION DESIGN

Whether or not the director is the main visualizer for a film, the development and implementation of the visual plan is the responsibility of the production designer and his staff. This organization of the creative forces is necessary whenever storytellers hope to control the time and setting of a picture, even when the subjects are simple events set in the present. The notion of designing the mise-en-scène of a film, rather than photographing available reality, first evolved in part because of the needs of fiction, but also because of the economic considerations of production—the twin engines of evolution and change in the Hollywood studio system from its very beginnings.

The emergence of the art director as a creative and key organizational position began early in the silent period when movies were still greatly influenced by the theater. Typically, the art director was a scenic designer, and the early sets were little more than painted backdrops and some furniture. The move from stage flats to constructed sets was inevitable— Griffith, with his refinement of multiple viewpoints, had seen to that. But it was the short-lived influence of the Italian cinema that challenged Griffith and the rest of the American movie industry to match Italian production standards.

Two Italian productions, *Quo Vadis?* (1912) and *Cabiria* (1913), were the most ambitious and technically sophisticated films of their time. Both used fully constructed and meticulously detailed sets, artificial lighting effects and limited moving camera. Their enormous success briefly overshadowed Griffith's work during this period, but inspired to a considerable extent the scope of his most innovative mature films, *Judith of Bethulia* (1913), *Birth of a Nation* (1915) and *Intolerance* (1916).

The rapidly increasing complexity of the physical production of a movie during the mid-teens, including constructed sets and the greater mobility of the camera, required greater cooperation between the art director and the cinematographer. Art directors discovered that the graphic illusions they were expected to provide were dependent on the camera. They learned to use partial sets to exploit the camera's limited view, and matte shots and models to replace scenic backdrops. By necessity, art directors were involved in the photographic decisions required to implement these new cinematic techniques and in so doing made the transition from theatrical to screen design.

As the feature became the dominant form in the movies, survival for any company meant producing films rapidly and efficiently. The practice of shooting scenes out of sequence became common, and craftspeople might work on several movies simultaneously, making props, sets or costumes in the newly built studios at Universal City, Inceville or Culver City. Following nineteenth century principles of mass production, jobs became specialized, and departments were established for each phase of production, including scriptwriting, set construction, properties, costumes, cinematography and editing.

By 1915 scenery, props and costumes built for one movie were being stored for later use on another. The departmental system in the studios required greater organization and communication between departments, and because the most complex, expensive and labor-intensive areas were related to construction, the art director became the logical choice to administer much of the production process. Unlike the cameraman and director, the art director possessed a language in the form of blueprints, concept sketches and models that the craftspeople in other departments understood. At the same time, the pictorial possibilities of the frame, suggested in the work of Griffith and a few other leading directors, raised the visual ante in the industry. Always on the lookout for new talent, the studios began recruiting magazine illustrators and architects to inject new ideas into the fledgling art departments and handle the increasingly ambitious productions that audiences expected. It was because the art department was able to plan a production that Hollywood became a successful movie factory capable of turning out hundreds of features and shorts throughout the silent period.

The next stage of development in the art department occurred in the '20s with the rise of the German cinema. During World War I several of the smaller production companies in Germany were combined into Ufa (Universum Film Aktien Gesellschaft), a single studio with mammoth stages and considerable state funding. This support, and the magnificent studios at Potsdam-Badelsberg, made technical and stylistic innovation driven by German Expressionism and the Kammerspielfilm possible. These two movements, one featuring fantastic subjects and the other naturalistic and somber subjects, were both darkly psychological and dependent on highly stylized settings and camera technique. In many ways Ufa, and its most important directors, writers and craftsmen—Karl Mayer, Karl Struss, Fritz Lang, F.W. Murnau, G.W. Pabst and A. E. Dupont—set the pace for film design in the '20s, contributing advances in mobile camera, subjective viewpoints and more sharply angular compositions.

Ufa incorporated the staging tradition of Wagnerian opera with its colossal and complicated sets in many films, not only showcasing the talents of the art director, but establishing that an artificial setting could add enormously to the emotional power of a film. It also proved that movies, even those with considerable exterior scenes, could be shot entirely in a controllable studio environment, which, when sound arrived at the end of the '20s, became an even more important factor in art direction.

Hollywood wasted no time in borrowing the aesthetic innovations of Ufa, first in coproductions, and later by importing the best European directors and cameramen while moving closer to the total studio environment approach to movie-making. By the end of the silent period the studio system in Hollywood was fully in place, with the art director now the head of a department that was largely responsible for the *mise-en-scène* of every film produced at a given studio. This resulted in the highly recognizable visual styles of the major studios during the sound period, each style generally attributed to the tastes of the supervising art director. The

Twentieth Century Fox look was shaped by William Darling, Richard Day and Lyle Wheeler; Warner Brothers had the gritty realism preferred by Anton Grot; MGM had the luxurious, high-key look of Cedric Gibbons; Paramount had the European sophistication of Hans Dreier; Universal, the moody darkness of Herman Rosse and Charles D. Hall. And at RKO, Van Nest Polglase oversaw the styling of the Astaire-Rogers musicals and *Citizen Kane*.

The ascendency of the art director continued throughout the sound period until a new title was invented for his expanded responsibilities. In 1939 William Cameron Menzies accepted an Academy Award for the newly created position of Production Designer for *Gone With The Wind*. Only ten years earlier he had received the Academy Award for art direction at the first Awards ceremony.

Though the production designer's specific responsibilities may vary slightly from film to film, he has a far more comprehensive role than that of the art director. In addition to designing the overall style of the sets, props and costumes, he is also intimately involved with the shot flow and dynamic elements of film design as well. A good example of this is Menzies' contributions to *Gone With the Wind*, for which he drew thousands of elaborate continuity sketches detailing the composition, staging and editing points for each shot of the film. Menzies helped elevate the production designer to the inner circle of the production team, joining the director, camerman, editor, and, in some instances, the writer, as one of the prime shot and sequence designers of a film.

Production Illustration

Today, the centralized art departments of bygone studio days no longer exist and production teams are assembled for each film. Still, a production designer will try to work with people he has worked well with in the past, and the producer usually permits him to assemble his own team, lending at least some continuity to working relationships. Included in the team are the key positions of art director, prop stylist, draftsman, production illustrator and costume designer.

Each member of the art department contributes illustrations that fall into three basic categories:

> Concept and Final Design Illustrations: These are used to describe individual elements for a production, including sets, props, costumes, makeup and special effects. These are individual illustrations intended to establish a style and visual direction and do not necessarily depict a shot or sequence in the film.

> Plans, Elevations and Projections: These are the highly technical descriptions that give the exact specifications needed to manufacture or fabricate whatever is depicted more evocatively in the design illustrations.

Continuity Sketches and Storyboards: These are the sequential panels that describe the individual compositions of each shot and their order in each scene of a film.

Concept and Final Design Illustrations

Many production illustrations are no more than quick sketches, thumbnails or roughs—whatever is necessary to get an idea across quickly during the early stages of production. These are ultimately developed for more formal presentations and precise communication into finished design illustrations, which are fully realized renderings, some as big as 30 X 40 in. Their purpose is to indicate the mood and feeling of a set, location, costume or makeup. Therefore, color, lighting and style are more important than a technically exact physical description. For this reason, a dramatic presentation is best, and finished conceptuals are usually executed in a traditional illustration medium like gouache, tempera, oils, watercolor, colored inks, acrylics or mixed-media. A fully rendered illustration is usually employed for each of the basic locations or environments of a film.

In the case of *Star Wars*, production illustrator Ralph McQuarrie initially made detailed paintings of eight major scenes, which established the pictorial tone for the entire movie and helped sell the project to a studio. Though many hundreds of additional drawings and paintings were made by other artists after McQuarrie's initial ideas, they were largely faithful to his original concepts.

An example of a concept illustration by production illustrator Joe Musso (now the president of the Matte Painters and Production Illustrators Union) is seen below. This gouache painting was used for Hitchcock's *Torn Curtain* and depicts the office of a Communist East Berlin Security Chief who is speaking with a U.S. scientist (Paul Newman) and his girlfriend (Julie Andrews). Outside the window are the bombed-out ruins of

Concept illustration by Joe Musso for *Torn Curtain*.

ONE ANGLE ON GREAT HALL

"Citizen Kane"
Orson Welles Production for R.K.O. Hollywood.
1941.
Art Director: Van Nest Polglase.
Associate: Perry Ferguson.

Production sketches for *Citizen Kane.*

The Purple Rose of Cairo: Set sketches by Production Designer Stuart Wurtzel.

old Berlin, which Hitchcock included to contrast with the modern office interior as a reminder of the historical context of the story. The ruins were eventually added in a matte painting by Albert Whitlock.

Two rare concept sketches for *Citizen Kane* appear on page 11. The first is an interior of the great hall in Kane's estate, Xanadu; the second, the empty pool and deteriorated awnings of the bathhouse outside.

Another example of concept illustration, set sketches for two beautifully realized scenes in *The Purple Rose of Cairo* by Production Designer Stuart Wurtzel, appear above and on page 13. Accompanying the illustra-

The Purple Rose of Cairo: Set sketches by Production Designer Stuart Wurtzel.

tions are the photographs of the sets as they appeared in the films. Both were filmed on location in upstate New York. Since *The Purple Rose of Cairo* featured a film within a film, Wurtzel had to create both the real world of the mid-thirties and a convincing recreation of a studio set for a drawing-room movie comedy of the same period.

Following these illustrations are two set sketches by Richard Sylbert, the production designer for such films as *Chinatown, The Graduate, Catch*

Set sketches by Production Designer Richard Sylbert. Top: *Reds*; bottom: *Splendor in the Grass.*

22 and *Dick Tracy.* His set sketches for *Reds* and *Splendor in the Grass* are examples of an assured and illustrative style.

Architectural Drawings

When the concepts for sets, costumes and props depicted in the finished illustrations are accepted, technical design work begins. This means determining the actual materials and mechanical solutions needed for

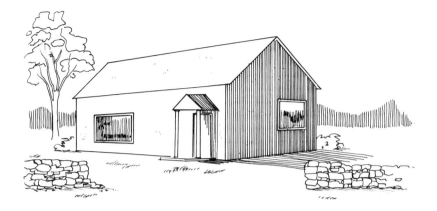

Diagram 2.1: A typical concept sketch.

construction and describing them in dimensionally accurate line drawings. Plans of this type are completed by draftsmen working for the art director and production designer, and in the case of the set design, this must conform to theatrical building codes and accepted architectural standards.

There are four basic types of architectural illustrations used in production design: the plan, the elevation, the section and the projection. The first three types of drawings are related views. Taken together they provide all the information the building crew needs to understand the construction of an object, building or set.

Plans, Sections and Elevations

A PLAN is a top view of an object, looking down at a cross-section as though a knife had cut across the entire building and the uppermost half had been removed. A building plan can be a floor plan, ceiling plan, roof plan or site plan (the land on which the building is located) depending on where the cut is made in the building. In film or theatrical work one works most often with floor plans, since a full-building structure is rarely required. Plans are drawn to scale and include precise dimensions.

A SECTION VIEW usually refers to a profile (side view) of an object or building as though one end had been sliced off to reveal a cross section. A plan can also be considered a section view.

ELEVATIONS are front and side views of an object. They are included alongside plans and drawn to the same scale.

Diagram 2.2 shows a typical layout for a plan, section and elevation of the house in the concept sketch (Diagram 2.1).

Unlike a concept sketch in which receding surfaces converge at the

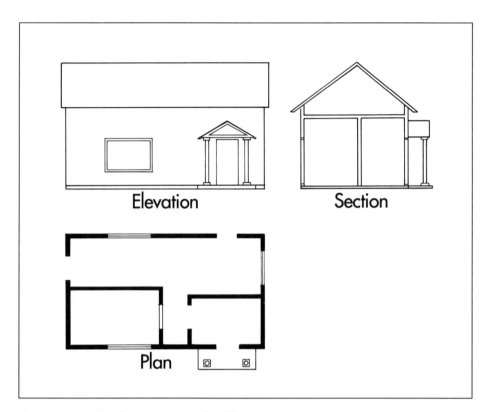

Diagram 2.2: The three views used in blueprints.

horizon to indicate perspective, plans, sections and elevations are drawn using orthographic projection. This means that the surfaces parallel in the object are also drawn parallel on the drawing.

Projections

It is possible to use the plan and elevation for a set as a basis for a perspective drawing illustrating how the finished set will appear to the camera for any combination of lens and camera positions. This type of drawing is called *camera angle projection*.

Here is how this type of illustration is useful: A scene in a movie calls for a plane to burst into flames in an aircraft hangar. A suitable location is found in a real hangar, and a false wall is built that can be set on fire. The new wall cuts the shooting space in half. The director had hoped to get a full shot of the plane, but that may be difficult now that the false wall has eliminated so much room. A very wide lens could be used to include the entire airplane within its view, but unfortunately this causes displeasing distortion.

Had the production designer used camera angle projections, the director would have seen all the problems on paper before the set was built. At the same time, the set designer might have learned that he only needed to build half the wall, since that is all the camera could view from any

Set projection sketch by Camille Abbott for *Flashdance*.

position in the hangar. In addition to previewing sets and interior locations, camera angle projection is particularly useful for effects shots such as glass paintings or matte shots, miniatures or forced perspective sets.

Harold Michelson has told me that when he first began in the art department in the late '40s, camera angle projection was routinely used and known by every illustrator in the art department. Projections were created for nearly every set that was constructed, helping to cut down on "overbuilding" and refining the proportions of set designs by taking into account the lens used to photograph them. Today the opposite is true, and many of the younger production illustrators are not familiar with this excellent tool.

Appearing above and on page 18 are two projection sketches based on plans and elevations provided by a production designer. The first is by Camille Abbott for the attic set in *Flashdance*. Abbott is a versatile and experienced production illustrator. She is particularly knowledgeable in projection drawing and is frequently consulted as a specialist for complex set projections.

The *Flashdance* art is drawn wider than the 1.85:1 aspect ratio because a pan shot was anticipated for the scene. Using Abbott's projection, the production designer, director and cameraman would know precisely how the set would look to the camera for the lens specified in the drawing. A change in lens or camera position would require a different projection drawing.

The second projection sketch is by Mentor Huebner for the movie *Harlem Nights*. In addition to being a projection for a set that exists only on paper, it is also a fully worked out conceptual drawing showing the lighting, staging, costumes and the character of the scene. A director would not only have a very accurate idea of what his set will look like from a particular angle, but would also gain from the many visual suggestions inherent in the detail that has been included. The original art was drawn 18 x 24 in. in charcoal and is typical of Huebner's wonderful draftsmanship. He has earned a reputation as one of the premier artists in his field. Indeed, his highly finished conceptual illustrations and continuity illustrations have earned Huebner the specialized title of primary production illustrator or primary visual conceptual artist.

Projection sketch by Mentor Huebner for *Harlem Nights*.

When a projection drawing is rendered as fully as the *Harlem Nights* conceptual it is one of the most powerful tools available to the art department and the director. (If you're interested in learning to project from plans and elevations or from photographs, Appendix I features a complete explanation of the Michelson method.)

Models

Scaled models are another visualization tool borrowed from the field of architecture. Unlike storyboards or concept sketches, models are used to visualize the three-dimensional space that the camera records rather than the two-dimensional space that the audience will see on the screen. They are an excellent visual aid for determining staging and camera setups but also help with planning what goes on behind the camera. Models that include the space surrounding a set or the on-camera location can be used by the production manager to find the best way to move crew, cast and equipment when large numbers of people appear in a scene.

Models are built in many materials. Cardboard, foamcore, balsa wood and modeling clay are the most common, but toy soldiers, cars and model railroad accessories are an excellent resource for ready-made buildings and foliage in a variety of scales.

Continuity Sketches and Storyboards

The detailed use of continuity sketches (as they were originally called in live action) probably began with Walt Disney in his first animated films. Webb Smith is the Disney animator credited with the invention of the storyboard in the early '30s, but this is a specialized use of the term. Continuity sketches (six to a page) showing the important action and cutting points in Disney's *Oswald the Lucky Rabbit* series were used as early as 1927. The following year continuity scripts containing key panels and typed descriptions of action for *Steamboat Willie* were also routine at Disney. What Smith contributed a few years later was the display of dozens of continuity sketches that were pinned up on a single wall-board—hence the term storyboards—allowing animators, especially the story-conscious Disney, to get the overview of an entire story.

Elsewhere in the movie industry at this time storyboards were still not the accepted norm for planning live-action movies, though art departments drew set designs and individual concept sketches that indicated camera angles. But by 1932 Disney was an international success and already the supreme animator of the day. Live-action art directors working in Hollywood would certainly have been aware of some of the innovations going on at the Disney Studios, including the use of storyboards. Even without Disney's influence, storyboards' nearest kin, the comic strips, were an established tradition for most Americans in the '30s, and the idea that a movie could be visualized in individual panels was probably an inevitable development.

Art director and production designer Gene Allen (the first President of the Storyboard and Matte Painters Union in 1953; now president of the Art Directors Guild) began his career in the Warner Brothers art department in 1937. Allen told me that continuity boards were already an established method of mapping out scenes in the mid-'30s and that at least eight full-time continuity sketch artists were working in the art department under the supervision of department head Anton Grot. In the studio system, the physical design of a movie was handled entirely by the art department. The art director worked out set designs and costumes and the continuity of the picture, aided by the staff artists. Only after the picture had been designed on paper (and with many sets built as well) would the director and cameraman join the picture. This procedure was extremely efficient, and if it resulted in generic graphic solutions much of the time, it also permitted major stars and directors to make as many as three pictures a year. When John Huston began directing at the height of this system, he knew the value of preplanning. Years later Huston would say, "I completely storyboarded *The Maltese Falcon* because I didn't want to lose face with the crew: I wanted to give the impression I knew what I was doing."

While the studio system and its organizational methods are gone, storyboards are still in far greater use than is generally acknowledged.

The myth that movies are made up by directors on the set frequently begins with the director and is perpetuated by critics, reviewers, film historians and the publicity departments of the distribution companies. A director may, in fact, be the main visual architect of a film, but the invented-on-the-set description of the production process is largely false. Only in experimental and independent film can one find completely self-sufficient hyphenates—the writer-director-cameraman-editors—and even their working method might include a great deal of planning and careful preparation before shooting.

Of the several types of production illustration, the storyboard is the most useful tool the filmmaker has for visualizing his ideas and the one most directly related to his responsibilities.   In the next chapter we will look at the work of individual continuity artists and the wide range of styles and approaches they use in planning the shot flow of a film.

An example of storyboard art for the movie *Her Alibi* begins below. As you will see, Huebner draws the entire scene of the action and frames the subject afterward as a cinematographer might. Not all storyboard artists use this technique, but it is particularly useful in indicating panning shots and camera movement.

Storyboard by Mentor Huebner for *Her Alibi.*

Storyboards by Mentor Huebner for *Her Alibi*.

Storyboards by Mentor Huebner for *Her Alibi*.

3 STORYBOARDS

Maurice Zuberano, one of the most respected production illustrators and art directors in the trade, has called the storyboard the "diary of the film." If so, it is a diary written about future events. What he was getting at, though, is that the storyboard is the private record of the visualization process, one of the reasons so few of them survive intact. Frequently, it is the evidence that the look of a film was the work of someone other than the director. For directors without a strong visual sense the storyboard illustrator is the shot-flow designer, essential to the structuring, staging and composition of shots and sequences.

Of course, there are directors who are as visually sophisticated as any member of the production staff and, in the narrative sense, perhaps more so. Hitchcock, who is probably associated with storyboarding more than any other director, used elaborate boards to refine his vision and control the filmmaking process, ensuring that his original intention was translated to the screen.

For Hitchcock, who began in films as an art director, it was also a way of making sure that he was credited with the design of his films. He liked to say that his movies were finished before they were ever made, before the cinematographer or editor touched a piece of film. This is confirmed by the fact that he rarely looked through the camera viewfinder on the set, since it was merely a photographic equivalent of a storyboard that had been finalized earlier.

Hitchcock influenced a whole generation of filmmakers in the '60s who already had affection for continuity graphics in the comics, which, like jazz and the blues, were beginning to be recognized as an American art form at that time. The most famous filmmaker of that generation, Steven Spielberg, generally recognized as the premier visualizer of the entertainment directors, has published collections of production art from his collaborations with George Lucas, bringing further attention to the use of storyboards and production illustration. Without storyboards, Spielberg's complex staging and kinetic effects would not have the lapidary polish that has become the hallmark of his work and the goal of many young filmmakers.

It would be easy to dismiss the current interest in storyboarding as further proof that today's Hollywood filmmakers have little knowledge of fiction outside comic books and that they are more comfortable with storyboards and action than ideas. But the truth is that many films are storyboarded regardless of subject matter. It may even be that films without a great deal of action benefit more from storyboards than kinetic subjects. Even Jean-Luc Godard, who throughout his career discarded or subverted the continuity devices shared by comic strip illustrators and classical Hollywood films, used storyboards at times to work out the connections between shots. Storyboards are merely a tool and need not reflect any style or content besides that which the individual filmmaker cares to show.

Storyboards serve two purposes: First, they allow a filmmaker to previsualize his ideas and refine them in the same way a writer develops ideas through successive drafts; secondly, they serve as the clearest language to communicate ideas to the entire production team. Admittedly, the communication value of storyboards grows with the complexity of the production, but storyboards are not restricted to action scenes and big-budget productions. Even small, dramatic films can benefit from storyboards, helping the director to refine mood and dialogue.

The Director's Role in Storyboarding

Every film is a unique blend of talents and personalities, and the responsibility for the look of a film is shared in varying degrees by the production designer, director, cinematographer and editor. In recent years, the trend has been for the director to work directly with a sketch artist, shifting some of the responsibility for continuity away from the production designer. It's important to remember, however, that a highly visual director has always been able to take charge of a picture despite the working system of the studio. Now that there are no longer studios to impose a house style, this is even more true.

Directors with some training in the graphic arts or a penchant for drawing—Hitchcock and Ridley Scott are two examples—may furnish rough storyboards of their own to be refined by the regular storyboard artist. Sherman Labby, a production illustrator much in demand, worked with Ridley Scott on the film *Blade Runner* and spoke of the evocative line drawings (affectionately named ridleygrams) he received for many scenes from director Scott. Director/artists have also included such stylists as Eisenstein, Fellini and Kurosawa, all of whom have storyboarded sequences or contributed elaborate conceptual sketches to their films. Even directors without a particular skill in drafting, such as Steven Spielberg and George Miller, occasionally make stick figure drawings to explain a specific composition or staging. Even when the director has a clear plan in mind, however, he will encourage the storyboard artist to contribute ideas.

Paul Power, one of the newer production illustrators with experience in comics and film, enjoys collaborating with the director working out each scene in long brainstorming sessions. Sometimes this includes reading the dialogue and acting out scenes page by page from the script with the director stopping only to make rough sketches. Later, these will be turned into more refined drawings for further discussion. His involvement in the staging and dramatic concept of a film has led Power to describe the type of illustration he does in the panels as "acting with a pencil." Power's defines the production illustrator's responsibility as helping the director find the means to express his vision. In fact, the primacy of the director was a consistent theme with all the production illustrators I spoke with. In a way, the very craft of storyboarding teaches an illustrator to be flexible. Since they are accustomed to refining a sequence through constant revisions, production illustrators recognize that there are many solutions to any problem. The challenge of collaboration is interpreting the director's view of the script.

Schedules

Production illustrators may work on a film for 2 weeks or for more than a year, depending on the complexity of the production and the needs of the director. While it is hard to pin down an average schedule, the thorough storyboarding of an entire film, as opposed to select action sequences, usually requires a minimum of 3-4 months. For large productions with elaborate sets and effects several sketch artists may be needed and in some cases, the production designer contributes continuity sketches as well. Even when more than one artist is at work, a complex film may require a year to storyboard. It should be mentioned, however, that this longer schedule does not reflect drawing time as much as the necessity of waiting for each element of the production (locations and sets) to be designed before storyboarding work can proceed.

Skills Required by Storyboard Artists

A production illustrator must understand staging, editing and composition and be thoroughly familiar with the use of lenses in cinematography. He should be a facile draftsman adept at drawing the human figure in a variety of poses without resorting to models or photographs. He also needs to be able to work quickly under the pressure of deadlines and to adapt to the look and feel of different historical periods and exotic locations. This doesn't mean research material isn't used. A sketch artist isn't expected to know period clothing or what the interior of a submarine or the skyline of Nepal looks like. But a good visual memory is invaluable since he will have limited time to find references for any series of sketches.

Reference and Research

In the later stages of design, the sketch artist will base his illustrations on photographs of the actual locations chosen by the director, production designer and cinematographer, or he may visit the location in person and photograph his own reference shots. In the case of the film *La Bamba*, the biography of rock and roll musician Ritchie Vallens, storyboarder Paul Power immersed himself in Mexican culture, visiting the locations where Vallens actually lived and meeting with members of his family. Power worked on the boards for several months before shooting and stayed with the production during actual shooting to make adjustments to the boards as filming progressed. An excerpt from Paul Power's opening storyboard for *La Bamba* begins on page 26.

For a relatively low budget film, Power's experience on *La Bamba* was enviable. In general, the storyboard illustrators in today's moviemaking environment have less time to refine their boards than in the past. Perversely, this excellent tool, which can save producers a great deal of time and money, is one of the first items in the budget to be reduced or

Storyboard for *La Bamba* by Paul Power.

Storyboard for *La Bamba* by Paul Power.

eliminated. Several production illustrators have told me that there is a general tendency to use less refined boards for fewer scenes, though the directors who know that this is penny-wise and pound-foolish demand the time for proper storyboarding.

In the days of the studio, when storyboard artists were on staff, the average level of execution in production illustration was probably higher. While there are illustrators today who are capable of producing work equal to the best of the past, the general shifting of money from below-the-line to above-the-line expenses has begun to adversely affect production illustration and ultimately the productions themselves.

Style

Beginning on page 29 are five storyboards from *Citizen Kane*. These are good examples of how continuity sketches can convey the visual flow and mood of a sequence and are typical of the type of work produced at the studios in the '30s and '40s. Credit is given at the bottom of one of the drawings to director Orson Welles, art director Van Nest Polglase and his associate Perry Ferguson. This is somewhat misleading and one of the many unattractive aspects of the studio system. In actuality, Ferguson was the art director on *Citizen Kane*, and Polglase was head of the entire RKO art department. Ferguson did the actual design work for *Citizen Kane* while Polglase's responsibility was largely managerial; he was not involved in most of the specific creative decisions. Unfortunately, under the studio system, production illustrators were not allowed to sign their work, making it difficult today to assign credit to individual drawings.

Ferguson worked in close collaboration with Welles on the conception of the scenes, which was then turned into sketches, set drawings and storyboards by illustrators in the RKO art department. According to credits listed in *The Making of Citizen Kane* by Robert C. Carringer, there were five illustrators on *Kane*: Charles Ohmann is listed as Principal Sketch Artist, while Al Abbott, Claude Gillingwater, Jr., Albert Pyke and Maurice Zuberano are listed under the heading, Sketches and Graphics. There may have been other artists who contributed sketches, and often-times more than one artist would work on a drawing or storyboard. In the studio system it was not unusual for illustrators in the art department to work on projects thay were not assigned to when the work needed to be done.

The first storyboard on page 29 is a four-panel sequence of the Thatcher Library. These charcoal sketches are a better example of set design and mood than of editing continuity, and the gothic lighting is very close to the way the scene appeared in the film.

The second sequence pictured is a more conventional continuity board and shows a scene deleted from the script. The sequence is a recollection by Kane's guardian, financier Walter Thatcher, of a trip to Rome to see Kane on his twenty-fifth birthday. Descriptions below each panel describe the basic action of the scene, transitions and camera movement.

In the next series Kane meets Susan Alexander for the first time outside a drugstore. The basic action of the scene is quite close to the

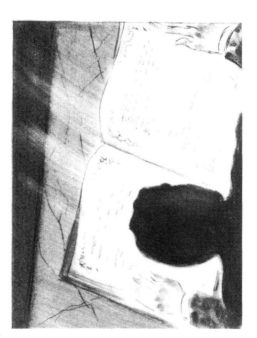

Storyboard for the Thatcher Library scene in *Citizen Kane.*

· 1ST ROME SEQUENCE ·

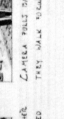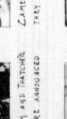

Rome

AS WRITTEN WORD "ROME" TRAVELS ACROSS AND OFF SCREEN WE SEE

SHADOW OF HORSE DRAWING BAROUCHE COME ACROSS SCREEN FOLLOWED QUICKLY

BY THE CARRIAGE. AS THATCHER AND PARKER QUICKLY ALIGHT AND START

TOWARD US. CAMERA PULLS BACK AND SHOWS GRILLED DOORWAY THRU WHICH WE WERE LOOKING BY

HAND COMES IN AND OPENS GRILLE FOLLOWING IMMEDIATLY BY

THE OPENING OF

A DOOR INTO ROOM AND THATCHER AND PARKER ARE ANNOUNCED

CAMERA PULLS BACK AS THEY WALK FORWARD TO

KANE AT FIREPLACE

WHERE DIALOGUE TAKES PLACE AND A DISSOLVE SHOWS US

KANE, THATCHER AND PARKER SIT IN A DIMLY LIT RICHLY DECORATED LIBRARY THAT NIGHT. WHEN DIALOGUE IS COMPLETED DISSOLVE

TO THATCHER SEATING HIMSELF IN CARRIAGE AS IT PULLS OUT FOLLOWED BY

SHADOW AGAINST BLANK WALL WHICH IN TURN IS FOLLOWED BY WRITTEN

I had

WORDS IN THATCHER'S MEMOIRS.

Storyboard of the Rome sequence deleted from *Citizen Kane*.

Kane meets Susan Alexander. Storyboard for *Citizen Kane*.

CRANE SHOT DESIGN.
"Citizen Kane"
Orson Welles Production for R.K.O. Hollywood.
1941.
Art Director: Van Nest Polglase.
Associate: Perry Ferguson.

Storyboard of the El Rancho cabaret crane shot from *Citizen Kane*.

"El Rancho" Cabaret

WILL READ 'EL RANCHO' & SO ON.

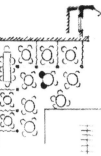

UPSHOT OF ROOF OF BUILDING- (MINIATURE)-SIGN-RAIN-THUNDER-LIGHTNING-CAMERA

TRAVELS UP AND THROUGH SIGN THEN

DOWN TO SHOW SKYLIGHT ON ROOF-RAIN BEATING DOWN CONTINUE ON

CLOSER TO SKYLIGHT AND BELOW CAN BARELY BE SEEN SUSAN SEATED AT TABLE

AS WE GET VERY CLOSE TO RAIN COVERED GLASS MATCH BLURRED SHOT WITH

SHOT MADE ON SET AS CAMERA CONTINUES TO CLOSE—

UP OF SUSAN-THE BUSINESS WITH THOMPSON AND HEAD WAITER

UNTIL THOMPSON DECIDES IT IS USELESS AND

LEAVES AS HEADWAITER ORDERS ANOTHER DRINK FOR SUSAN—

Storyboard of the El Rancho cabaret crane shot, including roof sign, from *Citizen Kane*.

filmed version, but the camera angles and staging are very different.

The last two storyboards show how a scene develops through successive drafts. The sequence depicted is one of the most famous shots in *Citizen Kane*: the crane move through the skylight of the El Rancho cabaret down to Susan Alexander and Kane seated at a table. The shot is actually a combination of a miniature rooftop set and the full-scale interior of the nightclub joined by a dissolve as the camera moves through the rain-covered glass of the skylight.

The first treatment of the crane shot on page 32 is wonderfully rendered in a style of illustration evoking the lighting of the German Expressionists of the '20s, though the framing of the scene is quite different from the way the sequence eventually turned out.

The second version is virtually identical to the original sequence as the camera approaches the skylight. But as the camera descends to the floor the storyboard again diverges from the filmed version. There may have been other storyboards of the scene, but a look at just these two should indicate how valuable they are as a method of developing ideas.

Notice that the storyboard also includes a schematic diagram of the scene drawn on the right-hand side of the board. This is helpful for both the designer and the cinematographer to communicate the technical requirements of the scene. This clarifies the layout of the set when unusual or disorienting perspectives are illustrated.

Similarly moody are Harold Michelson's storyboards for Hitchcock's *The Birds*. The six panels featured show how the economical use of line can convey all the information the cinematographer needs to understand the framing continuity of a scene. Without spending a great deal of time on specific detail, these energetic sketches establish mood, locale, composition, staging of action and the selection of lens for each shot. The six frames on pages 35 and 36 depict the attack of the birds on the children running from the schoolhouse in Bodega Bay after the birds have gathered in force.

The production designer for *The Birds*, Robert Boyle, collaborated with Hitchcock on five films beginning in 1942: *Saboteur, Shadow of a Doubt, North by Northwest, The Birds* and *Marnie*. He reaffirms Hitchcock's reputation as a methodical planner, but also as a director who was interested in the ideas of the talented people with whom he worked. Their usual way of working together began with meetings early in the production schedule to go over each scene. Hitchcock might furnish rough thumbnail sketches to elaborate a sequence, but this process was also intended to allow his creative team to elaborate on each other's ideas. From these meetings a general plan was devised for each scene, some more detailed than others, and Boyle would begin to oversee the storyboards, set designs, costumes and special effects necessary to turn ideas into cinematic fact. Boyle would contribute some of his own drawings for the sets and storyboards, but much of this work was handed over to storyboard illustrators who would receive instructions based on Boyle and Hitchcock's meetings.

Following Michelson's drawings on page 38 is an extremely rare page

439 *melanie – Run – Run.*

near Bodega School.

440 *Children – (foregnd against Sodium Screen) Backgnd Bodega school with michelle and 2 or 3 children*

Art - 12

440A *continuation of 440. – melanie runs past camera*

Storyboards for *The Birds* by Harold Michelson. Production design by Robert Boyle.

Storyboards for *The Birds* by Harold Michelson. Production design by Robert Boyle.

of notes and storyboard panels drawn by Hitchcock himself for the 1943 production of *Lifeboat*. The page is three-hole punched for use in a binder and includes notes describing action and the lines of dialogue that accompany the panels. The specific dialogue cues mean that Hitchcock was cutting in the camera, greatly limiting the manipulation possible during the editing process. The first panel shows that Hitchcock made a slight adjustment in the composition, moving closer and to camera left. Notice also that the direction "Repeat all with closer lens" appears on the far left of the second panel. This may refer to the dotted frame line around the oarsman, indicating that Hitchcock intended to get coverage of the same action, only closer.

Materials

Since the only criteria they must meet is ease of execution and reproducibility, most storyboards today are rendered with a fast, easily controlled medium such as pencil, ink and charcoal dust or dry markers for color work.

Pencil

The pencil, either graphite or charcoal, is one of the illustrator's basic tools, and even when a drawing is completed with ink, the undersketch is usually laid down in pencil. Photocopied, the contrast becomes sharper, though a tentative line tends to become scratchy. More than anything else the pencil's virtue is its erasability. It is the word processor for the artist. I used pencil for the storyboard demonstration of a crane shot in this chapter, and as you will see, the blacks are never quite as stunning as those possible in ink or charcoal.

Ink and Charcoal Dust

This seems to be a medium peculiar to storyboards. No other medium lays down a broad stroke of tone faster than a cotton ball dipped in charcoal dust, one that can be later erased with a kneaded eraser for corrections or creating highlights (see Harold Michelson's drawings, pages 35 and 36). It tends to reproduce better than pencil and is capable of deeper tones. It's probably the favorite medium of storyboard artists, and you will see it used by many of the illustrators featured in this book.

Markers

Madison Avenue has made the dry marker the medium of choice in the advertising art department. Dry markers are inexpensive, dry instantly and do not require the preparation or cleanup necessary with other color media. In the hands of a good comp artist they can produce remarkably realistic effects, though for finished conceptual drawings they are frequently combined with colored pencils, pastels and inks. They are virtually the standard comp material for studio artists, illustrators, product de-

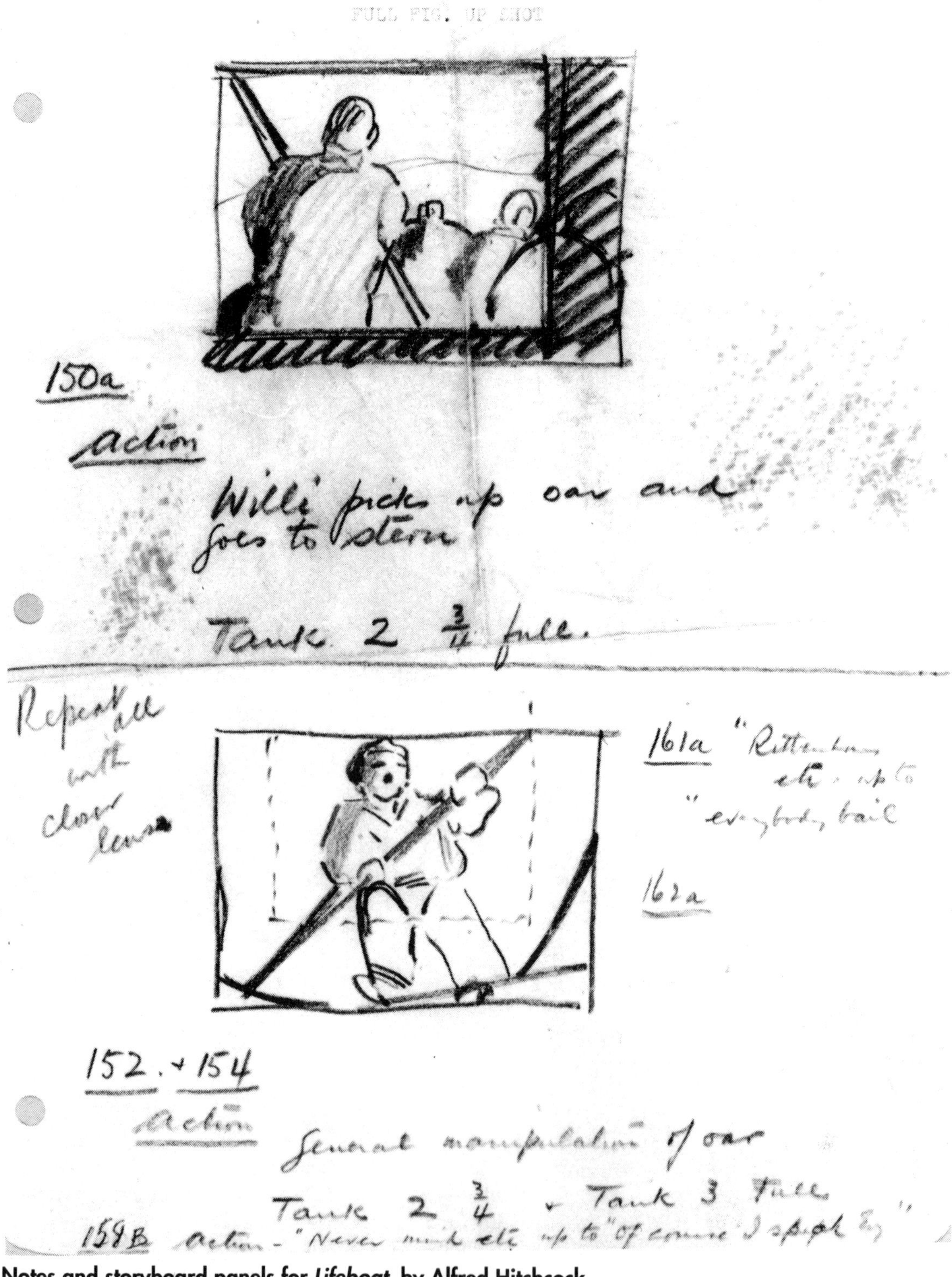

FULL FIG. UP SHOT
150a
action
Willi picks up oar and goes to stern
Tank 2 3/4 full.
Repeat all with close lens
161a "Rittenhouse etc. up to "everybody bail
162a
152. + 154
action
General manipulation of oar
Tank 2 3/4 + Tank 3 Full
158B action - "Never mind etc up to "Of course I speak Eng"

Notes and storyboard panels for *Lifeboat*, by Alfred Hitchcock.

signers, architects and interior designers—anyone who needs a brilliant, fast medium to communicate basic design concepts. Markers are not for timid sketchers and demand a bold touch. They do not blend easily and a misstroke can scar a delicate drawing. In most cases state-of-the-art marker technique is more elaborate than is necessary for feature storyboard work and a simple marker style is preferred. If you decide to use markers be sure to work in a well-ventilated studio—the solvents give off fumes, which many find unpleasant. One last point: Markers are not lightfast and will fade with time. The more ultraviolet light (primarily sunlight) they're exposed to, the faster they will fade. In prolonged bright sunlight noticeable deterioration will begin within a period of a few weeks. If you are saving your work for posterity keep this in mind.

Illustrating Camera Techniques

The most obvious limitation of the storyboard is its inability to show motion—not merely action within the frame, but more importantly, the movement of the camera. Optical effects like dissolves and fades are also beyond the scope of the illustrator, as are most manipulations of depth of field and focus. The most obvious solution is to use captions and schematic drawings to describe what cannot be drawn. There are also several techniques used by animators to show camera movement and extended space that can be adapted to live-action subjects.

The first element we need to consider is the border of the storyboard frame. Its purpose is to indicate a viewpoint, selected from the whole of space. Therefore it is permissible (and frequently valuable) to allow the drawing to extend beyond the edges of the frame. Actually, many artists begin a drawing without frame lines. After they have sketched in the basic elements of the drawing they use loose sheets of paper to mask off portions of the picture to find the exact composition they are looking for. Because both the camera and subject can move in film, the filmmaker will find that placing a storyboard frame within a larger drawing is a useful technique for illustrating the fluid compositional qualities of the medium.

In this next series of panels, I will use different drawing styles while showing several methods of illustrating camera movement and transitions.

The Pan Shot and the Tracking Shot

This first wide panel in Figure 3.1 illustrates a man running down a street in pursuit of a rooftop sniper. The man in the street is shown at important

Figure 3.1

positions in the action with an arrow to show his path. This type of panel can be used to indicate a pan or a tracking shot. In this version, specific framing is not indicated, however, the camera position and staging of the action is quite clear.

It is possible to show actual framing, as in this next example of a car chase in Figure 3.2. A frame within the frame indicates the composition of the shot as the camera will see the action. In this case left-hand frame (A) is panned in with the car. The arrow below the frame indicates that the

Figure 3.2: A storyboard pan shot.

camera zooms down to the size of the smaller right hand frame as the car moves right to left. There is no standardization in any of this iconography; you can pretty much design things the way you want as long as you get the idea across.

The third panoramic storyboard in Figure 3.3 is a vertical pan and shows how a multiperspective can indicate panning over a large expanse. The diver is seen first in an up shot and followed until the camera is tilted down to the pool.

Dolly and Zoom Shots

In animation it's possible to draw a large panel and then frame smaller portions of the whole picture to obtain medium shots, close-ups (CUs) and extreme close-ups. This is called a field cut in animation and is used to get the maximum number of shots from a single piece of artwork by photographing it in several frame sizes. A field cut is indicated as a frame within a frame, and the iconography is also used for live-action story-boards to indicate a dolly or zoom as shown in Figure 3.4. To indicate the direction of the dolly or zoom (in or out), arrows are added connecting the two squares. This shows that the change in shot size is obtained through movement rather than cutting.

A more conventional way of indicating an on-axis cut, dolly or zoom shot is shown in Figure 3.5. The problem, of course, is that the figure has to be drawn twice and requires additional explanation with captions. The advantage of the additional frame is that the impact of the CU is conveyed more effectively.

The frame within a frame can also be used to show erratic camera motion as in Figure 3.6.

Figure 3.3: Multiperspective views like this one are a good way to show a pan shot that pivots over a great distance. With this type of illustration it is hard to tell if the framing of the shot is a wide, medium or close-up shot. However, the alternative type of representation, which uses several individual frames of the diver's action, would not convey the main characteristic of the shot—smooth motion and the angle of view.

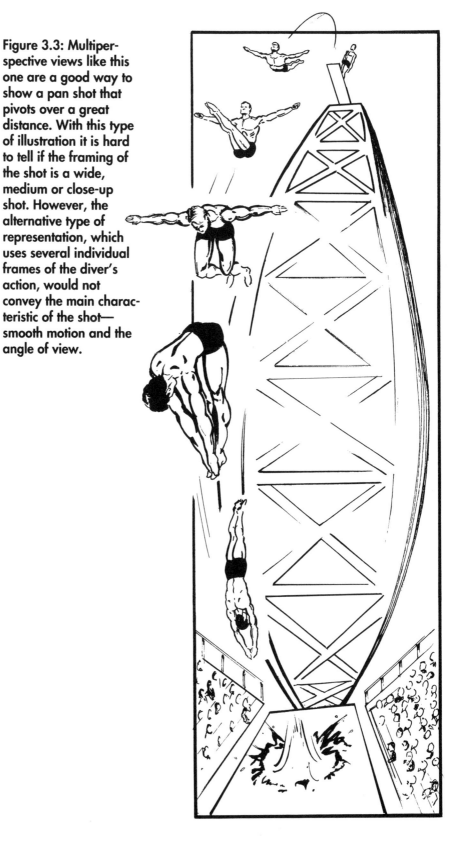

Figure 3.4: The drawing on the left uses a frame within a frame to indicate a zoom or dolly move. If the lines connecting the inner frame to the corners of the outer frame were removed this would mean that a change in shot size is accomplished with a cut to a new shot.

Transitions Between Shots

In the next few panels (Figure 3.7) we'll see how transitions like dissolves and fades can be handled. This particular type of layout is borrowed from animation storyboards. Styles vary slightly depending on the animation studio, but Figure 3.7 shows a typical use of the space between panels.

The Crane Shot

This last example of continuity and editing illustration techniques (Figure 3.8) is a full sequence shot using a crane move. Though there are 11 panels in the storyboard, it represents a single, unbroken shot.

Format and Presentation

There are several different ways to display storyboards, depending on the size of the individual panels. The average size is approximately 4 x 6 in., but this is largely a matter of the artist's preference. Some like to work on a larger scale if greater detail is required. Then the boards can either be used this way or reduced to a more convenient presentation size during duplication.

Storyboards are usually made available to several of the production departments during preproduction. The format of the presentation depends on how they will be used. Some production designers place the

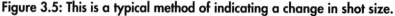

Figure 3.5: This is a typical method of indicating a change in shot size.

Figure 3.6: Camera movement used to simulate the movement of the ground, the pitching deck of a ship or any other movement of subject or space can be shown using a frame within a frame.

storyboards on a wall or bulletin board in the art department, following Disney's example, so that a great many panels can be seen in group meetings. This makes sense for getting a logistical overview of shooting requirements but is inconvenient for visualizing precise shot-to-shot flow and timing. Smaller boards containing 6 to 20 panels can be carried in a portfolio case, while some directors prefer seeing the panels book style, one large (8x10 in.) panel to a page in a loose-leaf binder. The advantage of the notebook-flip pad presentation is that each panel is seen individually as a page is turned into view. This allows the art director to preview how the completed sequence will look on the screen. He can vary the speed at which he turns the pages of the notebook to simulate editing rhythms. In addition, individual panels can be easily added, removed or

Figure 3.7: Animators use the space between frames to show transitions between shots.

APT. BUILDING IS IN FLAMES—
PAN DOWN WITH FALLING DEBRIS
TO ——

—WOMAN AND BABY IN EXTREME F.G.
ON APT. TERRACE ON FOURTH FLOOR.
IN B.G. FLAMES EXLPLODE FROM
WINDOW.

CAMERA PULLS BACK TO REVEAL
WOMAN ABOUT TO LOWER BABY
IN BASKET TO THE GROUND.

CAMERA BEGINS TO CRANE DOWN
BELOW BASKET AS IT DESCENDS.

Figure 3.8: The first of three panels illustrating a continuous crane shot.

reordered in much the same way an editor makes changes in the actual film.

Simplified Storyboard Illustration

Storyboards basically convey two kinds of information: a description of the physical environment of the sequence (set design/location) and a de-

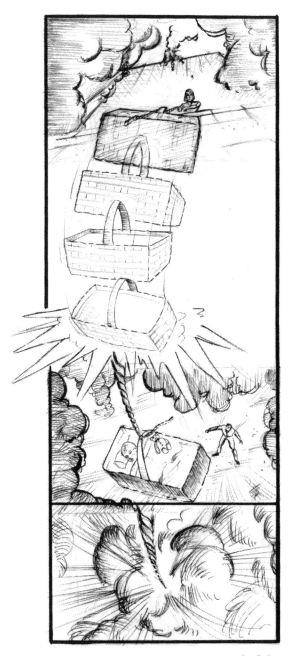

CAMERA CONTINUES TO MOVE DOWN BELOW BASKET UNTIL WOMAN IS FAR AWAY IN B.G.

BASKET DROPS FASTER GAINING ON CAMERA. BASKET PASSES CAMERA.

CAMERA PANS WITH BASKET INTO DOWN SHOT.

FATHER IS WAITING BELOW, WHEN FLAMES AND SMOKE BURST FROM WINDOW BELOW BASKET.

SMOKE ENVELOPES BASKET.

Figure 3.8: Second of three panels.

scription of the spatial quality of a sequence (staging, camera angle, lens and the movement of any elements in the shot). While a storyboard illustrator is expected to convey mood, lighting and other aspects of the environmental design, a director can convey his ideas for the basic setup of the camera with simpler drawing methods.

Shown next are several types of graphic representation that are fast and easily mastered. They can be combined in any way necessary to pre-

FRAME GOES BLACK WITH SMOKE.

CAMERA EMERGES FROM SMOKE MOVING DOWN TO FATHER.

FATHER SHOUTS --
"KEEP THE BASKET COMING, I CAN'T SEE IT!"

SMOKE BLOWS IN HIS EYES AND HE CAN BARELY SEE.

FATHER'S EXPRESSION SLOWLY CHANGES TO RELIEF AS BASKET SWINGS INTO EXT. F.G.

HE TAKES HOLD OF BASKET.

Figure 3.8: End of sequence.

sent the director's concept for a shot or scene. Our scene shows a woman running into the street and into the path of a car. In Figure 3.9 we begin with the most basic method of communication using written description and arrows to indicate screen direction of the subject of the shot or the movement of the camera. While this might seem so rudimentary as to be little help in designing a sequence, a director with editorial experience will be able to read the board and get a sense of the pacing.

Two types of schematic drawings are shown in Figure 3.10. First is an aerial plan that clearly shows the camera placement and the direction of action. The second pair of frames in Figure 3.10 are elevated schematics that show the height of the camera. Schematics are helpful in planning the order in which shots are photographed on the location, since many lo-

WIDE SHOT—WOMAN + CAR   M.CU. — WOMAN

Figure 3.9: Written descriptions in boxes are the simplest type of storyboard.

gistical problems are revealed. Usually this has to do with finding the best way to move equipment and people. An aerial schematic might show that if dolly track is laid for the last shot before lunch break, it blocks the path for cars that must be moved at that time. While schematics describe camera placement exactly, they give little indication of shot size or the emotional or kinetic quality of a shot.

One alternative is to use stick figures that convey figure placement and the direction of action. Two versions of these are shown in Figure 3.11. What stick-figure illustrations do not show is the height of the camera, since perspective is not indicated. Still, for all their crudeness, these four panels are really quite informative. These panels can be drawn in less than a minute, and yet they tell us a great deal about how each pair of frames would cut together. A director could greatly refine the shot size

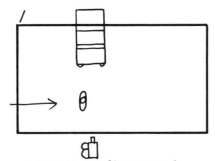

WOMAN ENTERS LEFT   WHEELS AROUND, STARTLED BY HEADLIGHTS.

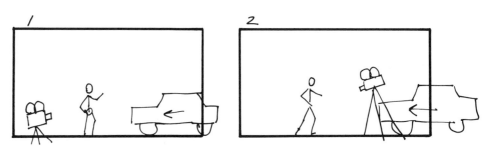

Figure 3.10: Schematic drawings.

FULL SHOT

MED. SHOT

WIDE SHOT— WOMAN

MED. SHOT — DOLLY INTO CU

Figure 3.11: Stick-figures without perspective.

for a sequence using drawings no more complex than these. With a little extra work arrows drawn in perspective can tell a great deal about the angle of view the director would like to see, as shown in Figure 3.12.

Arrows are a versatile sign and easily mastered. A wide selection is shown in Figure 3.13. They can be used to illustrate the motion of the camera or the subject of a shot or both. Arrows can show the complex path of a runaway car or can be used in schematic drawings to show the path of the camera in a sequence shot.

Another variation is the arrowheads in Figure 3.14, describing a whole range of angles. To help visualize these quickly a director might keep a page of arrows like the ones here or have his art director supply him with an assortment that he could copy when drawing stick figures. This will save the director time when he tries to figure out the perspective.

The frame itself can be used as an arrow to show the path of the

MED. HIGH ANGLE —
WIDE SHOT OF WOMAN.

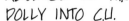

REVERSE TO M.C.U.
DOLLY INTO C.U.

Figure 3.12: Arrows can be added to indicate perspective.

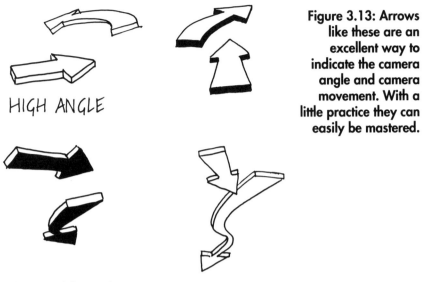

HIGH ANGLE

LOW ANGLE

Figure 3.13: Arrows like these are an excellent way to indicate the camera angle and camera movement. With a little practice they can easily be mastered.

camera over a scene. Overlapped frames can serve the same purpose. If the lines between overlapped frames are left in, this may mean that the camera stopped during the movement and moved on again. Figure 3.15 shows representative examples of these ideas.

Returning to the problem of showing perspective with stick figures, one way is to enclose them in simple three-dimensional boxes to describe the camera angle. Figure 3.16a shows two low-angle shots that, without the boxes, would not indicate the height of the camera. A variation in Figure 3.16b shows an extreme low-angle and a high-angle CU. As you can see, the car has been treated as a box to help define the perspective. Even in these simple drawings, the box technique helps tell us where the camera is placed. Even if you have no drawing experience whatsoever,

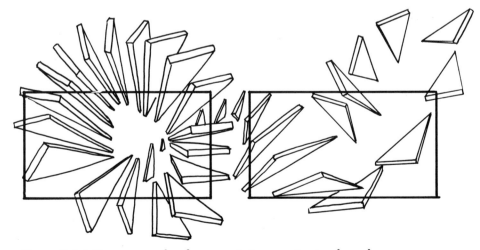

Figure 3.14: Keep a supply of arrows to trace onto storyboards.

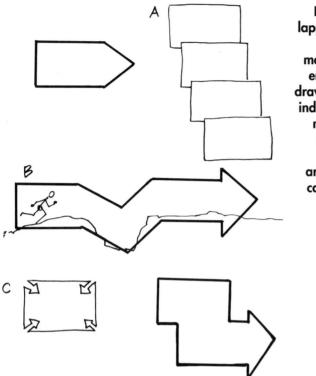

Figure 3.15: Overlapped panels can be used to indicate a moving shot (A). The entire frame can be drawn as an arrow to indicate the path of a moving subject (B). Illustrator uses the frame border for arrows to indicate a camera move to the subject (C).

learning to control the angle of a simple box like the ones used here is simple to master. Again, a single page of cubes in varying angles can be used for reference and can be provided by the production designer.

By adding form and volume to simple figures we get a better sense of spatial relationships. For instance, Figure 3.17 shows us how a director might try several versions until he was satisfied with the staging of the car and the woman in the frame.

The most important point to be made in this chapter is that storyboards are helpful to the director whether he follows them during shooting or not. For instance, after large portions of the script are boarded the director is able to see the dramatic flow of the story in a way that the screenplay fails to reveal. Moreover, the process of visualizing on paper is a technique for generating ideas, not just establishing the plan for the production team to follow on the set. This process is even more beneficial when the director works on his own drawings. There is really no way to overestimate the importance of rolling up your shirt-sleeves and working directly with images if you are directing a film. No matter how crude the drawings, the thought process and state of mind required to compose shots on paper is invaluable.

Director Brian DePalma draws his own stick-figure illustrations on a Macintosh computer using the software program Storyboarder®, but simple as the drawings are, it is likely that they serve as mnemonic devices, each frame an icon that brings to mind a familiar and detailed shot with all the perspective elements left out. Of course, what works for DePalma may not work for you. You may find a different type of representation that

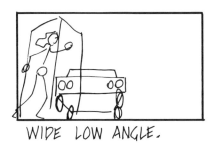

WIDE LOW ANGLE.

LOW ANGLE CU –TILTED FRAME.

Figure 3.16a

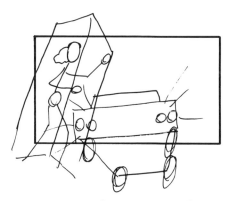

Figure 3.16b: Perspective boxes drawn over stick-figures help indicate camera angle.

suits your needs better. One of the pleasures in acquiring the storyboards for this book was discovering the many individual approaches to storyboarding that each illustrator developed.

Draftsmanship

If you can draw, there is no reason not to carry your storyboards to a higher degree of execution. While it is clearly beyond the scope of this book to teach drawing it is possible to convey one thought that is particularly valuable to storyboard artists: *It's what you leave out that counts.* Actually, I first heard this truism while playing music, and it seems to crop up whenever you're around seasoned artists of any kind. For a storyboard artist simplicity is more than a matter of taste. It is also a matter of necessity. Only in rare cases is the time available to make detailed drawings for every storyboard panel in a film.

Illustrator Noel Sickles' line work is a model of simplicity and is an object lesson in economical drawing. Though never a storyboard illustrator, his highly innovative work in the comics and later as a nationally recognized commercial illustrator is still an influence today. Appearing on page 53 are frame enlargements of his early work on the *Scorchy Smith* strip to show how only a few lines are needed to convey all types of

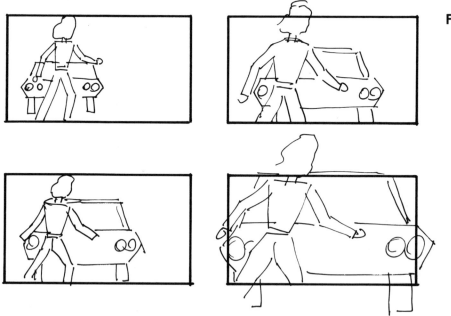

Figure 3.17: Adding volume to stick-figures conveys a great deal of compositional information.

surfaces and locales. The background details are particularly useful to study if you're looking to develop a practical storyboard style.

Even the simplest drawing style is useful to help the director shape a scene. Appearing on page 54 are very quick sketches drawn by Sherman Labby for *Beverly Hills Cop II*. These types of ink and tone thumbnail sketches are typically drawn in meetings with the director, each frame taking only 1-3 minutes. That means that an entire sequence can be talked out and drawn within an hour. However, it would be wrong to think of storyboarding solely in terms of the drawing. Actually, it is often the time spent working out the concept for a scene that determines how quickly a sequence is rendered on paper. Usually, drawings like the ones for *Beverly Hills Cop II* are used by the storyboard illustrator as notes for more finished renderings, which are submitted later.

Mood

Another series of storyboard panels by Sherman Labby appears on pages 55 to 63 and shows his fine sense of pictorial narrative in an opening scene from *Blade Runner*, one of two scenes that was never filmed. This is a beautiful example of the use of mood to establish the tone of a film, in this case, the ironic use of a calm, pastoral setting. The opening shows the Harrison Ford character, Decker, landing his Spinner vehicle on a farm. These first few elegantly composed frames contain only a few simple shapes evoking a sense of wonder typical of '40s science fiction.

Character

The next storyboard panels by Fred Lucky show how expressive characters help to make the comedic intention for each setup clear. Fred refined

Noel Sickles began drawing comic strips in 1933 at the age of 26 and quickly invented an impressionistic black and white inking style that achieved a highly realistic photographic look.   After five years, Sickles left the comic field and went on to become one of the foremost illustrators of his generation in magazine and book illustration.

These frame enlargements from Sickles' strip, *Scorchy Smith*, show how a few well placed lines and shadows can convey a great deal of visual information. His work is filled with graphic solutions and innovations that are a storehouse of ideas for storyboard artists. A reprint of his work will soon be available from:
Kitchen Sink Press, Inc.
Number 2 Swamp Road
Princeton, WI 54968.

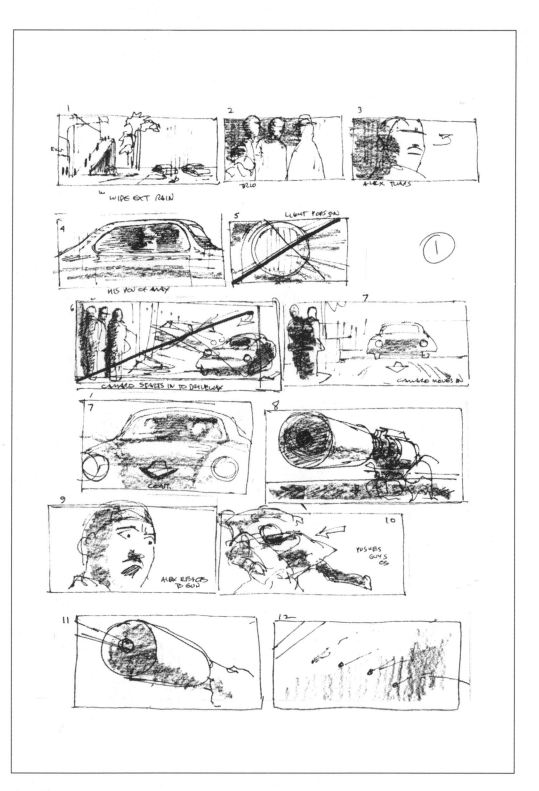

Sherman Labby's thumbnail sketches for a scene in *Beverly Hills Cop II*.

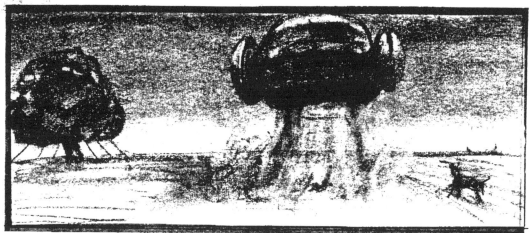

SPINNER KICKS UP DUST..

SPINNER LANDS - DOG BARKS AT IT AS D. RAISES HATCH

WIND BLOWS - D. WALKS TO FARMHOUSE - ⟵ CAM PAN

This version of the opening of *Blade Runner* was never shot. The beautifully conceived continuity is by Sherman Labby.

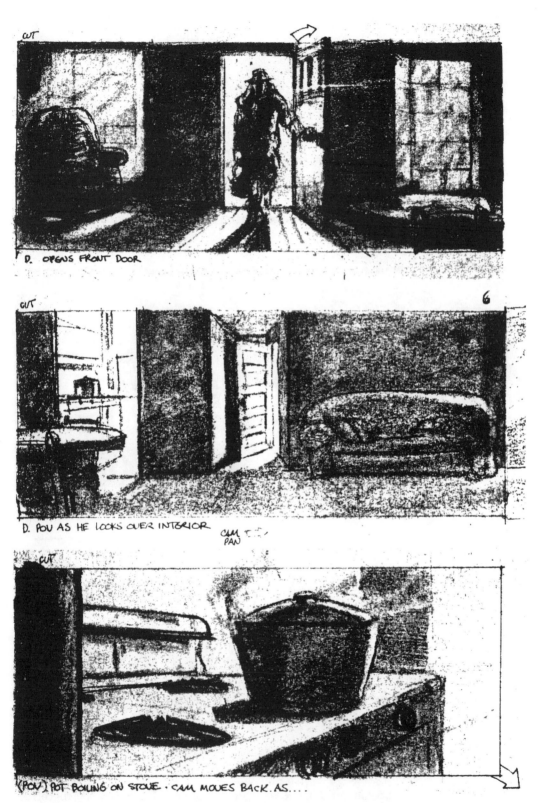

D. OPENS FRONT DOOR

6

D. POV AS HE LOOKS OVER INTERIOR CAM PAN

(POV) POT BOILING ON STOVE · CAM MOVES BACK. AS....

Sherman Labby's storyboard for *Blade Runner.*

... RVL D. LOOKING AT POT.. HE TURNS TO RIGHT.. CAM FOLLOWS

D. SITS - LOOKS OUT WINDOW

HIS POV OF GIANT TRACTOR MOVING TOWARD HOUSE

Sherman Labby's storyboard for *Blade Runner*.

MAN ENTERS - SEES DECKARD - DIALOGUE

MAN TAKES TAKES OFF GOGGLES..

MAN MOVES TO KITCHEN - D. CROSSES FRAME (DIALOGUE)

Sherman Labby's storyboard for *Blade Runner*.

RESOLUTION COMES TO DECKARD'S FACE

MAN COMES FROM KITCHEN WITH BOWL OF SOUP (DIALOGUE)

14

D. FIRES GUN AT MAN

Sherman Labby's storyboard for *Blade Runner*.

RUS. AS MAN IS HIT - HE FALLS.. DROPS SOUP BOWL.

HE FALLS OS AND OUT OF FRAME

17

D. STANDS OVER FALLEN MAN

Sherman Labby's storyboard for *Blade Runner*.

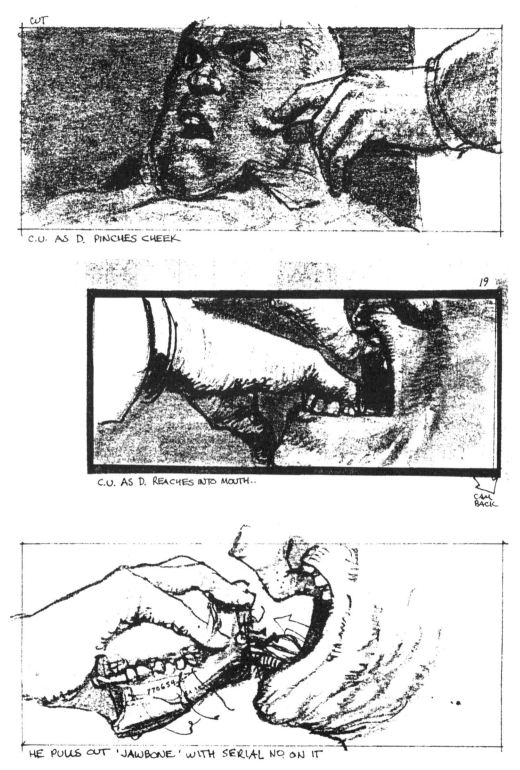

C.U. AS D. PINCHES CHEEK

19

C.U. AS D. REACHES INTO MOUTH..

CAM BACK

HE PULLS OUT 'JAWBONE' WITH SERIAL NO. ON IT

Sherman Labby's storyboard for *Blade Runner*.

HOLD AS HE TURNS- WALKS OUT OF HOUSE

CUT

HE WALKS ACROSS YARD- DOG FOLLOWS

D. WALKS TOWARD SPINNER FOLLOWED BY DOG- GIANT TRACTOR STANDS SILENT

Sherman Labby's storyboard for *Blade Runner*.

CAM FOLLOWS D. - HE ATTEMPTS TO PET DOG - DOG BACKS OFF - D. ENTERS SPINNER

POV DECKARD · SPINNER INT. RISES / MONITORS SHOW DOG TREE + FARM

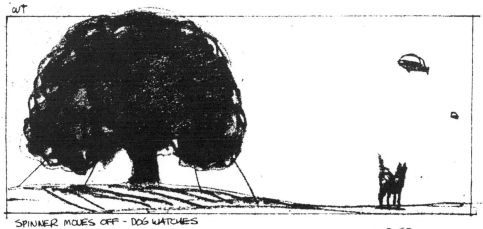

SPINNER MOVES OFF - DOG WATCHES

END SQ

Sherman Labby's storyboard for *Blade Runner*.

his drawing and cartooning skills in the animation department of Disney Studios before moving into their live-action division as a gag writer. For several years now Fred has been doing free-lance storyboarding on four or five films a year and is much in demand for his ability to interpret and write comedy and action sequences.

Interpretation

Above all, the storyboard conveys the shot flow of the scene, which is the combination of dramatic and graphic design. In the case of the best production illustrators it also conveys mood and tone, but practically speaking, the use of viewpoint, lens perspective and narrative motion are para-

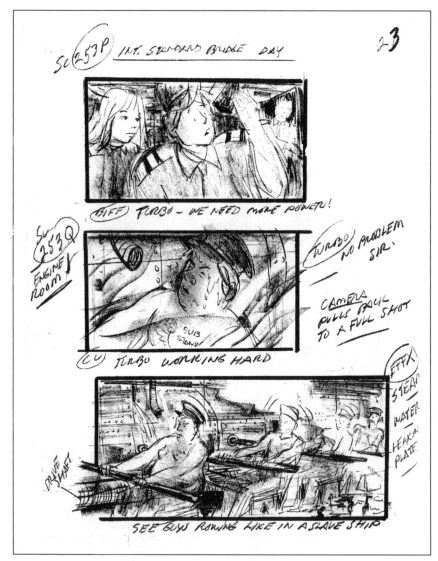

A storyboard by Fred Lucky. First of three panels.

mount. An excellent example of all of these qualities is seen in Harold Michelson's storyboards for *The Graduate* , beginning on page 67. The production design is by Richard Sylbert.

Even without a knowledge of the story, the action of the boards is easy to read and the cutting rhythm is clearly established. The individual and continuity design of panels 7, 8 and 9 is particularly elegant, with several effects cooperating to determine our relationship to the characters and to express Ben's point of view and daydreaming. The angular use of the frame is subtle and fully motivated by the staging, as are the dramatic backlighting and shadow effect on the water. This is visual storytelling of a very high order. Declaration of line and compositional statement are never used as an end in themselves, but are in complete harmony with the

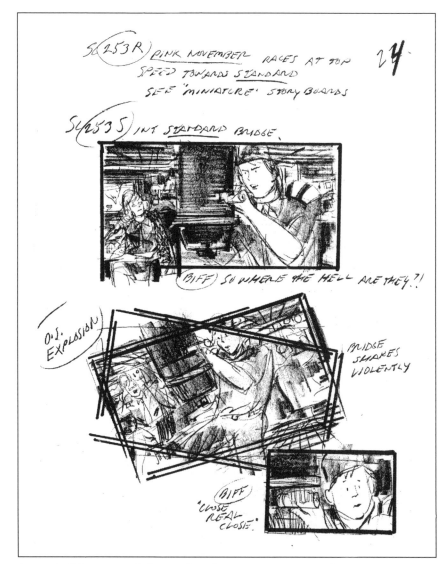

Second of three panels by Fred Lucky.

subject and narrative intention. This could very well serve as an object lesson in continuity illustration.

Adaptation

In a sense, all storyboards are adaptations, since they are transposed from a screenplay. Unlike a play or a novel, however, a screenplay is conceived as an intermediary form, a blueprint for the actual medium in which the narrative will appear. A screenwriter strives to be visual, to write drama that can be seen and heard, in fact, that needs to be seen and heard to be fully understood. In theory, the storyboard artist merely pictorializes the ideas in the screenplay, but in practice the storyboard may come very close to being another draft of the screenplay if only to polish some of the ideas. In the same way that screenwriters describe visual elements, some

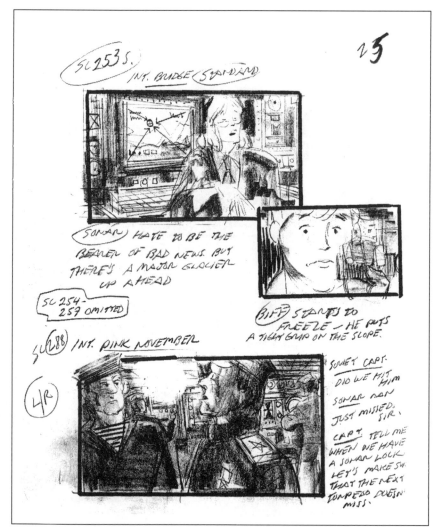

Third of three panels by Fred Lucky.

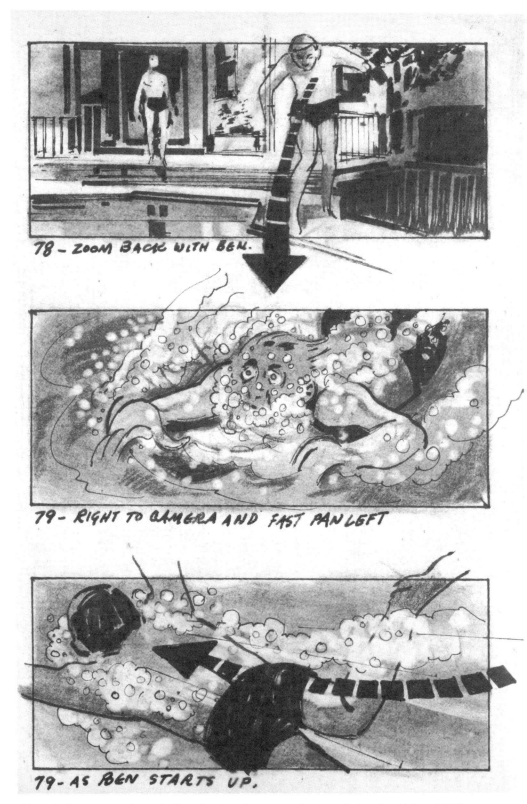

78 - ZOOM BACK WITH BEN.

79 - RIGHT TO CAMERA AND FAST PAN LEFT

79 - AS BEN STARTS UP.

Harold Michelson's storyboards for *The Graduate*. Production design by Richard Sylbert.

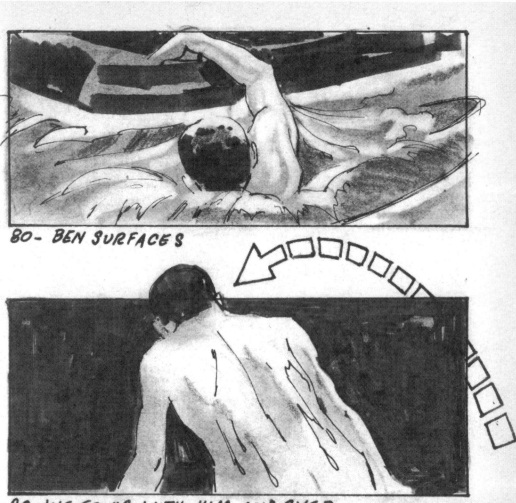

80- BEN SURFACES

80- WE GO UP WITH HIM AND OVER

81- INT. TAFT HOTEL ROOM

Harold Michelson's storyboard for *The Graduate*.

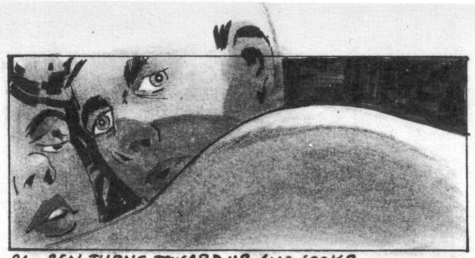

81- BEN TURNS TOWARD US AND LOOKS

82- P.O.V. SHOT... MR. BRADDOCK AT POOL.

83- BEN ON RAFT.

Harold Michelson's storyboard for *The Graduate*.

83- ... "GETTING OFF HIS ASS..."
   "THE ROBINSONS ARE HERE."

83

83- HI, BEN...

Harold Michelson's storyboard for *The Graduate*.

83- SAY HELLO TO MRS. ROBINSON, BENJAMIN

84- HELLO, MRS. ROBINSON

84- HELLO BENJAMIN.

Harold Michelson's storyboard for *The Graduate.*

storyboard artists suggest literary ideas, restructure scenes, add story elements and contribute dialogue.

To get a better sense of how a story can be shaped for the screen we can take a look at the way filmmaker Steven Spielberg adapted two scenes from J. G. Ballard's autobiographical novel *Empire of the Sun*. In this case, Spielberg is largely responsible for the conceptual content of the storyboard. Fortunately, we have several stages of the process to compare: The novel; two drafts of the screenplay, the first draft dated January 7, 1986, by playwright Tom Stoppard and the revised third draft dated September 12, 1986, by Menno Meyjes; and, of course, the storyboard. The storyboard by David Jonas begins on page 73.

The Novel

The story follows the exploits of an eleven-year-old British boy, Jim, living in Shanghai with his wealthy parents. The year is 1941, at the moment the Japanese invade Shanghai. Our first scene opens at dawn in Jim's room at the Palace Hotel. In the novel he is already awake and dressed in school clothes. He goes to the window overlooking the Shanghai waterfront along the Yangtze river. Jim watches two picketboats filled with Japanese marines and a motor launch of officers leave a Japanese gunboat. They board an American ship and a British ship. The launch flashes a message by signal lamp to the gunboat. Jim tries to signal back moving his arms in semaphores that he never quite learned in the scouts. Within seconds the gunboat fires a shell at the British ship and the shock wave rocks the hotel. Startled Jim jumps back to his bed. This is the beginning of the invasion of Shanghai and within minutes panicked guests are fleeing the hotel. Jim's father comes into his room and tells Jim that they are leaving in three minutes. Sitting on the bed Jim considers that he is responsible for the Japanese attack.

> He realized that he himself had probably started the war, with his confused semaphores from the window that the Japanese officers in the motor launch had misinterpreted.

The Screenplay

Here is Tom Stoppard's adaptation of the same scene from the novel. The scene opens in Jim's hotel room. This time Jim is asleep. He is awakened at dawn by the sound of a close flying plane. He gets out of bed and goes to the window.

The prolonged action of the Japanese marines boarding ships that appears in the novel is condensed in the screenplay to Jim's watching the Japanese gunboat moving in the river. He backs away from the window and turns on the bedside light. An exterior shot of the hotel lets us see the light in the window of the generally dark hotel.

We cut to a short time later and Jim is dressed in school clothes. He picks up a Latin Primer, which is near a small toy plane on a table alongside the bed, but is soon attracted to the action outside the window. The

Japanese gunboat in the middle of the river is sending a message to another boat with a signal light. Jim returns to his bedside and picks up a flashlight. Cut to a new shot outside the hotel. This is a wide shot of the hotel, the river and the gunboats. In the dim predawn light Jim's flashlight blinks in the window of his hotel room. After a moment of signaling, the gunboat cannons roar and Jim's room is lit up with a brilliant flash of light. Jim falls backward. Within seconds Jim's father rushes in calling his name.

JIM

I didn't mean it! It was a joke!

As it turns out the first and revised third drafts of the screenplay are essentially identical. We can compare this with the storyboard, which is a fairly straightforward staging of the screenplay. The major changes, the ones that make the scene truly cinematic, are added in the film. Beginning below is a condensed version of the storyboard.

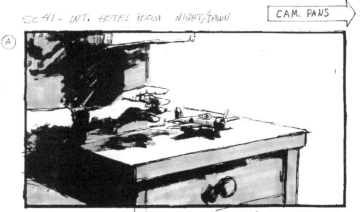

David Jonas' storyboard for *Empire of the Sun*.

SC 41B

HE LOOKS OUT OF THE WINDOW - CAM. PUSHES PAST
JIM TO REVEAL ---

CH-1c

SC 42

JIM'S VIEW OF THE RIVER. A FEW BOATS ARE MOVING -
A LITTLE EARLY MORNING TRAFFIC ON THE BUND - A FEW
RICKSHAWS ETC. CUT TO

CH-1D

SC 43 EXT. CATHAY HOTEL DAWN/DARK

JIM CAN BE SEEN LOOKING OUT OF THE WINDOW. WE
CAN HEAR THE SOUND OF A PLANE.

CH-2

David Jonas' storyboard for *Empire of the Sun*.

SC. 43A - EXT. SKY   DAWN/DARK

JIM'S POV - A JAPANESE FIGHTER   CUT TO -

SC 44. EXT - HOTEL - WINDOW.

JIM   NAKAJIMA -
    CUT TO   CH-4

SC 45. INT. HOTEL ROOM   DAWN

JIM IS DRESSED FOR SCHOOL - TYING HIS SHOE. ON A
TABLE IN F.G. IS A FLASHLIGHT AND KENNEDY'S LATIN PRIMER.
                                        CH-5A

David Jonas' storyboard for _Empire of the Sun_.

SC 45 A

JIM MOVES TO THE TABLE, TAKES THE BOOK, BEGINS
TO READ. BUT IS ATTRACTED BY LIGHTS BLINKING OUTSIDE.

CH-5B

SC 45 B

HE MOVES TOWARD THE WINDOW -   CUT TO

SC 46

LOOKING OUT THE WINDOW, JIM SEES A JAPANESE GUNBOAT
IN THE DISTANT B.G. SIGNALLING (FLASHING LIGHT) TOWARD A
BRITISH NAVAL VESSEL WHICH IS ALSO SIGNALLING.

CH-6A

David Jonas' storyboard for *Empire of the Sun*.

SC 46 A

HE TURNS BACK. CUT TO..

SC 47

JIM RUNS TOWARD CAMERA IN A WIDER SHOT.

SC 47A

CAM BOOMS DOWN

HE PICKS UP THE FLASHLIGHT. CUT TO..

David Jonas' storyboard for *Empire of the Sun*.

SC 47 B

THE JAPANESE VESSEL SIGNALS ... (CUT TO)

SC 48 EXT. CATHAY HOTEL DAWN

THE FLASHLIGHT BLINKING IN JIM'S WINDOW. CUT TO

SC 49 INT. HOTEL ROOM DAWN

JIM IS AT THE WINDOW, ENJOYING HIMSELF, LAUGHING
QUIETLY AS HE BLINKS THE FLASHLIGHT. THE LIGHT
FLARES AGAINST THE WINDOW GLASS. CUT TO

David Jonas' storyboard for *Empire of the Sun*.

SC 49A - EXT. CATHAY HOTEL

(A)

JIM LAUGHING, BLINKING THE FLASHLIGHT.

SC 49 B

(B)

THERE IS AN EXPLOSION. JIM'S WINDOW CRACKS - OTHERS
SHATTER. STONEWORK BREAKS LOOSE AND TUMBLES DOWN
THE FLASH IS REFLECTED IN THE WINDOWS

CUT TO —

SC 49 C

(A)

JIM IS THROWN TO THE FLOOR, STILL CLUTCHING
THE FLASHLIGHT.

CH-12A

David Jonas' storyboard for *Empire of the Sun*.

SC 49 D

JIM'S FATHER (VO)   JAMIE!

JIM (TURNING)   I DIDN'T MEAN IT!   IT WAS A JOKE.

CUT TO — —   CH-12ᴮ

SC 49 E

JIM'S FATHER .   GET DRESSED!

JIM   I AM.

JIM'S FATHER   WE'RE LEAVING   CH-13ᴀ

SC 49 F.

David Jonas' storyboard for *Empire of the Sun*.

Now that we have looked at all the sources for the scene—the novel, screenplay and storyboard—we can consider how the scene was actually shot.

The Sequence as Filmed

The scene opens with various shots of the Shanghai waterfront at dawn. Cut to the shadow of a plane on the ceiling of Jim's darkened hotel room. The camera pans with the shadow made by a toy plane Jim holds in the beam of his flashlight. Continue the pan down the wall and over to Jim who is dressed and lying in bed. The mournful sound of a ship's horn draws Jim's attention to the window overlooking the river.

New angle at the window with Jim. He watches the Japanese gunboat signaling the shore with a light.

Cut to three exterior medium shots of the Japanese crewman sending signals.

Cut to a wide shot of the river, the hotel and gunboat in the background. In this shot we see the two Japanese ships signaling back and forth. Suddenly a third light begins signaling in one of the upper floor hotel windows.

Cut to Jim's hotel room with him signaling with his flashlight.

We can pause here to review how the cinematic structure evolves. First, there is the use of the spotlight and the toy plane. Spielberg has condensed two story elements into a single image that graphically moves us to Jim. It's a choice evocation of childhood and it introduces the flashlight and the toy plane, which will become important in later scenes.

Another visual decision substitutes the flashlight for the semaphore signals described in the novel for the obvious reason that the light can be seen from a distance. This opens up new possibilities for shots. It is also far more plausible that Jim would imagine that he had inadvertently sent some provocative signal to the Japanese gunboat with the flashlight than with semaphores.

In the filmed sequence, unlike the screenplay and the storyboard, we never see Jim return from the window to pick up the flashlight. By introducing the flashlight in the opening shot with the toy plane, it is unnecessary to show Jim taking it from the nightstand. By omitting the in-between shots of Jim picking the flashlight up and going to the window, the scene is streamlined and the audience is surprised (but not confused) when Jim's signal light appears above the Japanese signal in the wide shot of the river.

Spielberg adds a final variation on the storyboard in the filmed staging. When Jim is startled by the gun blast and throws himself backwards onto the floor, the camera pans with him but leaves him in midair, panning quickly to record the moment he hits the ground in the reflection of three standing mirrors that are connected by hinges. One of the panels shaken by the blast swings inward and frames the doorway in time for us to see his father enter the room. Jim is reflected in two of the mirrors and his father is reflected in a third. In this way three shots are combined into one. This is so adroitly executed that the effect is all but invisible.

Empire used the talents of two production illustrators, David Jonas and Ed Verraux, who worked on the project for nearly a year. Using photographs shot in Shanghai, the illustrators worked at the art department in Spielberg's Amblin' Entertainment complex in Universal City. Like many of the production illustrators I spoke with, Jonas began working in production illustration in the Disney animation department, honing his drafting and storytelling skills before moving to live-action.

The *Empire of the Sun* boards, originally drawn to fill an $8^1/2$ x 11 in. page, are exceptionally detailed and show Jonas' wonderful compositional sense and figure drawing. This level of execution is as complex as storyboard illustration ever becomes, particularly since nearly every scene of the movie was illustrated with the same craftsmanship. Jonas and the other production illustrator on the movie, Ed Verraux, worked full time for nearly a year on the project.

Seeking a Career in Production Illustration

Storyboarding is a highly specialized skill offering little of the personal recognition artists in other fields can expect. To a great extent production ilustrators are hired to work out someone else's ideas and are then under great pressure to complete the work in a short time. For some, the collaboration with a good production designer and director and the opportunity to see their sketches turned into a great movie is sufficient reward.

Instruction

One of the reasons for this book is that there are so few film courses that include production design and production illustration. Though production illustration, in general, and storyboarding, in particular, are of value to directors, producers and writers, the subject is not offered at most film schools. Camille Abbott, the production illustrator whose work was included in Chapter 2, teaches a popular storyboarding course at UCLA called "Understanding Storyboards for the Motion Pictures," probably the most thorough training available at the present time. Unfortunately, it is the only course in the country dedicated to live-action production illustration.

Students are far more likely to find storyboarding instruction in the area of animation. The American Animation Institute in Los Angeles offers noncredit courses in storyboarding, life drawing, background painting and other aspects of animation techniques. The Institute is associated with the animators union, Motion Picture Screen Cartoonists Local 839, and the courses are generally taught by working professionals. Even if you are interested in production illustration for live-action, you will probably have better luck finding instruction in the related areas of animation, since at least some art schools now offer courses in this field. There are also a few dedicated animation schools in the United States that include design courses.

The good news is that traditional training at a fine arts or commercial art school is still a very good foundation for production designers, art directors and production illustrators. Many art schools offer courses in advertising art, which include television commercial storyboarding in the curriculum. However, the focus is usually on illustration technique and materials such as marker and mixed media rather than on motion picture technique. Though drawing skill is important, a production illustrator is primarily a film designer whose concern is really cinematography and editing. Courses in film history, technique and basic photography are, therefore, a necessity no matter how strong your illustration skills are.

Unions

There are only two organizations that specifically represent storyboard illustrators, both of them in California. First is the Illustrators and Matte Artists Local 790 I. A. T. S. E. (International Alliance of Theatrical Stage Employees) whose jurisdiction includes live-action storyboard art and production illustration. Most of the storyboard art appearing in this book is by members of this union. The major argument for craft unions in the motion picture industry is that they preserve the highly specialized skills of a small group of artists and technicians by providing some degree of job stability in a volatile business. Without the unions, many artists would have left the field to find work elsewhere during the slow periods, taking with them knowledge and experience that is unique to the field. To a large extent, some of this has already happened since shooting in the studio began to decline in the late '50s. In the past, the various trade unions prevented many new artists from entering the field, but today, the chief difficulty in finding work in any industry craft is the scarcity of work, not the pressure of the unions.

Today, the craft unions in the motion picture industry exert far less control than in the past, particularly since there are so many independently produced nonunion pictures made outside of Los Angeles. While the cost of making a picture goes up much faster than the rate of inflation, the main reason why even small motion pictures cost millions of dollars is due to the extraordinary salaries of producers, directors and stars, along with the expense of marketing a picture. Comparatively speaking, the cost of skilled union personnel is a bargain.

Local 790 is quite small with approximately 70 active members. Entrance into the union is not actually determined by the union, but is first dependent on the industry seniority system known as the producers' industry experience roster. To be eligible to enter the union, an illustrator must have worked 30 days under the terms of a union contract. The jurisdiction of local 790 is Los Angeles County, and while there is a San Francisco local as well, production illustrators are not represented by their own union in other parts of the country. Therefore, it is possible to obtain work on union and nonunion pictures throughout the United States without meeting the requirement of the production roster.

Finally, there is the Motion Picture Screen Cartoonists Local 839, also affiliated with the I.A.T.S.E., but this union only represents animators. Some production illustrators belong to both unions, and though there is a considerable overlap of skills, each has techniques and methods that are unique.

If you are interested in further information on these unions they can be reached at the following addresses and numbers:

Illustrators and Matte Artists Local 790 I. A. T. S. E.
14724 Ventura Boulevard
Penthouse B
Sherman Oaks, CA 91403
(818) 784-6555

Motion Picture Screen Cartoonists Local 839
4729 Lankershim Boulevard
North Hollywood, CA 91602-1864
(818) 766-7151

American Animation Institute
4729 Lankershim Boulevard
North Hollywood, CA 91602-1864
(818) 766-0521

4 VISUALIZATION: TOOLS AND TECHNIQUES

Photoboards

Storyboarding is not the only way to visualize your ideas before committing them to film. Another approach is the one taken in this book: photoboards. Their advantage is that they are easy to create and they share the optical and graphic properties of motion pictures. Depth of field and focal length decisions can all be accurately compared in photoboards, and lighting values can be evaluated. The disadvantage of this method is that models are necessary and scenes must be staged, however simply. The relative merits of storyboards vs. photoboards have a lot to do with the sequences being prepared: A small dramatic scene with a limited cast is ideal for photoboards, while an action sequence featuring large groups of people is more easily created with illustrations.

Video

The development of home video technology in the past decade has provided excellent opportunities for filmmakers to preview their ideas in very nearly the same format in which they will ultimately be filmed. Relatively inexpensive camcorders and home editing systems that permit clean edits are now available so that rough-cut sequences can be easily assembled, and, of course, the results in many ways are more refined than would be possible with a storyboard. Like photoboards, however, scenes must be staged for the video camera and shooting the videotaped version is certainly more difficult for the filmmaker than turning the storyboard work over to an artist.

Visualizing with videotape is particularly applicable to nonunion, independent filmmaking because actors are available to rehearse without significant expense. While your actors are rehearsing you can test visual ideas at the same time. If you don't already own a camcorder you might consider buying one. Camcorders are useful to the filmmaker in so many ways that you will not regret the investment. However, if you can't afford the hefty $750-$1,200 price for a new one you can probably justify the expenditure as part of the design budget for your film.

To take the previewing process one step farther, you can edit the test shots on your tapes into sequences. "Cuts only" (that means no dissolves) editing systems can be rented by the day, week or month. VHS, Super VHS and 8mm formats are available. Rental prices range from $800 to $1,200 per week. If this is beyond your means, the public access channel at your local cable system probably has an editing system that is available free of charge for nonprofit use. At one time, federal law required that cable companies provide an access channel with equipment and training for the citizenry. Since deregulation, cable companies don't have to comply unless a separate contract was worked out with the local municipality. Today, each cable company is a separate case, but with the rising cost of most cable services many companies have opted to continue public access to offset consumer dissatisfaction over rate increases.

Desktop Video

Multimedia has become the hot subject in personal computers (PCs). Sound, image and words are the media referred to, and while this may sound like the type of prediction heard at world's fairs, it's going to change the way we communicate. Following in the steps of the desktop publishing boom, desktop video (DTV) is the sound and image wing of multimedia. While desktop publishing was made possible by the laser printer, desktop video is really the confluence of new digital technologies—like computer graphics and compact discs—adapted from expensive dedicated computer systems to the personal computer.

Just what can desktop video do? Well, according to the visionaries at Macintosh computers (the current front-runners in DTV), just about everything. Since music, photography, video, illustration and film can all be digitized into a single numerical language that the computer can manipulate, the personal computer can be an editing console, a music synthesizer, a drawing board and a printing press.

Original art can be created on the computer or imported from various other sources, such as video, film, compact disc, photography, illustration and text. Once captured, preexisting art or sound can be manipulated with any of the dozens of multimedia software programs now available. If you have a VHS tape you can fly it into the computer, add titles or enhance the image with special effects or animation. Presently, the quality of affordable PC-generated video is not broadcast standard, but it is getting closer all the time. A wrinkle in the timetable might be the arrival of high-definition television, which will only widen the gap between PC quality and the new higher standards.

Articles in computer trade journals continually tout the latest television commercial created on a Macintosh. On closer inspection you usually find that the $6,000 personal computer was expanded with $15,000 (or more) worth of add-ons, and that the commercial was completed with far more expensive dedicated graphic equipment. It is true, however, that many major special effects houses, including Industrial Light and Magic and R. Greenberg Associates, are using Macintosh computers throughout the production and design process. This is where the PC is carving out a very practical niche—as a storyboarding and blueprinting system for film and video. A real advantage of this application is that the PC can generate very specific timing information that can be used to control more sophisticated graphic systems or motion-control devices once the creative decisions are nailed down. This is very useful for special effects and animation, where precision is crucial.

The state of the art in multimedia is changing so rapidly that predictions become fact every few months. Still, several products represent the basic capabilities of desktop video. Here are a few of them:

Storyboard/Animation Programs

Animation programs are designed to create presentations in business and education but are adaptable to more entertainment-oriented applications like storyboarding for motion pictures. There is a certain amount of overlap in these two uses, but differentiation falls along the axis of conceptualization vs. presentation.

Two major products, Storyboarder® by American Intelliware and Director® by MacroMind, represent the difference. Storyboarder was developed as a joint venture by the Cambridge Media Lab and the American Film Institute, which ultimately became American Intelliware, an independent California-based company specializing in computer programs for the motion picture industry. Storyboarder is designed to be a conceptual tool for filmmakers and it permits easy editing of sequences created in the program or taken from existing art. A comprehensive image library, or "clip file" as illustrators call it, includes line drawings of people, props and various settings. Fades, wipes and dissolves of varying length are possible as well as simple "animatic" type animation. Aspect ratios can be varied either to standard proportions or custom sizes. Storyboarder permits customized page layouts of individual panels and ac-

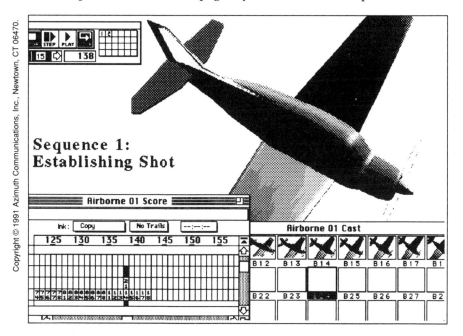

MacroMind Director can be used for storyboards, or corporate work. Here, an aircraft that was modeled in Swivel 3D Professional and imported into Director is being animated in a full-color presentation for a jury in a lawsuit. Windows open on various tools of the animator/director.

companying descriptive notes if desired. Selected images can be assembled on a spreadsheet-like master list, edited and time-coded for playback. Storyboards can be printed out as hard copy or shown in motion on the computer screen. There are many other features in this powerful program, which has been used by Brian DePalma to design *Casualties of War* and *Bonfire of the Vanities.*

Getting back to the difference between conceptual programs and presentation programs, Storyboarder was designed to be viewed by the production team but does not produce an extremely persuasive color presentation for an uninitiated audience. Macromind's program, Director, was developed for just this type of audience at sales meetings or for client presentations at an advertising agency. Director incorporates the refinements necessary for slicker business or industrial presentations, including full sound track capabilities. Text can be scrolled, rotated, skewed and manipulated with sparkles and other "wow 'em" type effects (suited to a corporate audience), and several typefaces are built into the system. The level of animation possible in Director and Storyboarder is fairly simple. Disneyesque human and animal locomotion is not yet available with these programs. Creative animators and filmmakers will find, however, that Director is flexible enough to storyboard television commercials, title sequences and scenes for films. Frames captured from video, storyboard art and photographs can be imported so that a sophisticated sequence can be preedited against a musical score and sound effects.

Both programs can create storyboards for motion pictures, and each has advantages. Storyboarder is considerably simpler to use and sequences can be assembled fairly quickly. Director, since it aims to compete with full corporate communication productions, is necessarily more complex and time consuming for the artist. The ability to import sounds and music is valuable, but then the soundtrack has to be created. This, by itself, is a skill apart from storyboarding and complex in its own right.

Storyboarder is better suited to the needs of the individual filmmaker and is sufficiently fast to be a realistic alternative to conventional storyboards. This, however, is not true of Director, which is more appropriate to the ad agency or corporate communication department where a full-time user is turning out presentations with the resources of a department behind him. Realistically, both programs work best when used with additional hardware such as laser printers and scanners, as well as ample memory in the computer and video output cards. These qualifications, like everything else in this field, are tied to the technology, so we can expect that computer storyboarding will continue to improve rapidly.

CAD Programs

CAD technology (computer-aided design and drafting) is well-established in engineering, architectural, graphic and motion picture special effects applications and is making inroads into set design in film and theater. CAD type technology and related rendering and design programs are responsible for the high-tech graphics we have been inundated by on television logos and opening credits for sports programs and many commercials. Basically, CAD permits a designer to construct a 3-D perspective view of any object he can imagine, then rotate the object in any direction. If the object is a house and the interior space has been mapped out, the designer can "enter" the front door and move freely through the rooms, seeing on the computer screen what he would see if the house were real. Since 3-D models of this type are constructed using architectural plans and elevations, simplified models appear as outlines without continuous form or texture. However, all this can be added so that every detail of an interior space can be rendered in full color, from wallpaper and furniture to the direction of light entering a skylight in the late afternoon. Given this capability, it is possible to use CAD technology to construct moving shots in sets that have not yet been built, or at locations that are thousands of miles away based on location photographs and measurements. In this respect, CAD is a highly advanced version of camera angle projection.

But even after these technologies penetrate the movie work place, traditional mediums like paint, pencil and ink will still be used since their particular tonal and emotional ranges are each unique and valuable. Ultimately, the finished drawings will be scanned into the computer to take advantage of its remarkable ability to manipulate an image in deep space.

The potential for this type of technology for motion picture design is obvious, and there are new computer companies who are adapting existing programs to the needs of the production designer. A leader in this area is ITAL, a California-based software and hardware reseller. In 1990 ITAL made presentations to the motion picture industry introducing CyberSpace, a new concept in 3-D design and presentation. Cyberspace is being developed by Autodesk, developer of the Academy Award-winning program, Renderman, and a major developer of other CAD products. One innovation of CyberSpace is the use of stereo head-mounted displays, which permit the wearer to move about in the computer-generated universe.

A related use of this technology has been developed by the designers at the Disney theme park. Extremely detailed scaled models of rides are constructed in three dimensions and then recorded (photographed) by a special computer rig. The computer interprets the information and makes topographical plans and elevations, complete with dimensions.

One of the most exciting of the new programs for filmmakers is Virtus WalkThrough, created by the Virtus Corporation. Product literature describes this new genre of software as CAV, computer-aided visualization. The designer begins by drawing a plan and elevation of a building or landscape in the program. In a matter of seconds this is projected into a three-dimensional color drawing that can be brought up full screen. Now here's the exciting part: You can enter the three-dimensional drawing in real time, literally walking in and around the room or building you have designed. You can change your speed, direction and angle of view while moving continuously. You can walk into the furnished room of a house and turn to look out the window to see a car in the driveway. As you move inside the room, the perspective through the window changes in accordance with your movement. If your house is set in the middle of a fully worked out lawn plan, you can go to a rear window and see the pool you designed. Stepping outside, you can go into the pool and look back at the house from a viewpoint just above the water level.

Of particular interest to the filmmaker is that the "lens angle" of the view can be changed within a wide range (15mm and 500mm). This can be done in a matter of seconds. Changing the dimensions of the rooms on the plan is equally simple. Let's say you have just strolled through the three rooms of a ranch house you have designed. You have scoped out dozens of angles but would like to make the living room wider. To make the adjustment all you have to do is return to the plan and alter the dimensions to make the 15 x 20 ft. room 20 x 25 ft. When you return to the perspective view, the room is rendered in the new dimensions with the perspective properly adjusted. You can add a window or move furniture just as easily. CAV technology is a major breakthrough and in time will certainly change the way films are designed.

Production Management

Programs are now available for every phase of the production process: scripting, budgeting, scheduling and the coding and organization of film for postproduction. These separate programs can be tied together so that scene numbers in the script will correspond to script notes taken by the continuity person on the set and sent to the lab and the editor. Similarly, budget information can be tracked relative to these other activities.

These products are only a small sample of the computer hardware and software available. The 1990s will most certainly be the decade when the computer becomes standard equipment for commercial designers and artisans of all types. If you're concerned that handmade work will disappear, consider the period in the late nineteenth century when many painters predicted that photography would make their craft obsolete. That of course didn't happen, although photography did alter the direction of the graphics arts. I will not argue that it has all been for the best, but in the final analysis, individuals of skill and talent are always at work carving out their view of things no matter what tools they have to work with.

An appropriate way to end this chapter is with an extended example of visualization using the storyboard from *Empire of the Sun*. This is a continuation of the several panels by production illustrator David Jonas included in the last chapter. Apparent in every panel is Jonas' ability to depict just the precise moment in the action to convey the editing and dynamics of the shots.

It is clear, however, that the storyboard serves to convey Steven Spielberg's visual style, and filmmakers familiar with his work will recognize some of his favorite effects. For instance, the reflection of Jim's face in the interior car window appears as a semitransparent image through which we can see the scene outside that Jim is looking at. This simple effect combines the shot, reverse shot editing pattern in a single shot.

The sequence begins moments after the last one (page 80), which concluded with the beginning of the Japanese invasion of Shanghai. Our new storyboard begins when Jim's parents leave the hotel and try to escape the city by car.

SC-51 J-

WIDE LOW ANGLE FROM STREET   AS YANG HUSTLES JIM AND
HIS PARENTS INTO THE PACKARD... (CUT TO)

TB-11

SC 52-

INT PACKARD~ ANGLE ON IGNITION SWITCH — YANG TURNS KEY~
STARTS ENGINE — (CUT TO)

TB-12

SC 52-A-

Ⓐ

EXT PACKARD... ANGLE THRU WINDOW AS JIM LOOKS OUT AT
THE CROWD STREAMING BY--- THEIR REFLECTIONS ON THE
GLASS...

TB-13A

David Jonas' storyboard for *Empire of the Sun*.

SC 52 A (CONT)

(B)

CAR EXITS FRAME .... (CUT TO)

TB-13B

SC·52 B

INT CAR ~ JIM'S MOTHER .. "WHAT ARE WE GOING TO DO?"
JIM'S FATHER "PERHAPS THERE'LL BE A BOAT ~ I'M SORRY YOU TWO...
MAX WAS RIGHT." (CUT TO)

TB-14

SC 52 C

EXT... ANGLE ON PACKARD AS IT CRAWLS ALONG WITH THE CROWD...
(CUT TO)

TB-15

David Jonas' storyboard for *Empire of the Sun*.

SC 52 D

EXT... ANGLE ON REAR WINDOW — JIM PEERS OUT —

SC 52 D (CONT)

HIS CAR PULLS AWAY FROM CAM FOLLOWED BY A SECOND CAR — (CUT TO)

TB-16~

SC. 53

AS THE CAR FOLLOWING JIM'S PACKARD PASSES UNDER CAM, SURROUNDED BY THE CROWD, A CONTINGENT OF JAPANESE MARINES ROUNDS THE CORNER BEHIND, FOLLOWED BY A TANK —...

TB-17A

David Jonas' storyboard for *Empire of the Sun*.

SC 53 (cont)

(B)

~. WHICH IS ITSELF FOLLOWED BY TWO MORE TANKS AND TWO
ARMORED CARS ~. (CUT TO)

TB-17ᴮ

SC 54   ←[CAM WHIP PANS LEFT]

(A)

CLOSE ON JIM'S FATHER, SWEATING NERVOUSLY — HE
HEARS A TAPPING ON THE WINDOW —
CAM WHIP PANS TO ~.

TB-18ᴬ

SC 54 (cont)

(B)

~ AN ENGLISHMAN AT THE WINDOW ~.
" THERE'S MEN IN THE WATER ~ BRITISH ~.

TB-18ᴮ

David Jonas' storyboard for *Empire of the Sun*.

SC.54 (cont)

(—)

THE ENGLISHMAN MOVES AWAY TOWARD THE RIVER. THERE
ARE MEN STRUGGLING IN THE WATER BEYOND, OTHERS HELPING
THEM, MORE CROWDED BY THE WATER'S EDGE, STANDING IN THE
MUD. SHELLS BURST IN THE WATER, THROWING UP GEYSERS

SC.54 (cont)

(D)

JIM'S FATHER'S FACE IS REFLECTED IN THE WINDOW AS
HE MOVES TO GET OUT OF THE CAR.
"JAMIE, LOOK AFTER YOUR MOTHER."   CUT TO—

SC.54 A

(A)

EXT PACKARD. THE DOOR SWINGS OPEN AND JIMS
FATHER LEAPS OUT INTO THE CROWD AND HURRIES
TOWARD CAM.   CAM PUSHES IN.

TB-19A

David Jonas' storyboard for *Empire of the Sun*.

SC 54 A

Ⓑ

~ TO JIM'S MOTHER AS SHE LUNGES PAST JIM,
CALLING OUT TO HIS FATHER –
"STAY WITH US!"   CUT TO ~

TB-19 B

SC 54 B

THE CAR BEHIND SMASHING INTO THE REAR BUMPER
OF THE PACKARD ~   CUT TO ~

TB-20

SC 54 C

INT. PACKARD REAR SEAT AS JIM AND HIS MOTHER
ARE HURLED BACK INTO THE SEAT.   CUT TO ~

TB-21

David Jonas' storyboard for *Empire of the Sun*.

5 THE PRODUCTION CYCLE

The production cycle for a film is like a long train pulling car after car of equipment and passengers. Once the train leaves the station—which is equivalent to beginning principal photography on a film—changes in the schedule are almost impossible to make. The only time a director is free to alter the direction of a film without penalty is before considerable money and personnel are committed. In general, this is the time when only the director, producer, screenwriter and production designer are at work on a project. At this point, the director must rely on visualization to determine the production decisions that will be increasingly difficult to change as shooting approaches. Just as important for any director is understanding how to integrate your personal visualization skills into the collaborative process of the production cycle.

More than anything else, live-action film is unpredictable. This is a creative virtue and a logistical liability—a virtue in that the unexpected is exciting for the artist and ultimately the audience; a liability because the expense and complexity of filmmaking can become a tremendous obstacle when things do not go as planned. Visualization is one way to reduce the obstacles even if the filmmaker takes his work to the edge. By developing ideas and planning their execution before shooting, the filmmaker is able to free his time and attention so that he can respond to the unexpected opportunities that arise throughout production from the first days of writing to the final cut.

Feature film production schedules, whether independent or mainstream, are relatively similar, though the specific schedule and creative assignments vary with the project and the amount of involvement the director has in the visualizaton process. In general, the director is responsible for the visual decisions that determine staging and camera setup. The theatrical environment of the film, including set, costume and prop design, is the responsibility of the production designer guided by the director's overall conceptual and thematic plan.

Most importantly, a filmmaker should devise his own method of working to implement his particular skills and strengths. That's why this chapter presents the production cycle as a flexible framework that filmmakers can adapt to their individual needs. It is also a practical guide to the creative process, since filmmaking is a supremely practical craft (even though a little impracticality may be a filmmaker's greatest asset).

Visualization works in two ways: first, as a process of inclusion in which the subject of a film is explored and ideas are collected and stored away, and secondly, as a process of simplification as the vision is honed, leaving only the best and most pertinent ideas. Whether your project is a big-budget feature or a small independent film, these two types of visualization can be adapted to the five phases of preproduction:

Scriptwriting

Production Design

Script Analysis

Cinematography

Rehearsal

The time allocated to each of these categories varies with the type of film and the budget. For instance, an action picture requires more design time than a small dramatic film. There is also the question of distribution and market. Any major release that winds up in the local cineplex is a fully budgeted union film with an ample (if not distended) budget and at least one full year of production time from the time the project is green lighted to its theatrical release. Independent filmmakers working outside the Hollywood system make do with fewer resources, particularly in the area of production design. For their trouble they gain a great deal of direct experience in every aspect of the filmmaking craft and a measure of freedom many star directors envy.

Former novelist and short story writer, John Sayles, earned the money to direct, write and produce his personal work, *The Return of the Secaucus Seven*, by writing witty, low-budget horror films. Working on a shoestring budget, he edited the film himself without any prior experience. This type of hands-on experience is worth any number of sessions with a professional editor doing the work for you. Many of the film school-trained filmmakers today have learned their craft this way and understand the filmmaking process from script to release print. This alone does not make a great filmmaker, but whatever other qualities are necessary, they are better served by a full knowledge of the craft.

PHASE ONE:
SCRIPTWRITING

The screenplay has remained a remarkably consistent form, following the division-of-labor mode of studio production by separating narrative and visual elements. For all the good reasons that can be given for following this accepted practice, in the final analysis there are no hard and fast rules for how a screenplay should be composed or its function in the making of a film.

The following quote from David Byrne's introduction to his published screenplay and storyboards for the film, *True Stories*, is a good description of the way in which the visualization and writing processes can be combined.

> The way this film framework was constructed was inspired a little bit by my work with Robert Wilson, by his working process. He often begins work on a theater piece with mainly visual ideas and then layers the sound and dialogue on top of that. I used a similar method. I covered a wall with drawings, most of them representing events that could take place in one town. Then I reordered the drawings, again and again, until they seemed to have some sort of flow. Meanwhile I assigned the characters inspired by the tabloid newspaper articles to the people represented in the drawings.

This approach is very personal and is dependent on the fact that Byrne was the principal writer and the director of *True Stories*. His script was not written in a style intended to convince a studio to buy the project, so he was free to compose his story in a way that was more cinematic, putting visual and verbal material on an equal basis. The film is not a conventional narrative (by Hollywood standards), and this is as much a result of the compositional method as the cause of it. Observation is the key word. Throughout the making of *True Stories*, Byrne sought material that was strongly reportorial and placed it in his stylized framework. The point is that the traditional approach to screenwriting, in which words precede the image, is not the only way to write a script. On page 100 are some of the storyboard panels drawn by David Byrne that helped shape the screenplay.

Memory and Research

The filmmaker who writes his own scripts can keep a file or scrapbook of images for each scene during composition. This material can be used as reference to specific locations or, in a more general sense, to evoke memories and feelings. This is useful in developing the dramatic content of the story and later as source material for design ideas during preproduction.

For example, if a story involves children, photos of a child's bedroom will contain ideas and images that will convey that world in a way that words in a script cannot. The pictures do not have to represent shots that the filmmaker expects to use in the film, but can be used to communicate the spirit and tone of a scene to the production designer or cinematographer. Shots of a child's toy box, posters on a bedroom wall or the general chaos of a boy's closet will contain details that are easily forgotten without the photographic record. Writers often develop back stories, or biographies, for their characters that describe their lives before the time frame presented in the story. By creating fully rounded characters with pasts, writers can create the present more easily, predicting in a sense the behavior of characters whose history they know. Photographs, pictures from magazines, newspaper headlines, postcards or a page photocopied from a

David Byrne made drawings like these to develop his script for the movie *True Stories*.

high school yearbook can form a visual back story. These real life details will help you imagine the grit and texture of your story during the long hours spent in front of a typewriter or word processor.

Connections

One tried and true method of organizing the structure of a script is the index card layout. Rows of cards, each representing a scene in a story, are displayed on a bulletin board. This permits the writer to see the overall structure all at one time. A similar layout can be made using images to go along with each scene. The images you find can be any kind of picture that sets the tone and spirit of the scene. You might use a David Hockney painting or a Polaroid you have made of friends at the beach or a 1958 cover of *Boy's Life*. If it stimulates other images and feelings that bring the scene to mind, it's doing the job.

A similar technique uses images that represent the idea of a scene from your script, but not the specific look of the scene itself. John Huston used this indirect type of communication while giving Katharine Hepburn direction in *The African Queen*. Dissatisfied with her conception of the role of Rosie, the spinster missionary, he suggested that Hepburn play the role as if she were Eleanor Roosevelt. This was far more useful advice than lengthy conversations searching for ways to make an individual line or gesture funny. A picture or photograph can be an equally evocative way of describing the tone and atmosphere of a scene. For instance, if your script contains two men in a mid-western bar in the 1950s, a photograph of the selections on a jukebox from that time and region will set the mood in a way a script could not.

Sound and Music

Visualization isn't just images; sound and music are also part of the process because they elicit images. Many filmmakers I know write to music. This helps them visualize the mood and tempo of a scene. Some film editors cut sequences to music they have selected even though it will be replaced by an original score later on.

Music is also an excellent way of communicating the rhythm and pace of a scene to the production designer or editor. This works even if you do not anticipate using music in the scene. A cinematographer and production designer may instantly grasp the feeling and even the cutting plan you're after from your choice of music. Could Stanley Kubrick have found a better description of how the opening space sequence in *2001: A Space Odyssey* was to look than the Strauss waltz that ultimately accompanied the languorous movements of the spacecrafts?

Sound effects are also valuable, and the street traffic and echo of a far away siren can help conjure images of city streets for a writer typing away in his suburban home. Cassette recorders are so small and lightweight nowadays that it's easy to carry one around to capture regional accents, snatches of dialogue, office sounds or the summer hum of the woods. An actor would call these sounds sense-memory cues, and one part of learning how to act is to heighten one's sensitivity to the world through observation. Filmmakers should do the same thing.

A Visual Sketchbook

Since a filmmaker must turn observation into images and sounds, spending time looking through the viewfinder of a camera is one way he can hone his skills. For me, filmmaking is a commitment to discovering how experience can be transformed into images. Being behind the camera is a necessity, so I'm always surprised how infrequently some filmmakers shoot films on their own. Super 8 cameras, camcorders, cassette recorders and still cameras for all budgets are so convenient to use that a filmmaker has no excuse for not getting out in the real world to practice his craft. The sounds and images recorded can serve as research, but are also useful exercises for sharpening your eye. Apart from any practical value they may have, image sketches are an end in themselves, documents of your way of seeing and, most importantly, of the things seen.

PHASE TWO:
PRODUCTION DESIGN

While scriptwriting answers many of the "what" questions of the story, production design answers the "where" and "how" questions of execution. The visual and aural research that the filmmaker gathered while writing becomes raw material for the plastic elements of film design. All the unconnected pictures and sounds that the filmmaker accumulated in his sketchbooks can now help to establish the mood and atmospheric detail of the actual film.

In rare cases, such as extremely low-budget or animated films, a filmmaker will do his own design work, but most of the time he collaborates with a production designer. The filmmaker begins the preproduction process by having conferences with his production designer, explaining each scene of the script as he sees it. If the filmmaker has researched his material while writing, he already has a great deal of material for the designer to look at.

Script Breakdown

Filmmakers frequently spend as much time finding ways to shoot things economically as they do perfecting the dramatic and visual elements of their films. Professionals in feature films are so accustomed to hearing the meter running that they are often unaware of how many creative options they do not consider because of cost. But contrary to what you might think, the budget does not always take precedence over creative concerns, and films do go over budget because the producer, director and sometimes even the financing entity feel that spending more money will improve the picture. This, however, is not done without pain or penalty.

At the beginning of the preproduction process the assistant director and production manager will do a script breakdown, which is essentially a logistical and financial forecast of the film. The breakdown asks the basic questions: How long will it take and how much will it cost? The breakdown will change as the creative team works out the specific plan for the film, but the total cost will remain the same and an increase in one area of production will mean a decrease in some other category.

The script breakdown and production schedule are the best argument for visualization. In almost every case, films are shot out of continuity to save money. This is the logic that determines the breakdown: use any actor, set, location or other resource as much as possible on any given day. Since actors are paid a day rate, it is very inefficient to bring an actor to the set to recite a few lines of dialogue for three scenes each shot on a separate day. Often the breakdown/schedule will require that the actor say all his lines for each scene he's included in on one day. Therefore the director often finds himself shooting a scene from the middle and the end of a picture on the same day. The only guide through this jigsaw puzzle schedule is the script. Unfortunately, this tells the director practically nothing about the individual shots that are being photographed on separate days even though they are pieces of a single scene. The script supervisor will maintain a thorough record of continuity for each shot and scene, but this is a record of what has gone before, not of what is to come. This is why a storyboard or some other type of visualization is so important. Even if it only serves to inspire the director to create new shots on the set, the director will be able to see the total action of the story.

Pictorial Design

There are really two types of visual design that a filmmaker must consider: pictorial and sequential. Pictorial considerations include set design, costumes, props, makeup and any element that is layered on top of a location and must be built, manufactured or otherwise obtained. Pictorial design is the film's environment. It has a great deal in common with theatrical and architectural design and is usually the specific responsibility of the art director. This highly specialized craft is quite different from the sequential art skills of the writer, continuity artist, director, cinematographer and editor.

Every creative team for a film works differently, and the director and producer will set the tone for the collaboration and the division of responsibility. The director will have specific requests for pictorial design, but the art director is often permitted a great deal of latitude under the production designer's auspices. The basic creative direction of a picture is determined in an ongoing process by the director, production designer and art director. After a great deal of discussion, production illustration begins so that concepts can be evaluated within the group.

Patricia Von Brandenstein, production designer for many complex productions including *Amadeus* and *The Untouchables*, is a strong advocate for the primacy of the location, the physical reality of the space in front of the camera in the design process. Though she is an accomplished artist who produces fully rendered conceptual drawings when necessary, she prefers to work out the sequential design of a movie on the set, walking through a location with the director and cinematographer planning shots and staging. The decisions made during the location "walk through" might be recorded in the script as a shot list or in rough storyboards, but the cinematic aspects of the scene were already determined on location.

In low-budget independent films, the production requirements are usually kept to an absolute minimum and sets are usually prohibitively expensive. In this case, production designers are more likely to go out and find workable locations that can be used with a minimum of dressing. Directors tend to be more involved on a nuts and bolts level with production design decisions on very low-budget pictures, partly because there is not an overwhelming amount of specialized design, but also because low-budget films are often made by director/writers, filmmakers with considerable hands-on experience.

Continuity Design

Continuity design includes the composition of individual shots, the staging of action, the choice of lenses and the order of the shots in the finished film. My personal view is that these decisions are the responsibility of the director.

Continuity design usually begins in earnest when several of the location decisions have been made. At this point, the filmmaker can begin to use storyboards. Not every filmmaker likes to use detailed shooting plans. Some filmmakers feel that adequate coverage is all they need to record a scene; others do not want to inhibit their improvisational technique on the set. Still others simply don't want the responsibility for the visual look of the film and leave the continuity decisions to the production designer, cinematographer and editor. Storyboards are not necessarily in conflict with all these goals, but if you are not comfortable with this tool there is no reason to use them. Apart from their practical advantages, however, they can be fun to work with.

Location Scouting

The first step in continuity design is to determine where individual scenes will be shot, including the decision whether or not to shoot in a studio. During preproduction, a filmmaker spends a great deal of time driving around with his producer and production designer (and sometimes the cinematographer), looking at shooting sites preselected by location scouts for final approval. At the location the filmmaker walks through the basic action of the scene with the production team, which might include the cinematographer, production designer, producer and storyboard artist. Ideas that seemed to work in the ideal, imaginary setting of the script may be impractical at an actual location, and often new ideas arise out of the details and circumstances of a real place.

If the director is a visual stylist, rather than one who relies solely on his production team to create the look of the film, he can shoot stills at this point, testing angles, compositions and different lenses. The filmmaker may want to invest in a director's viewfinder (basically a lens and viewfinder combined) for testing angles.

Personally, I would rather carry a 35mm SLR and a couple of zoom lenses on location scouts so that I can test lenses and angles. In this case, it's possible to purchase Kodak motion picture films spooled onto cassettes for your SLR. What you end up with are slides that are shot on the same stock you expect to use in principal photography, bringing your visualization that much closer to the finished film. Another worthwhile addition to your director's kit is a compass, which can help you determine the movement of the sun for lighting. I'll talk about scouting kits in the next chapter.

The Illustrated Script

When most of the locations are secured, I think it's very important that the filmmaker develop an overview of the film. One way to do this is to place photographs and/or concept sketches in the script to depict the overall look of each scene. Because preproduction is made up of a tremendous amount of detail, directors tend to lose sight of pacing, mood and the visual arc of the story as it relates to locations. Locations seen separately may appear very different when placed sequentially in a script. The "illustrated script" is one way to help the filmmaker gain a sense of the visual continuity of the entire film.

Overview Meetings

I like the idea of having the creative team gathered in one place where the research material for a scene can be laid out on the floor or on some other large work surface. Everyone should be able to reach down to rearrange the order of the pictures. This is like having a movable collage of research material: coffee table books, magazines, posters, sketches, location photos and concept sketches. For some reason this way of looking at ideas encourages the team to find unexpected connections between them. Inevitably, these visual discoveries have a direct impact on the dramatic content of the film as well.

PHASE THREE:
SCRIPT ANALYSIS

Every filmmaker will devise his own way of working with the script before shooting. Some filmmakers use storyboards while others write out a shot list or an aerial view diagram of the location indicating camera setups. There are many ways of turning the script into sequences, and your way of working may vary with the project. The suggestions that follow represent several methods of devising a shot plan or storyboard for a scene. They could best be described as a series of daydreaming sessions based on, but not restricted to, the script.

Let's apply the different methods of planning shots to a hypothetical script, *Appomattox*, based on the surrender of Robert E. Lee to Ulysses S. Grant at Appomattox Court House at the end of the Civil War.

After reading the script many times and working on a final polish with the writer, the director has a general sense of how most of the scenes should be staged. He has written notes in the margin of the script detailing specific ideas and ultimately transfers these to a separate notebook, which includes photographs, sketches and other reference material he has gathered. Later, he visits Appomattox Court House and other location sites and takes photographs at each place. Now the director is ready to begin working out the shot by shot plan for each scene.

Creating a shot plan means describing the staging of the action, the size of the shot, the choice of lens and the camera angle. If the director uses a shot list, it might read: "Wide shot, using a long focal length lens to compress the foreground and background. The camera is looking down on the Union line from a modest high angle with trees in the immediate foreground. The camera pans with a horseman who enters the right side of the frame."

These are all traditional descriptions of the graphic quality and photographic quality of a shot. The director, however, is ultimately interested in how the photographic qualities of a shot determine the narrative effect of the scene. The following exercise is a good way to heighten your awareness of the relationship between visual and dramatic elements by rephrasing traditional shot descriptions in dramatic terms. In the four categories listed below graphic qualities are matched with equivalent narrative qualities, posed as questions.

1 Graphic — Where is the camera stationed?
  Narrative — Whose point of view is being expressed?

2 Graphic — What is the size of the shot?
  Narrative — What distance are we from the subject of the scene?

3 Graphic — What is our angle of view?
  Narrative — What is our relationship to the subject?

4 Graphic — Are we cutting or moving the camera?
  Narrative — Are we comparing points of view?

All these questions overlap somewhat, but answering them individually is a technique that forces you to see the material in new ways. Now we can see how they might be applied to the script excerpts from *Appomattox*.

Shot Plan—First Draft
After the director has visited the locations a second time and made preliminary production choices based on the budget, he makes a shot plan

that is more than wishful thinking. He begins by taking the location photos and any other research material and spreads it out where he works. Next, an image list is made (not a shot list), based on the ideas that come to mind when reading the script. He can write these on index cards, one image to a card. This exercise amounts to free association and can include the director's feelings about the characters, how they are standing or what they are looking at or the look of the location. Sometimes a personal experience comes to mind that is pertinent. For example, the director remembers losing a fight in elementary school and the sympathetic look on the face of a friend afterwards. He writes this on an index card. Finally, the director includes specific shot or compositional ideas or thumbnail sketches if he has drawing skill.

Second Draft
Now the director becomes more specific. We will use script sample 1 from *Appomattox* to show one way the director might work.

```
1. EXT.   NORTHERN LINE AT APPOMATTOX CREEK — MIDDAY
We are behind the thin line of battle of the Northern
troops. They are remarkably quiet as the entire line of
men  watches  four  horsemen  under  a  flag  of  truce
approach across an open field. One of the horsemen is
General Robert E. Lee.  The line slowly parts to let
the riders pass.  The soldiers turn and watch Lee
travel down the slope behind them into the trees that
line the creek.  Several of the soldiers walk a short
distance down the slope to see the horsemen disappear
into the mottled sunlight of the trees.
```

The action describes the first stage of Lee's surrender to Grant. The lines of battle during the Civil War were nothing less than the boundary between victory and defeat, so when the Confederacy's greatest general moves behind the Union line it is an incredible moment. The Northern soldiers know they are witnessing history and very probably the end of the Civil War.

It seems to be the screenwriter's intent in this scene to see the events from the Northern soldiers' point of view. This is a valid choice and answers the first of our four questions: Whose point of view is being expressed?

Next we need to answer question two: what is the size of the shot, wide, medium, or close-up? Or, in narrative terms, what distance are we from the subject? This requires some clarification. I prefer to think of shot size in terms of distance since it discourages thinking of the shot size as a picture frame surrounding the subject. Actually, the frame is a three-dimensional box with the camera at one end. While we *see* the four sides of the frame we *feel* the distance to the subject. Because the camera is our point of view, the size of the frame tells us how close we are to the action or subject. In narrative film, physical distance translates to *emotional distance*. When we speak of shot size we are really talking about our emotional relationship with the action on screen.

Since the director has decided to make the point of view of this first shot that of the Union soldiers, the shot size/emotional distance refers to the soldiers emotional separation from Robert E. Lee. He is at the dramatic center of the scene. Though they may feel great admiration for him, and even sympathy, he is still their mortal enemy. For this reason the director's choice of shot size/distance never comes closer than a full shot of Lee as he rides past. He must remain inscrutable. The audience must strain to see emotion on his face. To achieve this, distance is required.

Now the director considers the angle of view. Having determined the point of view and distance, he knows that the camera will be placed alongside the soldiers awaiting Lee's approach. If the camera is at a low angle, it may cause some practical problems because soldiers may block the camera's view. At the same time, the director considers the experience of the men on the line to be communal since they are all intently focused on Lee and share the same concerns. Therefore, the camera should treat the soldiers as a group. For both these reasons, the director believes the camera should be at a medium high angle, perhaps 7-8 ft. above the ground. In this way, the camera has a clear view of Lee while encompassing many of the soldiers in the shot.

Finally, the director comes to the question of editing (cutting vs. camera movement) and whether or not the point of view should change. The director's sense of the action is that it should develop slowly as Lee appears in the distance and moves towards the Northern line. There may be shots of individual soldiers as the word spreads that Lee is approaching, but the scene is solemn and should not be rushed. Therefore, a sequence shot on a crane with the camera dipping down among the men for a close look before moving up again as General Lee passes would be a good choice. With this last decision the director has determined how the scene will be shot.

This is how these decisions might be written in the shot list for script sample 1:

"The camera is placed among the Northern troops on a crane or long jib arm. Camera viewpoint is along the soldiers' line of sight to Lee approaching at a distance. The camera starts low among the men as their attention turns to Lee approaching. The camera follows the group of men to the line of battle. The camera slowly goes up to 8-10 ft. as Lee passes by. Pan with Lee and other horsemen as they pass. Additional shots: Shots of men at various activities behind the line as they learn that Lee is coming." Figure 5.1 would accompany the notes.

As you can see the schematic drawing can only roughly approximate a dolly shot combined with a crane move upwards when we are dealing with a sequence shot. The choreography of camera and the subject (timing of the pan and the position of the camera when Lee passes, etc.) cannot be shown without notes. The schematic, however, enables the production designer, cinematographer, production manager and assistant director to get cast, crew and equipment to the right place. This plan outlines all the problems that the creative and organizational team needs to know. This is our first plan for the script; now we can try another.

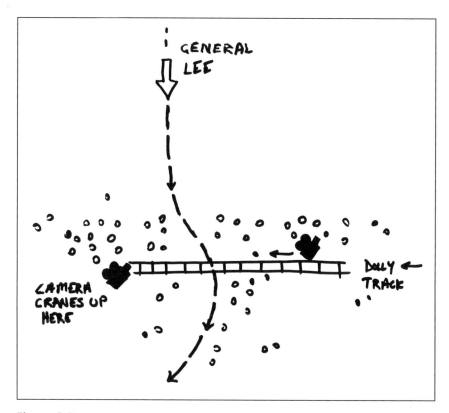

Figure 5.1

Moving on to script sample 2, the director shifts to another scene in a new location.

```
CUT TO:
```

```
2. EXT.   FIELD —  NORTHERN SIDE
We are on the side of the Union skirmishers who were on
the verge of clashing with Rebel pickets when a one
hour truce was called.  The advance line of graybacks
are seated in a field at the edge of a line of trees
facing the blue skirmishers who are seated in and on
both sides of a dusty road not quite 100 yards away.
The men on both sides can see each other clearly.  One
Union soldier sits near camera whiling away the time
poking his bayonet into an anthill.
```

This time the director doesn't analyze the scene but instead writes out the action written in the script. He plans to cut several shots together rather than use a sequence shot:

"Low angle of rebels in a field facing an equal number of bluecoats. Camera is on the Union side shooting past several of the Union soldiers. In the extreme foreground, a very young bluecoat passes the time by watching an ant crawl up the bayonet of his rifle, which he has plunged into an anthill. More and more ants come out. Across the field one of the rebels nearest the young bluecoat is watching him from a distance of about 60 yards. The young bluecoat looks up and the two soldiers make eye contact. Self-conscious, the bluecoat pulls his gun out of the ground, destroying the anthill. He then shakes the ants off. Cut to new shot from behind the rebel. The rebel sees the bluecoat raise his gun and thinking that it is some kind of boastful gesture, picks up his own gun and lays it

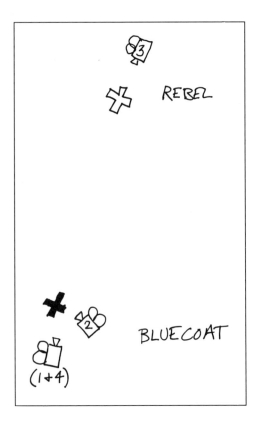

Figure 5.2: The schematic drawing at left uses numbers for each camera angle in the sequence. The numbers correspond to the storyboard panels that would follow this initial plan. The story-board panels appear on pages 115 and 116.

across his lap. He looks straight back at the bluecoat staring him down with a smile."

Shot list:
1) Profile of bluecoat alongside anthill. Rebel soldier in b.g.
2) CU anthill and bayonet.
3) Reverse wide over the shoulder (OTS) of rebel soldier and bluecoat in b.g.
4) Over the shoulder (OTS) of bluecoat and rebel in b.g.

Figure 5.2 shows how the schematic might appear for this scene.

Now we can move to script sample 3 and see how a dialogue scene might be handled. This time we are in a farmhouse with General Lee.

3. INT. PARLOR — BRICK FARMHOUSE — AFTERNOON
General Robert E. Lee, sits in a chair in a
corner of the room. He stares out the window.

Then realizing that he is staring, he begins
to look around the room, but this is nothing
more than a form of pacing. Even this is
studied, and no action or emotion is shown that
will betray his feelings. His military secretary, Lt. Col. Charles Marshall, a much younger
man, looks at a picture on the wall, taking his
cue from his general to remain impassive. From
time to time Marshall looks to see what Lee is
doing and finally takes a seat by the fireplace.

Standing in the front hallway is Lt. Col.
Orville Babcock of Grant's staff. He has left
Lee and Marshall alone in the parlor rather
than make small talk, which is uncomfortable
for all of them. Babcock is greatly relieved to
see General Grant and General Sheridan enter
the gate in the front yard. Babcock opens the
door and lets the officers in. Everyone stands.

                    BABCOCK
                   (to Grant)
              General Grant—

Grant barely acknowledges Babcock. His thoughts
are on only one man. He goes directly across
the parlor to Lee, who stands to greet him. The
two men shake hands.

                     GRANT
              General Lee.

Grant looks around for a chair and Lee sits in
his former place. Grant is distracted for a
moment as Babcock lets five other officers into
the room. They slowly file in and take places
around the room, and Marshall steps back to the
fireplace. Grant pulls a chair up and sits down
directly across from Lee. Grant tries to make
the moment less tense for both of them.

                     GRANT
I met you once before General Lee. I was
stationed in New Mexico, and you came to
inspect the brigade. I have always remembered
your appearance and I think I should have

recognized you anywhere.

>   LEE
> Yes, I know I met you on that occasion and I
> have tried to recollect how you looked. But I
> have never been able to recall a single
> feature.

This time the shot plan is not worked out in full. Since an interior scene with dialogue and restricted movement is more easily staged with the actors, descriptions consist of observations about the characters and how they might be revealed with the camera. The shot notes might appear as follows.

Shot plan:
1. Wide shot looking into room at Lee seated in the parlor of the farmhouse. In the foreground is Lt. Col. Babcock, a member of Grant's staff, who escorted Lee through the lines. Standing in the room near Lee is Lt. Col. Marshall, Lee's military secretary. Babcock is looking out the window, but he has also chosen to remain in the hall and leave Lee alone with Marshall. Babcock looks in at Lee who is adjusting his glove. We hear voices outside Off screen, Babcock straightens up.

2. Ext. Profile LONG SHOT of house and front yard. Slightly low angle. Grant is entering the gate with General Sheridan. He is walking fast and brushing dust off his rumpled uniform in a last minute effort to make himself presentable, but he doesn't break stride as he does so.

3. Int. Shot of Parlor. Camera is behind Lee at back of room. Lee has stood up to greet Grant. Grant enters the front door and walks straight to Lee. The two men shake hands. CUT TO:

4. REVERSE SHOT OF LEE AND GRANT as they shake hands. Marshall crosses frame and CAMERA PULLS BACK. Grant looks for a chair, Lee sits in his former place and Grant pulls up a chair for himself before Babcock can help him. Grant seems nervous. Lee is a study in composure. CUT TO:

5. MED. SHOT OF FRONT DOOR. Camera height 5 ft. Union officers enter quietly as if attending a funeral. All steal glances of Lee. Camera backs up with them, pans with one officer to —

WIDE SHOT OF ROOM. ANGULAR PROFILE OF LEE AND GRANT, FAVORING LEE. Camera height 4 ft. Hold this throughout the entire conversation between the generals (this is the master).

6. OTS LEE.

7. OTS GRANT.

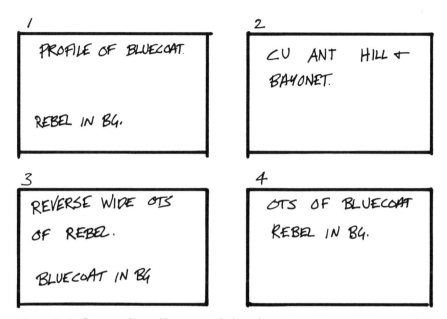

1 PROFILE OF BLUECOAT.

REBEL IN BG.

2 CU ANT HILL ↤ BAYONET.

3 REVERSE WIDE OTS OF REBEL.

BLUECOAT IN BG

4 OTS OF BLUECOAT REBEL IN BG.

Figure 5.3: This storyboard began with the schematic in Figure 5.2 (page 110).

8. CU LEE.

9. CU GRANT.

As you can see, there's no strict form. Notes, diagrams, shot lists—anything that clarifies what needs to be shot is useful. The only goal is to be concise and to the point while including all the important visual detail. Usually an overall description of the staging and visual action precedes the numbered shots. In this way, the cameraman, actors and crew will understand the general plan and purpose for the staging, so that when the numbered shots appear, the cutting and composition of the scene is clear.

Preparing a Storyboard

The shot plan the director just prepared is fairly precise. Now he's ready to turn this into a storyboard. One way to begin is to write out the shot plan in storyboard boxes but without drawings. This forces the director to think in sequence. For some reason, even a shot list seems to be more cinematic—closer to what will be seen on the screen—if each shot description appears within the borders of a frame. Storyboard frames of this type for the shot plan appearing on page 114 are shown in Figure 5.3, above.

Next, the director adds drawings or photographs. This could be thumbnail sketches or Polaroids. Figures can be drawn over any photos. The director has a supply of close-ups, medium shots and long shots of the principal actors. He uses these for his storyboard. He pastes the storyboard panels onto individual pages and places them in a loose-leaf binder so that the order of the shots can be changed. Figure 5.4 on page 114 is the

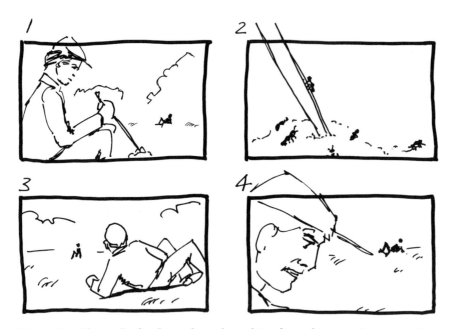

Figure 5.4: This is the final storyboard resulting from the script interpretation process.

type of drawing the director might make at this stage.

The director plays music while working with the storyboard and imagining the scene. Different music suggests different ideas. When working with a dramatic scene the director might record rehearsal dialogue and play this back while designing a scene.

It may take several films to greatly improve your visual memory by working with sequential art in this way, but your visualization skills will ultimately be sharpened. Longer and more complex sequences will eventually become easier to manage. You will find that your ability to judge what does and does not work (for you) has greatly improved.

Models and Miniatures

For a film like *Appomattox*, models are particularly valuable. The first scene in our sample script—Lee crossing the Union line of battle during a truce—involves hundreds of costumed extras, horses and special props like wagons and cannons. The logistical problem of staging a scene of this type is enormous, and visualizing what goes on behind the camera is as important as visualizing what the camera will record. The assistant director and the production manager might want to include access roads, generator truck, crane, dolly track and any other equipment that will be a factor in staging the action.

Planning the first scene of *Appomattox*, the director tries different groupings of the miniature figures, photographing each of them with a still camera. The director shoots several photographs, some with the framing he would like to see for specific shots, and other, wider framings to give an overview of the location. He also shoots bird's-eye views of the miniature set, which will be helpful in later discussions with the production team.

Once the director has the prints of the wide shot he can draw on them using a felt-tip marker. In this way he can indicate the motion of the camera or show what the camera sees in a pan shot. In fact, all the storyboard drawing techniques in Chapter 3 can be added to the photos to indicate motion, camera movement or staging.

The interior scene in *Appomattox* can be treated in the same way. The interior walls of the actual location or set can be photographed, printed and pasted on foam core like miniature flats. Figures and dollhouse furniture are added to the model. If you have a close-up lens, macro lens or a set of diopters, you will be able to photograph medium shots and even close-ups of the toy figures. Models are more easily adapted to large complex scenes, but the final judge of their appropriateness is whether or not the director has been able to perfect the scene without them. As with any visualization tool, its main function is provoking the imagination of the filmmaker.

PHASE FOUR: CINEMATOGRAPHY

It's not uncommon for a busy cinematographer to join the production team of a film only a few weeks before principal photography begins. This means he has to move quickly to learn the production demands of the film, which has probably been in preproduction for many months. Upon joining the team, the cinematographer immediately visits the locations with the director, reviews the storyboards, sets, props, costumes and makeup, possibly shooting tests of any of these elements.

Though it varies with each film, the cinematographer's major responsibilities are lighting, exposing the film and executing the framing and camera movement determined by the production designer, the director and the cinematographer himself. It seems strange to many people that the cinematographer does not have absolute control of the shot flow, but it is ultimately the director's call.

Communication between the director and the cinematographer is crucial. Some filmmakers show their cinematographers photographs, paintings, other films or any other visual source as a way of illustrating what they're after stylistically. Often an evocative description is all that's needed to give the director of photography the direction he needs. Naturally, this will provoke discussions and controversy out of which solutions and new ideas are forged.

In the final weeks before shooting, the director should have a precise understanding of the environment of his story, including sets, locations, major props, costumes and makeup. Evaluation of lighting and photography can be made at this time by shooting test footage of any of the design elements, making adjustments where necessary.

PHASE FIVE:
REHEARSAL

Among the pleasures of reading or watching fiction are the odd details and evanescent moments of everyday life that we often forget until we see them in a book or on the screen. Actors and directors store up these impressions through constant observation, and this is one of the things you hope to uncover while collaborating. Often the pressure of the shooting process gets in the way of tapping these small bits of behavior, which the actor must incorporate intuitively. When this happens, actors and directors tend to fall back on the obvious in their creative choices. It is the director's job to create an environment in which the actor can connect with his adventurous impulses and find the unexpected and unpredictable in their work together. It is this, more than anything else, that contributes to creative staging (and all other aspects of performance). Once the actor locates within himself the quirkiness of the everyday and makes it his own through action, the director has only to compose it within the frame.

Unfortunately, rehearsal time on most features is very short (sometimes nonexistent) as compared with live theater. If a full cast is assembled for two or three weeks before the film begins, this is considered extremely generous. By comparison, stage directors are accustomed to having three or four times as much rehearsal time.

Previewing Scenes

Once the actors are available to begin working on scenes, one visualizing tool stands out that is invaluable—video. Even a single viewpoint recorded during a rehearsal is tremendously informative. Placing a frame around the actors changes the way a scene plays, so the director will discover problems and opportunities that were not apparent before.

The structure and pacing can also be approximated with simple editing of master scenes. A rough cut of two or three consecutive scenes is easily assembled every few days using an inexpensive off-line editing system. Since the appropriate transitions (dissolves, wipes, etc.) and a temporary music track can be added fairly easily, the filmmaker can get a very good sense of the dramatic flow of the picture. Depending on the type of film, longer sections of the film can be assembled. Obviously, it's easier to simulate scenes in a small film than those in a sprawling action picture, but in any case the fundamental dramatic thrust of the performances can be previewed. The difficulty of honing a script and performances within the hectic schedule of a motion picture production was one of the reasons that MGM's head of production, Irving Thalberg, followed Groucho Marx's suggestion that the Marx Brothers test the routines for *A Night at the Opera* on stage before a live audience before filming began.

In addition to previewing dramatic elements, the specifics of camera angles and staging can also be refined. If possible, working at the location site is ideal but not absolutely necessary. If a rehearsal space is used, the floor can be marked off with masking tape indicating doorways and furniture so that the actors have the general sense of the layout of an actual location. If props are available, or the appropriate furniture can be found, this is better still. An actor is motivated by the detail of a place. Any prop that can be easily included to give the rehearsal space reality is a plus. If a scene takes place in a diner, go to a diner during off hours with the actors. Usually no one will object to your having an assistant set up a VHS camcorder. Scenes in cars, bedrooms, parks, a lawyer's office or any other relatively simple setting are easily recorded. Video previewing is also an excellent way to permit your actors to improvise ideas for the script. Once recorded, a new line of dialogue or a gesture is preserved and can be added to the script.

If you are using a sketch artist to do boards it might be useful for him or her to attend the rehearsals from time to time or to view the rehearsal tapes. If a rehearsal room is used to simulate a location not yet available—for example, a busy shopping mall interior—the artist will be able to add the background in his drawings.

This brings us to the final stages of the production cycle, and at this point you are into principal photography. Visualization continues, though by now the director has previewed so many versions of the script that he can fluidly improvise if he so chooses. Much of the time things will be shot according to a definite plan, and the director and crew will have the storyboard on set to refer to. Ed Verraux, a production illustrator turned art director, who storyboarded several of Steven Spielberg's movies, told me highly rendered boards for each shooting day were displayed on the set for the crew to see. As each shot was accomplished it was checked off.

Postproduction

Finally, the editor receives the storyboards and camera notes from the continuity person. (The editor may have been involved in storyboard conferences at some point.) In some instances, the editor is rough cutting during the making of the picture and may be on location with his flatbed. A 1-4 minute dialogue sequence, shot in one day, can often be rough-cut after the film returns from the lab. Electronic editing can speed up the assembly process; however, additional time is needed at the lab to transfer the footage to tape.

Storyboards can also be used in editing by drawing panels based on actual footage. I have used this method several times when cutting on a flatbed editing table. By placing a sheet of paper over the screen on the flatbed, I am able to quickly trace individual panels for each shot. The shots are then laid out on the floor in rows. I keep rearranging the order until the graphic flow seems to work smoothly. This saves an enormous amount of trial and error when splicing the actual film.

Research Tools and Materials

There are several basic tools a filmmaker should own for visualizing his film and as a way of keeping his technique sharpened. We've already spoken about several of them: the director's finders, video cameras and still cameras. Here are some further thoughts on the subject. The 35mm SLR is still the most indispensable tool a filmmaker can own. Nearly all the motion picture lenses described in this book have equivalents in the 35mm SLR format. If you own two zoom lenses in popular ranges such as 30-80mm and 80-200mm they will cover most of the situations you will encounter in filmmaking. If any additional lenses are needed, it will probably be at the wide end, and 28mm and 24mm primes will be the most useful. New and better zoom lenses are coming out all the time and you may find a range of focal lengths that is better for your needs. Since I have been a professional photographer for many years, my kit includes lenses from 17mm to 1000mm and a variety of close-up diopters and filters. Frankly, this is a heavy load for scouting, and because I usually know in advance what lenses I will use for a proposed scene, some of the equipment stays packed away as I hike around a set or location. However, at one time or another each lens I own comes in handy.

Polaroid cameras are useful for location work, and the amateur models are cheap and convenient. For more demanding work the 6OO SE professional model has three interchangeable lenses and manual aperture, shutter speed and focus controls. A few years ago, I resurrected an old SX 70 (now discontinued) because it could focus down to 1 ft., permitting instant, extreme close-up photography. Polaroids are also useful for storyboarding if you need a reference shot fast. You need only step outside into the driveway to get a shot of a car or a low angle of a house or a shot of a model or any other subject you require for reference.

If you're interested in an enhanced Polaroid camera for visualizing, you might want to contact the 4 Designs Company at 6531 Grosse Point Ave., Canoga Park, CA 91307, (818) 716-8540, for literature describing their complete product line. They specialize in rebuilding and modifying discontinued Polaroid cameras to accept the newer pack film. The advantage to the older Polaroid cameras is that they permit manual shutter and exposure control. Still photographers have been using these cameras for years for testing exposure and lighting, particularly for strobe sources. 4 Designs also builds additional features into the cameras, such as multiple exposure capability or fitting standard "PC" strobe connections to the shutter.

I like to shoot slide film, so a light box is a valuable way to look at a day's work. Fairly inexpensive $60 - $200 color-corrected boxes are available that permit the viewing of 25 to 150 slides. Light boxes allow you to easily arrange and rearrange sequences.

Scouting Kits

Your kit should include a compass, the camera or cameras of your choice, extra film, a minicassette recorder for notes, pad and pencil, measuring tapes (up to 50 ft.) and a plastic bag to cover your equipment in case of a sudden downpour (it's happened to me on horseback, miles from the stable). Art director, Harold Michelson, told me he carries an infrared measuring device so that he can calculate the height of tall ceilings or other inaccessible places.

Part II

Elements of the Continuity Style

6 COMPOSING SHOTS: SPATIAL CONNECTIONS

Shot Size

As we all know, the universal units of composition are the long shot, the medium shot, and the close-up. These shots are a development of the continuity system insofar as they are overlapping portions of a single space and only make sense in relation to one another. That is, they are used together to create a consistent spatial/temporal order. Though they can be used to describe spaces as large as the solar system or as small as the head of a pin, we always know approximately how large an area is being framed when these terms are used. That's because the shots are scaled to the subject and related to one another proportionately.

A long shot of the World Trade Center frames all of the twin towers and a generous piece of Manhattan; a medium shot of the building would lop off some of the lower floors. Moving in for a close-up, a single window might fill the frame. There are no absolute rules in the use of these terms and even the terms themselves vary. In Figure 6.1 on page 122 the basic framing heights are shown for the human figure.

The change of size from shot to shot varies but is determined by the limits of identification. As long as we recognize that each shot is an overlapping portion of the wide shot, the change in scale is permissible. Actually, even this definition must take into account the change in editing styles over several decades. The move from wide shot to close-up was considered too radical a jump for audiences during the first five decades of motion pictures unless a medium shot was used in between. Hollywood editors were forbidden to juxtapose a wide shot with a close-up lest they confuse the audience as to where the close-up was taking place. Today, after several decades of familiarity with Hollywood conventions, audiences easily accept extreme changes in scale. If anything, it is likely that the conservative editing rules of the past lagged behind audience understanding.

Visual recognition between shots, however, is only half the strategy of the continuity style. Most often the relationship between shots is one of implication or inference. For example, we see a wide shot of a man approaching a door. This is followed by a cut to an extreme close-up of the man's hand turning the doorknob. Even if the doorknob was too small to attract our attention in the wide shot, we *expect* that it is connected to the previous shot since it makes logical sense, even though we could be looking at another doorway in a different place and time. Narrative logic and the visual connection between shots cooperate to create a

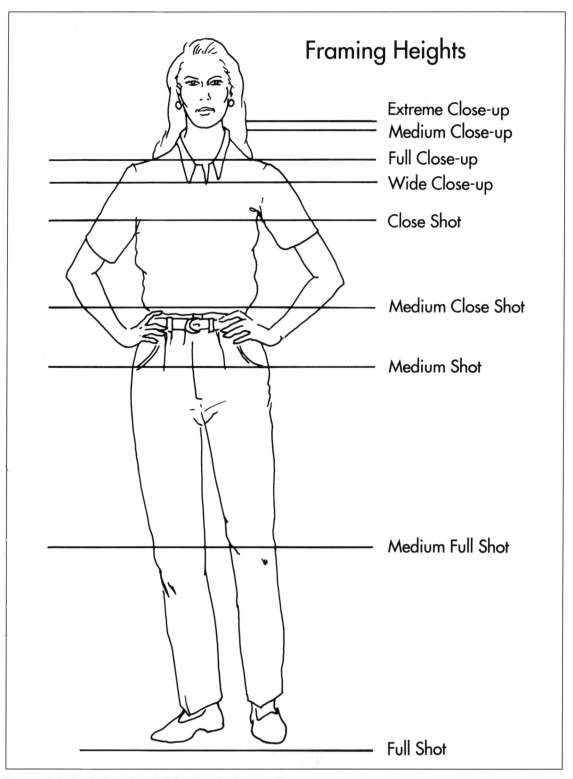

Figure 6.1: Basic Framing heights for the human figure.

sense of continuous space. This pair of ideas, cause and effect and spatial recognition, provide the organizational basis of the continuity style.

Long shots, medium shots, and close-ups can describe any subject or location but are most often used to describe the human figure. The terms take on special meaning in this connection. Here the change in scale between shots is not related by logic or visual recognition alone. Instead, framing is determined by conventions of post-Renaissance art or what are generally considered pleasing and balanced compositions.

The Close-up

Television has greatly increased the use of the close-up. To compensate for the small size of the screen, the close-up is used to bring us into closer contact with the action. For dialogue sequences the shoulder-and-head shot has become the predominant framing. Cost-minded producers like the tighter shots because they are easier to light and can be joined to almost any other shot, reducing the amount of coverage needed. The preference for the close-up has been carried over to feature films as more and more film directors graduate from television to the big screen.

In film the eyes have it. Jean-Luc Godard once said that the most natural cut is the cut on the look. The powerful suggestiveness of this gesture helps explain film's love affair with winks, glances, stares, tears, squints, glares and the whole range of language that the eyes command. The eyes are perhaps the most expressive feature of the human face, communicating silently what the mouth must do largely with words and sounds. A look can tell us that an object out of frame is of interest, and it can tell us in which direction the object is located. In the same way that the focal length of the lens and the angle of the camera can place the viewer in a definite relationship with the subjects on the screen, the eye-line of a subject clearly determines spatial relations in the scene space. Viewers are particularly sensitive to incongruities in the sight lines between subjects who are looking at each other and in most situations can easily detect when the eye match is slightly off. The use of lens-axis teleprompters has come about largely because audiences are aware when a performer is looking at a cue card that is only a few inches off center.

The close-up can bring us into a more intimate relationship with the subjects on the screen than we would normally have with anyone but our closest friends or family. Sometimes this capacity for inspection can be overdone, and the close-up becomes a violation of privacy by forcing a degree of intimacy that should only be shared by consent. The camera, however, does not require consent, particularly if it is equipped with a telephoto lens. Television news cameramen frequently pry into the lives of families during moments of grief, using extreme close-ups. Viewers may find themselves uncomfortable watching scenes that they would normally have the tact to turn away from in their daily lives.

In every culture there are customs of privacy, physical contact and accepted behavior based on the distances permitted between people in various situations. A filmmaker can use the camera to record these social distances in such a way that we react to them as if they were happening within our own personal space. Not only can the close-up reveal the intimate, it can make us feel as if we are intruding on moments of privacy or sharing a moment of vulnerability—as if the person on the screen has opened himself up to us. We can be made to feel detachment or an emotional involvement with events and subjects on the screen largely through the manipulation of space with the lens of the camera.

Figure 6.2 features a series of eight close-up framings in three aspect ratios, Academy aperture, which is the same as 16mm and television (1.33:1); wide screen (1.85:1); and the anamorphic Cinemascope process (2.35:1).

The images are shown in pairs as they might appear together in a sequence because the balance or imbalance of any frame is dependent on the shots that come before and after it. In the first two frames the subjects are positioned dead center. If you move your eyes over these frames, "reading" them as though they were edited, you will see that there is no rhythm in the shot change since the eyes remain focused on the center of the screen. Compare this with frames 3 and 4. Here the off-center compositions in alternate close-ups creates a left/right eye motion that is dynamic. This effect becomes more pronounced as the width of the screen increases. Here we have a good example of what is meant by sequential art, since compositions are not judged individually but by how they combine in a sequence.

Conventions in western art favor portraits that position the human face slighty off-center to avoid disturbing symmetrical compositions. The customary solution is to leave extra space on the side of the screen the subject is looking at and more space at the bottom of the frame than at the

Figure 6.2: Close-ups in three aspect ratios.

top. In film, the use of off-center compositions becomes more common as the screen widens. But don't let this stand in the way of experimentation. There is no reason for filmmakers to accept these limitations if they do not suit their sense of design. The following examples illustrate common and uncommon framing proportions.

Extreme use of screen width is possible as shown in Figure 6.3, illustrating unconventional treatments of portrait composition. Sharply off-center framing is possible in any aspect ratio though the effect becomes more pronounced the wider the screen. This type of composition has become quite common in television commercials recently, influenced by print graphics in advertising. This has had a subtle influence on the movies, which tend to absorb techniques from the other arts.

The eyes, mouth and ears are frequently given extreme close-ups of their own, usually to advance some specific part of the narrative. For example, a shot of a woman walking home alone at night on a lonely street might be followed by an extreme close-up of her ear, as faint footsteps are heard. A similar setup might utilize a close-up of her eyes indicating her fear. These are familiar devices and there are many more ways that you can utilize macro close-ups if you begin to experiment. Three versions of extreme and macro close-ups are shown in Figure 6.4 on page 128. In all cases, the viewpoint was from the front or side of the face

Figure 6.3

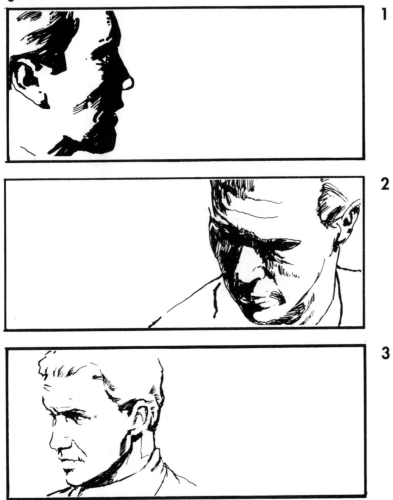

1

2

3

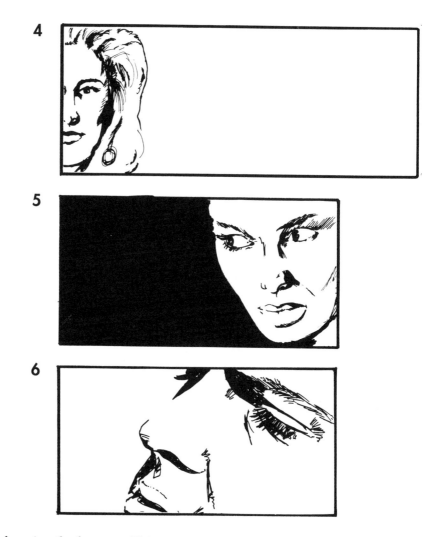

favoring the features. This is just one more convention that need not limit your individual style. Unconventional viewpoints, framing and shot size can be used to explore portraiture through texture, light and the infinite varieties of form. This does not mean that you have to give up traditional methods. They are by no means exhausted and can be as communicative, startling and moving as more experimental techniques.

The Medium Shot

Before television began emphasizing the use of the close-up and extreme close-up, the medium shot was the workhorse for dialogue scenes throughout the sound period. Combining valuable qualities of the full shot and the close-up, it is still widely employed in television and feature films. Like the full shot, the medium shot captures an actor's gestures and body language, but is still tight enough to include subtle variations in facial expression.

The medium shot is also the general range in which group shots are

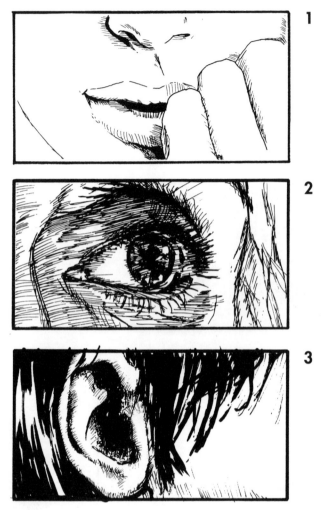

Figure 6.4

composed for dialogue scenes. The two-shot, three-shot, four-shot or five-shot are the typical groupings. With more than five players in the frame the camera often must pull back into the full-shot range to include everyone if the figures are not significantly overlapped. The medium shot shares the honors with the close-up for popularity at the present time but only insofar as it is used in conjunction with close-ups—not as the primary setup for a scene. We will pass over examples of medium shots in this section and cover them in depth later in the workshop section of the book.

The Full Shot

The full shot as an alternative to the medium or close-up has fallen into disuse in the last twenty years, relegated to the function of an establishing shot when it is necessary to connect a character and a location in a single shot. Filmmakers seem to be reluctant to play a scene wide if a close-up or medium shot can be substituted. One of the reasons the full shot is underused is that it requires dialogue scenes to be played in long takes. This is because the full shot usually frames all the speaking characters in a scene, making a cutting pattern of medium and close-up shots unnecessary. If the long shot is used with these two tighter framings, the editing pattern invariably moves in close and does not return to the full shot. While the medium and long shots can encompass the action in a scene without resorting to other shots to fulfill the narrative, a close-up generally must be accompanied by other close-ups, medium or full shots to fulfill the narrative requirements of a scene.

One of the full shot's most attractive qualities is that it allows the actor to use body language. This type of physical expression has all but disappeared from the movies since the silent period. Again, television and tight-fisted producers are to blame since there is nothing as inexpensive to shoot or to light as the close-up. This is most clear in the way dance is photographed in music videos, which rarely show the full figure in extended shots.

Compositionally, the long shot of a single figure offers many of the same opportunities for asymmetrical framing as the close-up. The vertical line of the standing figure easily fits into designs that stress graphic patterns particularly in the wider formats.

Figure 6.5 on page 130 features two full shots illustrating frame balance. Slightly off-center framing is so common today that a centered subject is nearly as powerful as a drastically decentered composition.

The Line of Action

The general approach in this book is to encourage the development of solutions that are adapted to the individual needs of the filmmaker. Many of the solutions that will be shown are part of recognizable strategies, but the filmmaker's personal vision can at any time overrule systems, accepted practice, traditional wisdom or convention. Having said that, we can look at the most basic rule of camera placement that the continuity system observes: the line of action.

The purpose of the line of action is quite simple: It organizes camera angles to preserve consistent screen direction and space. It's also useful for organizing the shooting plan. Because the set has to be relit every time the camera is moved to a new angle, it makes sense to gang shots sharing a similar angle of view together, so that they can be shot at one time. This avoids having to light any camera position more than once.

We can think of the line of action as an imaginary partition running through the space in front of the camera. It was originally devised to make sure that if multiple angles of a scene were shot, they could be cut together without a confusing reversal of left and right screen space. This way, subjects moving through the frame in one shot continue in the same direction in a subsequent shot. The line of action is also called the "180-degree rule" or the "axis of action," illustrated in Figure 6.6 on page 131. To maintain consistent screen direction of the two people seated at the table, the continuity system proposes that an imaginary line of action be drawn

Figure 6.5: Frame balance.

between them. The direction of the line can be anywhere the filmmaker chooses, but it is usually the line of sight between subjects featured in a scene. Once the line is determined, a working space of 180 degrees (the gray semicircle) is established. For any scene or sequence, only camera positions within the established semicircle are permitted. The result is that the screen direction of any shots obtained from one side of the line will be consistent with each other. This is illustrated in Figure 6.7, which shows the shots obtained with cameras A, B and C of Figure 6.6. Camera positions that are outside the gray working space are said to be *across the line* or *over the line*. Figure 6.8 shows what happens if we edit shots from both sides of the line together, in this case, cameras A and F. The result is that the man is looking at the back of the woman's head.

The Triangle System

When the line of action is in use, another convention, the triangle system of camera placement, is a shorthand way of describing camera positions on one side of the line. The system proposes that all the basic shots possible for any subject can be taken from three points within the 180-degree working space. Connecting the three points, we have a triangle of

Camera
A

Camera
C

Camera
B

Figure 6.6

A

B

C

Figure 6.7

A

F

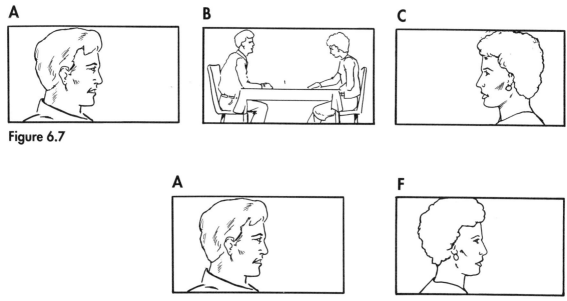

Figure 6.8

variable shape and size depending on the placement of the cameras. Any shot can be joined to any other shot in the triangle system of setups. The system includes all the basic shot sizes and camera angles used for dialogue scenes in the continuity style. The triangle system is employed for all types of situations, including single subjects and action scenes. It is used extensively for live television programs such as quiz shows, sports programs and sit-coms. Even though three cameras are pictured in the following examples, a single camera can be moved to each point along the triangle and the different setups obtained individually. This is often the case in feature films. However, the triangle system lends itself to the multiple camera setup as long as extensive staging or camera movement is not required. This would create the problem of one camera moving in front of another. There are five basic camera setups that can be obtained within the triangle: Angular singles (medium shots or close-ups), master two-shots, over-the-shoulder shots, point-of-view singles (medium shots or close-ups) and profile shots.

In Figure 6.9, camera positions A and C are angular shots of the two subjects seated at the table. Position B is a two-shot. The framings accompanying each camera position, of course, could be varied, and the shot size for cameras A and C can be any size from an extreme close-up to a full shot.

Figure 6.10 is the second triangle setup for over-the-shoulder shots. Cameras A and C are moved into the over-the-shoulder position. Camera

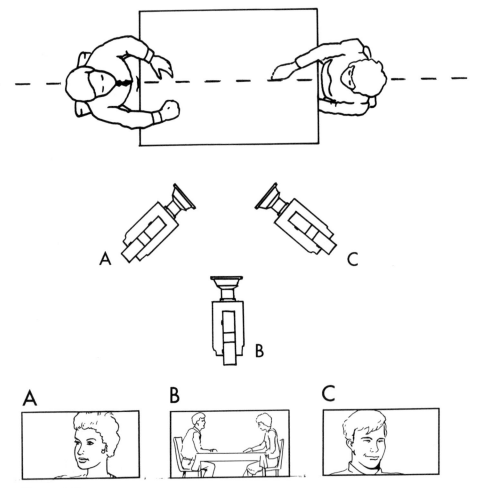

Figure 6.9

B always obtains the two-shot as in Figure 6.9 and so is not included in the subsequent examples. Variations are only obtained with the outside or wing camera positions.

OVER-THE-SHOULDER SHOTS

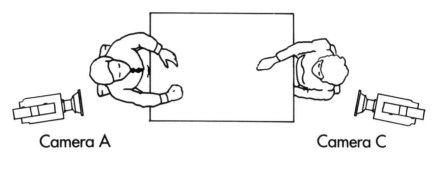

Figure 6.10

In the setup pictured in Figure 6.11, cameras A and C have been moved just inside the line of action or, more appropriately, the line of sight of the subjects. Camera positions A and C are now used to obtain close-ups from each subject's point of view. In this case, the subject not

POINT OF VIEW CLOSE-UPS

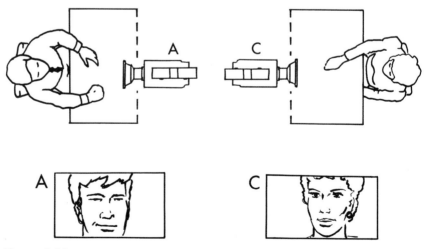

Figure 6.11

being photographed would be moved out of the way to place the camera in position. This is indicated by the broken line.

Figure 6.12 shows the last possible setup within the triangle method—profile shots using cameras A and C. Naturally, the exact angle of the shot, composition and shot size are infinitely variable within the triangle as long as the line of action is not violated.

PROFILE SHOTS

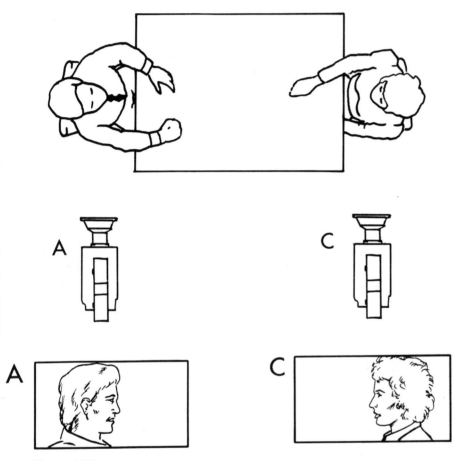

Figure 6.12

Establishing a New Line of Action With a New Sight Line

The only time the camera is permitted to cross the line of action is when a new line is established. One way to do this is shown in Figure 6.13. In this example, the old line is established between the couple seated at the table. A second man approaches the table and the seated man turns his attention to him. This new line of sight establishes a new line of action and a corresponding 180-degree working space for the camera. This is indi-

ESTABLISHING A NEW LINE

Figure 6.13

cated by the gray semicircle. The establishment of a new line is usually set up with a shot of a person who turns his attention to a new area or person within the frame. This *pivot shot* joins the two lines of action.

Once the new line of action has been set up, the camera can move across the old line of action anywhere within the new working space *as long as the sight line remains with the two men.* You will notice that this space also includes the woman. Even though it is permissible under the 180-degree rule, a camera will not be placed in quadrant X to photograph the woman. The next time she is seen in a shot, the camera will be located according to the *old line of action.* This is called a reestablishing shot. Conventional wisdom advocates reusing lines of action and the corresponding camera setups so that a consistent sense of space is reinforced through repetition. Once the basic editing pattern (and shot geography) has been established, a return to an old line of action does not have to be motivated by the pivot shot since the viewer has a general sense of the spatial relationships between actors.

The business of changing lines is considerably less complicated in practice. The shooting plan is arranged so that all the shots from a given angle are consolidated even if dialogue is shot out of order. Later, the shots are edited into the proper dramatic sequence. On screen, the changing line of action may appear to follow a far more complex scheme than was actually the case.

Establishing a New Line When a Player Crosses the Line

A second method of establishing a new line is to have one of the players in a scene cross his own line of action. This is shown in Figure 6.14 on page 136. As before, the line of action is between the seated couple; the working space for the camera is on the near side of the line (A). In Step One, the actor gets up from the table and moves to a new position over the line into

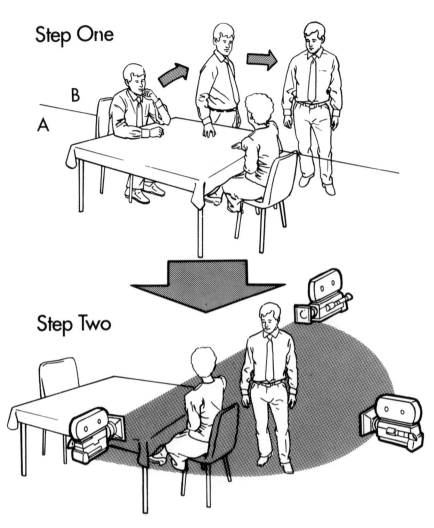

Step One

B

A

Step Two

Figure 6.14

space B. As soon as the man reestablishes eye contact with the woman in Step Two, the new line of action is established. The new line overrules the old line, which is no longer in effect. Again, a working space of 180 degrees is created. The only requirement for this strategy is that the actor's relocation must be seen clearly in a shot that permits the viewer to reorient himself.

Another factor to consider when establishing any new line is which side to use for the camera. Figure 6.15 on page 137 illustrates an alternative setup to the one in Figure 6.14. This time the working space for the camera is on the opposite side of the line. *Either choice is permissible as long as the new space agrees with the pivot shot taken from the previous line of action.* This is shown in Figure 6.16. Part One shows the line of action and corresponding semicircular working space for the camera. The line bisecting the semicircle is the new line of action that will be established when the

ALTERNATIVE WORKING SPACE

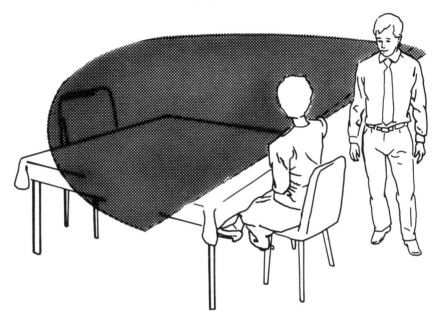

Figure 6.15

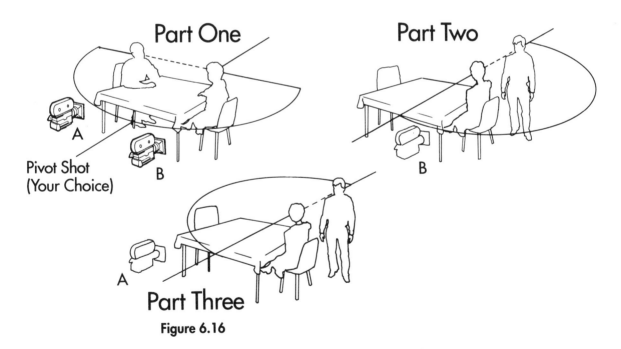

Figure 6.16

man moves to the standing position to face the woman. Cameras A and B represent the choices for the pivot shot used to record the man as he moves to the new position. Part Two of the diagram shows the 180-degree working space that you would use if camera position B were used for the pivot shot. Part Three shows the 180-degree working space if camera position A were used for the pivot shot.

As a rule, the working area chosen for each new line of action keeps the camera in the center of the group when shooting dialogue situations at a table or in a confined space.

Moving the Camera Over the Line

Not only can a player cross the line and establish a new one, but the camera can pan, dolly or make a crane move to a new space and a new line of action. This is easily accomplished as long as the camera movement is uninterrupted. In this situation, an eyeline does not have to be established and the camera can move from one side of the line of sight between two players to the other without confusion. Figure 6.17 shows

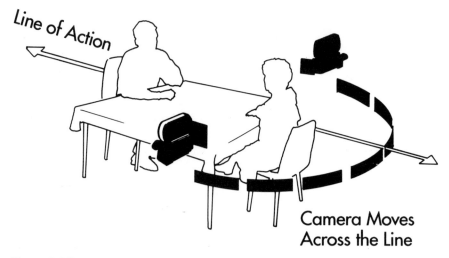

Figure 6.17

one version of this strategy with a curved camera path (black dotted line) crossing the line of action.

Cutaways and Bridge Shots

Another way to cross the line to another part of the scene is to interrupt the geography of a sequence with a shot that is clearly related to the action, but not the geography of the scene. For instance, let's say that we have established the line of action in a scene in the classroom of a school. We want to cross the line, but none of the strategies we have looked at in previous examples will work within the action of the scene. In this case, we photograph a close-up of a student's notebook or other pertinent detail. This cutaway serves the same purpose as the pivot shot. When we return to the main action, the camera can be moved over the line and a

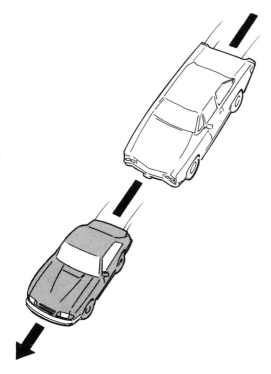

Figure 6.18: Line of action follows direction of motion.

new line established. This solution is generally used as a quick fix in the editing process when problems of continuity arise.

The Line of Action for Moving Subjects and Action

In my opinion, the line of action is most useful when used to organize the photography of multiple-player dialogue sequences. Though screen direction would seem to be crucial to understanding the relationship of fast moving subjects—for instance, cars in a chase sequence—unquestioning observance of the line of action may actually stand in the way of more interesting arrangements of shots. For one thing, continuity editing is not the only way of organizing film images: Other methods, such as kinetic or analytical editing, may be in conflict with strict continuity and yet provide better solutions to creative problems. For another, today's viewers are so visually sophisticated that they are able to "read" unconventional editing patterns with relative ease. Be aware that more dynamic results may be obtained in some sequences if the line is crossed and screen direction is reversed. Later we'll be looking at other types of editing more closely, but for now, as we continue to explore the line of action, keep in mind that there are alternative ways of organizing shots.

Action Sequences

In action sequences there is frequently no line of sight to establish the line of action. In this case, the line of action follows the dominant motion of the subject of the shot. If one car is pursuing another, the line is the path of the cars, as shown in Figure 6.18. If the two cars are alongside each other, an *additional* line of action can be established between the cars. I call this the *implied sight line* because even when the drivers of the cars are not prominent in the shot, the cars become the symbols of the drivers and their line of sight. This situation is peculiar to cars, boats, planes or any other conveyance that has a driver. Both lines are shown in Figure 6.19. Shots photographed from both sides of the line of motion (camera positions A, C and B, D) will result in a reversal of screen direction when cut together, as shown in the accompanying storyboard panels. The implied sight line is a special case and only overrides the line of motion temporarily. Otherwise, the line of motion is the prevailing rule. While this may seem like the type of situation that the 180-degree rule was devised to prevent, it is actually a common editing pattern even in dialogue scenes where there is a line of motion and an implied sight line.

This is the case in *The Godfather Part II* when the young Vito Corleone

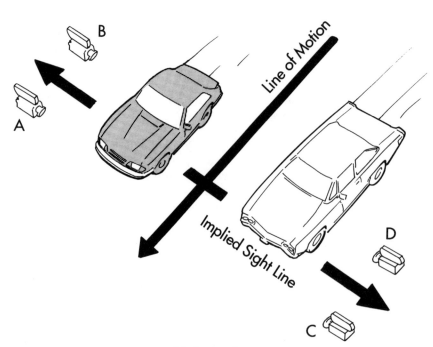

Figure 6.19, Part 1: Two possible lines of action.

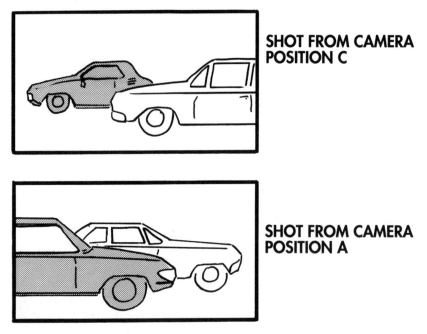

SHOT FROM CAMERA POSITION C

SHOT FROM CAMERA POSITION A

Figure 6.19, Part 2

is driving a small truck along crowded New York streets. Fanucci, the local crime lord, is seated next to Vito, and they have a conversation as the car moves along. Two tracking shots are used, one on each side of the car, framing a good deal of the car and the moving background. Cut together the shots form a pair of very wide over-the-shoulder shots. Each time there is a cut during the conversation, the background reverses direction. The abruptness of the cut could have been softened if the shots were tighter, so that Vito and Fanucci filled the frame. As it turns out, the shot change is not bothersome and so stands as an example of the latitude possible within the 180-degree rule.

Crossing the Line in Action Sequences

The strategies for "properly" crossing the line in nondialogue situations are essentially the same as those illustrated for dialogue scenes, beginning with Figure 6.13, page 135. The only difference is that the principal line of motion is substituted for the sight line. To recap, there are three basic ways to establish a new line of action/motion:

1) A subject (car, horse, person, etc.) can cross the line establishing a new one by the direction of his new line of motion.

2) The camera can cross the line either following a subject to a new scene space or merely traveling for graphic variety to a new viewpoint.

3) A new subject can enter the frame and become the dominant line of motion in contrast to the first. This is analogous to the situation in Figure 6.13 when a new character entered the scene establishing a new line of sight.

Crossing the Line While on the Line

The closer the camera is to the line of action, the more difficult it is to detect when the camera has crossed the line. In Figure 6.20 camera positions A and B are on the line of action, so when they are edited together there is a reversal of screen direction. This type of sequence would probably have been avoided 60 years ago; but today, audiences have no problem understanding the geography of the scene space in this editing pattern. This reversal is somewhat more startling than is sometimes the case when shooting on the line since the subject is in profile. When the subject's sight line is the same as the line of action, we get front and back views, which help the viewer differentiate the shots.

When actually filming, it usually turns out that it is rarely necessary to go through elaborate staging and logistical analysis to find a way of establishing a new line of action. My basic belief is that if the filmmaker has a solid understanding of cinematic geography, has a good overview of the scene, has kept thorough notes on what he is going to shoot and has already shot, then he will probably not encounter any major difficulties with continuity.

Conclusion

The 180-degree rule is only a rule if you accept it without question. My

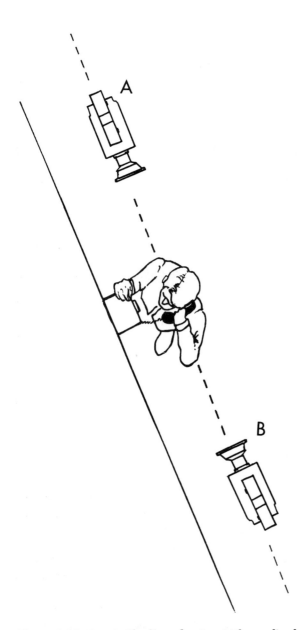

Figure 6.20, Part 1: The line of action. When edited together, shots obtained with cameras A and B reverse screen direction.

own feeling is that many of its assumptions are overstated. Audiences have turned out to be far more astute in understanding the spatial relationships in films than they are generally given credit for. Directors like Ozu, Bresson and Dreyer developed narrative techniques that frequently violate the conventions of continuity filmmaking to achieve their aims. While demanding in other respects, the viewer is not confused by their visual styles. Unlike Godard and the radical film movement, these direc-

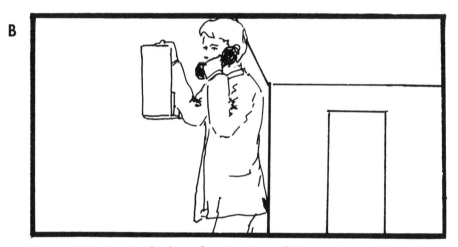

Figure 6.20, Part 2: The line of action. Any of the camera positions shown above can be edited together without disorienting the viewer.

tors were not reacting against the continuity style, and their visual solutions to thematic concerns are more varied and particular than the often mannered style of the left.

Ten years ago a defense of the line of action would have been considered reactionary, dismissed out of hand by virtually every film movement outside of mainstream features. It is probably still too soon for a fair reevaluation of the continuity style. But after four decades of concentrated criticism on the left analyzing the limitations of traditional narrative technique, it might restore some balance to the argument to state my own view that no style of filmmaking is superior to any other. If you feel that a particular style, or combination of styles, is appropriate to your work, there is no reason not to experiment. If anything is true of the arts, it is that there are no rules.

7 EDITING: TEMPORAL CONNECTIONS

In 1920 the Soviet filmmaker and theorist Lev Kuleshov performed a now famous experiment demonstrating that the meaning of shots in sequence can be created entirely through editing. Kuleshov used a close-up shot of the Russian actor Moszhukhin's expressionless face as a reaction shot in three different sequences. The actor is seen "reacting" to a bowl of soup, a woman in a coffin and a child playing with a toy bear. Audiences viewing the scenes marveled at Moszhukhin's sensitive performance in each situation, though in every instance it was the same close-up.

While the power of the editing process to shape meaning is undeniable, this type of wholesale invention is a special case. In most narrative films, shots are rarely neutral building blocks as Kuleshov used them, but have been composed to express an idea and tell a story according to the script. Each shot, together with the accompanying soundtrack, contains narrative and graphic information that predetermines key editing decisions such as the length and order of shots. This view of editing emphasizes the director's and the writer's roles in shaping the storytelling logic that provides the basis for any decision the editor makes.

When we speak of storytelling logic, we are actually referring to the structure of shots, sequences and scenes. Structure controls the order in which the story information is given to the viewer. It is as important to the storytelling process as the actual information being presented. Since structure in films can be presented in a storyboard in ways that a screenplay cannot convey, the visualization process can be considered part of the writing and, ultimately, the editing process.

The Narrative Impulse

Novelist E. M. Forster's often quoted definition of plot is a good place to begin understanding the kind of structural logic that motivates editing choices. Forster began by describing a series of events that were not a plot: "The King died and then the Queen died." But, as Forster observed, if we say "The King died and the Queen died of grief," we have described a plot because there is a causal connection.

In the course of any story this cause and effect relationship is the underlying scheme that involves the reader. It does this by asking the reader to become involved in making the logical connections between events. Forster's example is simplified to make a point and doesn't show us how an author might reveal the relationship between the King and Queen. For instance, in the early chapters the Queen might be portrayed as indifferent to the King's death. As the story progresses, however, the author might reveal small details that would explain that the Queen, having assumed the throne takes care not to reveal her feelings for fear of being seen as weak by her subjects. Or we might learn in chapter one that the Queen has died and not discover until the last page of the story that the cause of her illness was the King's death. In both cases, the reader is provoked into speculation by the order and manner in which the plot is revealed even though the same basic events are being related in each version of the story.

In fiction, cause and effect is frequently set up as a question and answer scheme that encourages the reader's participation. The cliff-hanger ending in a serialized story, where the answer to the question of what will happen next is withheld to create suspense, is an example of the most exaggerated exploitation of this device.

Stories that use a question and answer strategy may be set up in many ways. A question may be answered through the accumulation of detail over several dozen pages or it might be answered succinctly shortly after it has been posed. In fact, the question and answer presentation of information usually occurs on every page of a story operating on several levels simultaneously. This is as true for a screenplay or film as it is for a novel or short story. Continuity editing is based on these types of question and answer strategies, though we usually speak of them as connections. Listed below are the three most basic types of connections found in continuity editing:

> Temporal connections: We cut from a man dropping his drinking glass in one shot to the glass breaking on the floor in the second shot.
>
> Spatial connections: We cut from a wide shot of the White House to a recognizable detail of the White House in a closer shot—for example, the portico and front door.
>
> Logical connections: We cut from a wide shot of the White House to a shot of the President seated in an office. No temporal or spatial connection is necessary in this combination. If we recognize the White House and we recognize the President, then we make the logical connection that he's seated in an office in the White House, even though there is no actual information presented to tell us we are in the White House.

As you can see, these types of connections create the illusion of a real, physical world. We can probably think of them as background connections that establish the environment of a film, but they also can be used to shape the plot and dramatic content as well.

Narrative Motion

To advance the narrative it is necessary not only to ask questions but to set up expectations. For instance, in the example of the two shots used to show the man dropping his drinking glass, questions and answers are only used to depict action. If, however, we know that one of the drinks at the party contains poison, we will be provoked into asking all sorts of who, what, when, where and why questions about the poison. Since we bring all sorts of knowledge and experience to any story we read or watch, we will speculate about possible answers to all the questions raised. Nearly all editing strategies in narrative film are devised to set up a framework of expectations in a series of shots. The result is narrative motion.

This way of arranging shots is fundamental in film editing. Even dialectical montage, which Soviet filmmaker Sergei Eisenstein felt was an alternative to cause and effect editing, exploited narrative motion by setting up expectations and asking questions. In Eisenstein's dialectical shot pattern of thesis-antithesis-synthesis, the first two shots ask the question "What is the connection between these ideas?" The answer, supplied by Eisenstein in shot three, is synthesis. In this analysis, Soviet montage and Hollywood continuity cutting are not polar opposites but variations of the same principle of question and answer strategies.

Q&A Patterns

The simplest question and answer editing pattern requires only two shots—for example, a shot of a person looking offscreen followed by a shot of the object the person is observing. Patterns are not limited by length and may require dozens of shots to complete a question and answer cycle. Or, the patterns can be varied by changing the order of the shots. Though we do not speak of their storytelling in this way, much of what we appreciate in the films of directors like Buñuel, Hitchcock, Godard, Welles and Truffaut are the ways in which they develop question and answer patterns that challenge the viewer.

Context

The meaning of any given Q and A pattern can be further extended or modified by changing the context that frames it. For instance, in the Kuleshov experiment, our understanding of the man's reaction to the soup, coffin and child is framed by our assumption that the man is sincerely moved in each scene. If a new scene is added establishing that he is faking his responses, then we will interpret the original sequences differently. While this may seem like rudimentary plotting, the manipulation of these

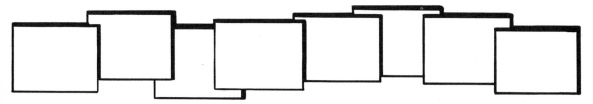

Figure 7.1: Question and answer relationship between shots links them into an overlapping chain.

types of narrative elements was crucial to the way Alfred Hitchcock created suspense or Buster Keaton constructed a gag.

Using the Patterns

For me, the main concern for the visualizer is not the pictorial elements of a shot or sequence, but the structure of the sequence—or, to put it another way, what the viewer knows and when. As it turns out, interesting compositional ideas are usually the result of narrative invention rather than daring pictorial experimentation.

This first series of examples illustrates how the narrative context and question and answer pattern determine how we read a scene.

A

Example One

Narrative context: Our scene takes place in the woods on a summer day. Laura, a teenager, is looking for her older brother Tom. At this point in the story we have not yet seen Tom and so we do not know what he looks like.

B

> Shot A: Laura enters the woods.
> Question: "Where is Tom?"
>
> Shot B: Laura stops short a few yards from a clearing.
> New Question: "What has she found?"
>
> Shot C: Tom and a girl lying naked on a blanket in a clearing.
> Answer: "Laura has found her brother."

C

This is a straightforward question and answer editing pattern, and the viewer can easily anticipate the outcome. If, in the next example, we change the context slightly so that we know what Tom looks like, then shot C becomes an answer to shot A and simultaneously raises a new question.

Example Two

A

> Shot A: Laura enters the woods.
> Question: "Where is Tom?"
>
> Shot C: Tom and a girl lying naked on a blanket in a clearing.
> Answer: "Tom is here."
> New Question: "Will Laura find Tom?"
>
> Shot B: Laura stops short a few yards from the clearing.
> Answer: "Laura has found Tom."

C

Now, if we were to prolong the time before Laura's arrival in shot B, the viewer would share a secret with the filmmaker by knowing that Tom is nearby in a compromising situation. This editing pattern places an answer before the question, thereby creating suspense. We can do this by changing the order of the shots and adjusting the context.

B

Example Three

Let's change the narrative context again. This time we know that Tom's

C

A

B

sister is looking for him. However, we have not seen her in the story at this point and do not know what she looks like. The context, set in a previous scene, leaves Tom's whereabouts unknown. As the scene opens we receive our first answer.

Shot C: Tom and a girl lying naked on a blanket in a clearing.
Answer: "Tom is here."

Shot A: A girl enters the woods.
Question: "Is this Laura?"

Shot B: Laura stops short a few yards from the clearing.
Answer: "This is Laura."

By revealing Tom in a compromising situation in the opening shot, a suspenseful situation is established for the remainder of the scene. When Laura enters the woods in the second shot, the fuse is lit, and we know that a potentially embarrassing meeting is possible. Hitchcock frequently sets up a scene this way by placing the audience in a privileged (and uncomfortable) position by providing them with information that the protagonist desperately needs but cannot obtain. A further embellishment of the same idea might undermine our expectations by letting Laura find other couples making love in the woods before discovering Tom. These earlier encounters would be designed to momentarily encourage us to believe that Laura has found Tom before revealing to us that the couples are strangers to Laura. This would make us unsure of our ability to second-guess the narrative and more susceptible to the surprise of the actual meeting.

In addition to the narrative context created by the filmmaker, the audience brings certain assumptions to their understanding of any scene that the filmmaker uses. These assumptions might include popularly held notions of morality or familiarity with storytelling conventions. The filmmaker can play with these assumptions by supporting or subverting them.

Hitchcock did this rather perversely in *Psycho* by killing off the person that for the first third of the film the audience believes is the protagonist. This was completely unexpected, breaking all the rules of conventional narrative. The result is that the audience feels completely abandoned, as indeed they were, by any kind of moral reason in the fictional world they are watching. The point of these examples is this: Editing patterns and the narrative context do not necessarily lay the events of a story out in simple chronological order.

More Q and A Variations

In addition to altering the order of question and answer patterns, the rhythm and timing of the patterns can be varied by withholding some or all of expected narrative information for a few shots or for several scenes. It is also possible to have more than one question or answer raised within a single shot or combined within a shot. Using a mini-noir scenario we can look at a few examples:

• A question can be raised in one shot and answered several shots later rather than in the following shot.

Sequence A

In this case the look in the first shot would ordinarily be answered by a shot of the gun. However, the answer has been postponed while shots 2 and 3 show the man turning on the light.

• An answer can be given in a shot and the question raised later.

Sequence B

In this version the cut on the look has been reversed so that we see the object of attention before the look.

• A question can be raised and elaborated on in a series of shots before being answered in a single shot or in a series of shots.

Sequence C

The question in these shots, of course, is who is the person coming through the door and why. The partial answer is that it is a man, and in frame 3 we see that he has one finger missing. In frame 4 we learn that he is there to find the gun.

• There can be more than one question raised in a shot or shots. Consequently, more than one answer can be given in a shot or shots.

Sequence D

In frame 1 two questions are raised: Who is coming through the door and whose hand emerges from behind the door? When the person enters the room in frame 2 we receive a partial answer, learning that the person is a man. But frame 2 also raises the question of the significance of the pool of black ink on the floor. In frame 3 the man puts his hand on the sheet of paper on the table. This answers the question of the man's identity since we now know it is the man with the missing finger, but a new question is raised: Why has part of the letter been carefully removed? Finally, in frame 3, we learn that the gun is on the floor. However, a new question is raised: Who is the woman standing over the gun?

Compared with the previous examples, this last series includes far more information in the same number of shots. This is an exaggeration of Q and A patterns, but the subtle use of these same strategies was exploited by Bergman, Kurosawa, Dreyer and many other filmmakers to shape psychological fiction and implicate the viewer in the moral dilemmas they presented.

If we try to imagine a graphic representation of the question and answer relationships we have been looking at, the shots do not appear connected end-to-end as the editor arranges the actual film stock, but rather they resemble a series of overlapping panels—like a deck of cards that has been fanned out. Figure 7.1 on page 147 shows the narrative relationship between shots in a series. Each is connected to the next by some cause and effect relationship. Some shots are more prominent narratively than others, while some shots remain in the background without answering questions or raising new ones, simply supporting existing information with additional detail.

The Limits of Clarity

Because question and answer storytelling techniques frequently relate information in a roundabout way, this indirectness may appear confusing to the uninitiated when described in a screenplay, shot list or storyboard. Screenwriters, directors and editors may be encouraged to avoid unusual Q and A patterns because it is mistakenly believed that the results will be clearer to an audience. An example of this is the classic establishing shot at the opening of a scene. For instance, a scene ends as we learn that an understudy in a play is on her way to the theater to replace the ailing lead. In the opening shot of the next scene we see the theater. This familiar pattern merely shows us what we already expect and does little to raise expectations or contribute to narrative motion. If, however, the introduction of the theater is composed of separate shots that raise questions, then the viewer is engaged in connecting these pieces to form a meaningful statement. Consider this sequence of shots as a way of introducing the theater location:

A CU of a few crumpled theater programs on the ground.
+ A CU of stage flats in a garbage dumpster.
+ A CU of an empty marquee with most of the letters taken down.
= A closed show.

This is a storytelling alternative to an establishing shot showing the front of a theater with a banner across the lobby doors with the word "closed" printed across it in big letters. Both versions are familiar strategies, and the lesson is not the specific solution, but the overall notion that storytelling should engage the viewer at every point.

As narrative editing patterns become more complex and syncopated, it is increasingly difficult to execute them without considerable planning. As we have seen, challenging patterns often mean that questions and answers overlap from shot to shot. This precise interrelationship between shots tends to limit the cutting options to a carefully designed plan. On the other hand, the cutting options that are eliminated are nearly always stock solutions. In a sense, business-as-usual editing strategies are easily inter-changeable precisely because they lack the connective relationships of complex question and answer strategies. This brings us to the subject of coverage of action.

Camera Cutting vs. Coverage

Theoretically, a fully developed storyboard can show a director all the shots he needs for a scene. If the director and cinematographer shoot the boards exactly as they appear on paper even the lengths of shots can be estimated. Later, the editor only has to trim shots here and there to make them all fit neatly together. This method of shooting is called cutting in the camera and presupposes a perfect script, perfect storyboard and the perfect execution of each shot. Optimism may be a virtue, but to disregard the things that can go wrong in filmmaking—and they are many—is foolhardy. Cutting in the camera is like working on a high wire without a net.

The alternative view supposes that perfection is unobtainable and, therefore, not worth pursuing in the first place. Directors who believe this, and who are unsure of how to visualize, shoot sequences by resorting to a programmed formula of camera setups. This system, usually based on the triangle system of camera placement, is called coverage and employs several camera setups for every action, ensuring that a logical sequence can be cut together in the editing process. A formulaic selection of wide, medium and close-up shots is usually sufficient for a basic rendition of any scene and places a great deal of emphasis on the editor's contribution. While coverage is an extremely safe way to shoot, it is also uninspired, because visual strategies designed for the specific needs of a scene are discouraged unless all the coverage shots have been obtained first. Unfortunately, there is often only enough time within the shooting schedule for the coverage with the result that many interesting visual approaches are never attempted.

Each method, camera cutting and coverage, has advantages and disadvantages and is rarely used exclusively in feature filmmaking. For this reason, "getting coverage" can refer not only to a system of camera placement but also to shooting extra backup shots (in addition to those storyboarded) if time permits or if the director has gambled on an unusual approach to a scene. Once a set is lit and blocked and the essential shots needed to convey the story have been photographed, the attitude of director and cinematographer is generally "We're here, so we might as well get some backup shots just in case." Any filmmaker will know how practical this is, since moving the camera to pickup extra angles can be done fairly rapidly in comparison with the time it takes to light a set and block a scene. Once the technical and dramatic needs of a scene are set, directors are often tempted to get as many shots as possible before tearing down lights and moving on to the next scene. Besides, film stock is relatively inexpensive compared with the total production cost for a full day's shooting. Even when using a storyboard, the same attitudes are at work, and just how many extra shots are filmed depends on the confidence and experience of the director. And finally there is the enthusiasm factor. Many directors just like to take pictures. Even after all the necessary shots are in the can, if the weather is right or the lighting and set are great, it can be very hard to call it a wrap.

One of the more useful aspects of coverage is that action is played out in full for most setups even if the director expects to use only a small portion of a particular take. This is most useful when filming dialogue. For instance, a scene consisting of a father speaking to his children is storyboarded so that the father does all the talking. In the storyboards the father is pictured in a three-shot that dollies past the kids and ends up in close-up on Dad. The entire scene is played in one long take. Though everyone on the creative team might agree that this is the way the scene should be photographed, it would be unwise to rely on this one shot and not get reaction shots of the children at the same time. The director would then be covered in case there is a problem with the tracking shot that doesn't become clear until the film is seen in dailies.

Now let's suppose that instead of using the long dolly shot indicated in the storyboard, the director elects to use camera coverage instead. He would probably shoot a medium shot and close-up of the father and the same setups of the kids. That would be six shots. He would probably also shoot a three-shot OTS of the kids and a reverse OTS of Dad. That would be a total of eight setups. The amount of time it would take to light and photograph all these shots could easily mean that the dolly shot would have to be sacrificed. That is the practical choice between coverage and camera cutting.

It should be clear from this example that the balance between the two methods depends on the situation. Some scenes are obviously easier to film than others for dramatic or technical reasons. Sometimes it's possible to get considerable coverage *and* complex dolly moves or other time-consuming setups. Be assured, however, that many of the shots will not be used in the edited version. Part of learning your craft as a visualizer is having a good sense of what will work before the camera rolls. All directors leave a margin for error and cover themselves, but knowing what works in advance translates into a high *average* of usable shots. The payoff is not the money saved by shooting fewer setups, but the extra time that can be used to take greater artistic chances with more ambitious staging, shots and performances.

Composing Action for Editing

So far this chapter has focused on editing for the visualizer, stressing storytelling and narrative motion. A full discussion of editing techniques for the film editor as well as editing room procedures can be found in several excellent books listed in the recommended reading section in the back of this book. However, a brief overview of these techniques is of value to any filmmaker visualizing a sequence.

Cutting On Movement

As mentioned at the beginning of the chapter, edit points are "placed" in the shot or at least anticipated by the director in the staging of action. There are three ways in which an edit can be made to preserve the continuity of action when two or more views of a subject are being combined. Suppose we have a shot of a boy running across the front lawn of his home and jumping over

Figure 7.2: Cutting ranges for action.

a hedge onto the sidewalk, as shown in Figure 7.2. The first shot runs the entire length of the action. Now we decide to cut to a new angle somewhere into the first shot. Here are the three options: 1) We can cut to the new shot at the point where the boy reaches the hedge and begins to jump. 2) We can cut to the new shot while the boy is in midjump. 3) We can cut to the new shot after he lands on the ground.

These are all acceptable edit points, but the common practice in the continuity style would locate the cut somewhere into the action rather than before or after the boy has left the ground. This tends to hide the cut and make the transition to a new shot invisible. The exact point of the cut is dependent on the subject and the editor's sense of movement.

Cutting on the action is found in virtually all types of sequences whether the subject of the shot is lifting a drink to his or her lips or merely turning his head or moving his eyes. Filmmakers mindful of this essential

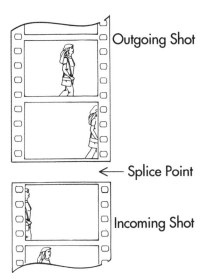

Outgoing Shot

← Splice Point

Incoming Shot

Figure 7.3

editing strategy will stage action so that it will overlap an anticipated edit point between camera angles.

Exits and Entrances

When the subject of a shot moves into or out of a frame it is common practice to make the cut while the subject is still partially within the frame. Figure 7.3 shows the position of a subject in an outgoing and an incoming shot. The effect on-screen is to make the cut smoother and to speed up the flow of action.

Clearing the Frame

This is an alternative strategy to cutting on movement when joining different angles of the same subject. Instead of cutting while the subject is within the frame, the subject is allowed to exit the frame before the cut to a new shot is made. It is customary in this strategy to hold on the empty frame of the outgoing shot for a moment. Figure 7.4 shows an example of this strategy. In the outgoing shot birds fly into the frame, which gives us action to view while holding the clear frame for a minimum of 1-2 seconds at the end of the shot (in our diagram the last frame is symbolic of what would be 24 or more actual film frames).

There are several options for cutting to the incoming shot after clearing the frame, depending on how long the clear frame is held in the outgoing shot. One option is for the incoming shot (A) to open without the subject in the frame. This opening can vary in length depending on the action in the shot before the main subject arrives. If we open on a busy park or a trickling stream in the woods the opening serves the purpose of an establishing shot and could be held for several seconds. A second option is for the incoming shot (B) to open with the subject already in the frame. This is not a common practice in the continuity style since it is somewhat abrupt. A third alternative would be to cut on the subject partially in frame, as shown in the previous figure (7.3).

Clearing the frame can be looked at in two ways. First, it is a method for joining shots of the same subject in different backgrounds. In this case it serves a function similar to that of the dissolve and indicates a passage of time. The second use for clearing the frame is as a substitute for the cut on action so that an ingoing shot and outgoing shot represent continuous time. In

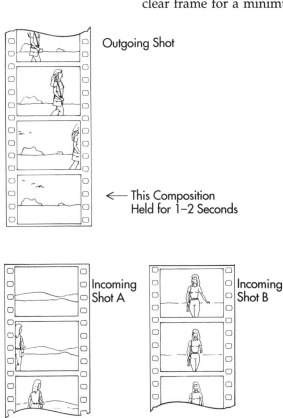

Outgoing Shot

← This Composition Held for 1–2 Seconds

Incoming Shot A

Incoming Shot B

Figure 7.4

general, clearing the frame is an easy out for directors who are timid about preserving continuity, since it is almost impossible to make a continuity mistake with this technique. In fact, it is such a flexible cut that it can be used to join shots on opposite sides of the line of action.

One last strategy is shown in Figure 7.5. In this version the outgoing shot ends with the subject clearly within the frame. The incoming shot begins before the subject appears and holds on a clear frame for at least a second before the subject enters (again the clear frame in the diagram is symbolic of many more clear frames).

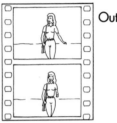

Outgoing Shot

Editing and Visualization

One of the values of knowing conventional editing practices is that it gives the filmmaker a point of departure when he is visualizing. Staging, in particular, is made easier by an awareness of the types of movement that provide opportunities for cutting. In any given scene, the filmmaker will visualize how long certain actions should be viewed before moving to another shot. He will then try to plan action at that point so that editing is motivated visually.

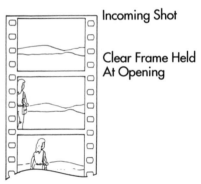

Incoming Shot

Clear Frame Held
At Opening

This may sound far more mechanical than it really is. If these rules sound overly restrictive it should be remembered that they can be broken at any time in favor of a better idea. The value of understanding editing practices is that it enables the director to visualize an overview of required camera setups for an entire sequence, allowing him to turn his attention to the dramatic needs of the scene.

Figure 7.5

Part III
The Workshop

THE BASICS APPLIED

Shot Flow

Shot flow is the name given to the kinetic effect of a sequence of shots. This is an apt description since it evokes the image of a river, which can be turbulent, tranquil or winding and can even turn back against itself in mid-course. A sequence of shots is often comprised of complex rhythmic and dynamic continuity relationships that, like a river, merge into a single, unified structure. But no matter how intricate the relationships between the shots, there are two sequential ingredients that are fundamental to our understanding of visualization: shot size and camera angle. There are also many other compositional elements familiar to artists from photography and painting that contribute to a sequence, but camera angle and shot size are the dominant physical changes that determine shot flow. In this chapter we will concentrate on shot size.

The basic relationship between wide, medium and close-up shots and angle of view becomes clear if we construct a sequence that establishes a subject within a location. By keeping our example simple we will be able to concentrate on the graphic design of the frame. The purpose of this first exercise is to increase our awareness of the range of kinetic qualities that can be produced with a few simple shots.

Before getting started let's establish standard shot descriptions and their abbreviations. These will be used throughout the book from this point on.

ECU	—	Extreme close-up
MCU	—	Medium close-up
CU	—	Close-up
MS	—	Medium shot
WS	—	Wide shot
LS	—	Long shot
ELS	—	Extreme long shot
BG (bg)	—	Background
FG (fg)	—	Foreground
OTS	—	Over the shoulder
POV	—	Point of view

Establishing a Location By Varying Shot Size

As basic as the change in shot size is to the continuity style, it is rarely studied in depth by filmmakers. Testing your ability to judge the effect of graphic variation in a sequence will help you to sharpen your perception of mood, point of view, rhythm, tempo, emotional distance and dramatic intent in narrative situations.

In the following series of photoboards we will establish the location of a house to examine the consequences of shot size. There are three basic continuity strategies that are possible to describe the location: The camera can move towards the house beginning in wide shot; the camera can move out from a close-up of some detail of the house to reveal the full location; or the camera can create a sense of the whole by using a series of close-ups.

VERSION ONE

In the first pair of sequences, frames 1-3 and 4-6, we can compare the graphic relationship between shots when we vary the scale. Each sequence creates movement, and you should be aware of the variation in velocity and acceleration in each version. Frames 1-3, for instance, show limited change between frames 1 and 2 until the house jumps forward in frame 3. The second sequence is more dynamic, largely because frame 6 fills the frame. We can also judge the effect of "pulling back" from a subject by reading the photoboards in reverse order from right to left.

Putting analysis aside for a moment, look at each sequence as a complete statement. Developing an intuitive sense of the overall perceptual effect of a sequence is one of the skills necessary for visualization. Try to imagine a story line for these sequences with sound and score. Move your eyes over them as you might imagine them being edited. This is essentially the skill you wil need to turn the text of a script into a storyboard.

VERSION TWO

Here we see a more fully extended range of shots. In the previous examples each sequence showed the house moving closer, but no new information was revealed. Now a true CU is added in frames 3 and 6, and we see a For Sale sign. The change in scale is extreme, with the camera moving approximately ¼ mile between shots. Now cover frames 2 and 5 with one hand and look at the resulting shot pairs 1-3 and 4-6. You can see just how wide a jump can be made through space while retaining spatial unity.

1 **2** **3**

4 **5** **6**

VERSION THREE

This next approach compares four sequences. First is a straightforward treatment of a change in shot size from an extreme high angle (frames 1-3). In frames 4-6 rotational movement is added but without the change in shot size. Next we combine these approaches, moving closer in a circular path as shown in frames 7-9.

1 **2** **3**

4 **5** **6**

7   **8**   **9**

Finally, in frames 10-12 we move in three planes: downward, closer and in an arc around the house.

10   **11**   **12**

VERSION FOUR

In these next two treatments we move from a CU to a wide shot, essentially a pullback move. In both cases the two straight-on angles end with an angular aerial shot, which results in a more dynamic editing pattern. This visual contrast in motion is a valuable graphic effect demonstrating the power of a simple change in angle. In both of the present examples the first two shots of each sequence set up a line of motion: In the third frame we expect to continue the straight line of motion back from the front door of the house, but instead there is a large jump in scale and angle.

1   **2**   **3**

VERSION FIVE

We will handle this next series of shots somewhat differently, composing a location from details from which the viewer will construct the whole. This relies on a more iconographic, abstract use of images. For this reason we will start with a list of shots— concepts of the house as expressed in individual images. To help focus our energies we'll give ourselves a narrative context. This is our story: A divorce has split a family in two and the house they formally occupied is now up for sale. Following is a list of images that seem to me to express this idea.

1) Rusted bike abandoned outside
2) Mailbox knocked over on ground
3) Uncollected junk mail piled on the porch
4) Broken window panes
5) Empty rooms viewed through the broken windows
6) For Sale sign
7) Disconnected cable television line
8) Empty doghouse turned over
9) Vandalism (graffiti on the side of house)
10) Moving boxes filled with trash

The following storyboard is based on some of these ideas.

As we have just seen, a basic three- or six-shot sequence can be handled in several ways even when using a static camera to record a simple subject. Part of the visualizing process is comparing "drafts" of the storyboard as we have just done, recombining new and old ideas until the sequence is exactly as you want it. The value of exercises like the ones we have just completed is to help filmmakers develop the ability to imagine a story in whole sequences by improving visual memory and the awareness of the many graphic elements that comprise any shot and sequence. In the next example we will view the design process through the eyes of a filmmaker. By personalizing the examples this way we will have a chance not only to see the results of the creative process, but to see the process itself.

NARRATIVE PROBLEM ONE: THE STATIC SHOT

A filmmaker is scouting a location for the opening scene of a film based on his childhood experiences. The scene calls for a suburban neighborhood. He passes a side street in which a line of trees and the way the sunlight falls on the pavement evoke familiar memories. He gets out of his car and walks down the sidewalk to a house that is very much like his family's first house. Standing at the edge of the front lawn he begins to imagine the opening scene of the film. He feels he does not have to follow the direction of the script in every detail in the first scene, but merely needs to introduce the period, characters and mood of the story.

The scene, as the filmmaker originally wrote it, described a weekday morning when, as usual, he was the last member of his family to wake up. Most of the action took place in the kitchen with very little dialogue. But as the filmmaker stands in front of this real house in the bright sunlight, new memories come to him. He remembers his parents' frustration over his forgetfulness, the jackets and sweaters lost at school or textbooks left on the bus. He remembers a certain morning when he was 10 . . . .

VERSION ONE

In this first sequence the filmmaker decides to restrict himself to static shots using limited panning to follow the action. He begins with a straight-forward wide shot of the house in frame 1. After a few moments the father exits the front door heading to the garage. A new shot in frame 2 shows the window of the boy's bedroom through which we can see a corner of the bed as the father passes by outside. The covers move and a sock falls off

1

DAD EXITS FRONT DOOR AND WALKS TO GARAGE

2

SOCK FALLS OFF BED WHEN BOY STIRS COVERS. DAD CROSSES BG.

3

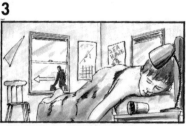

DAD PASSES BY WINDOW IN BG.

the bed. We cut to frame 3 with the boy in the extreme foreground and the father outside.

The filmmaker stops here, seeing that the staging is not working. He feels frame 1 should show the house within a wider context—that is, the neighborhood and the past. The filmmaker also feels the second frame of the window is too oblique, even though he likes the offhand framing that shows only a part of the boy's bed and not the boy. He tries a new staging.

VERSION TWO

The filmmaker begins the new sequence with a high-angle shot that removes him slightly from the action. He thinks the shot could be less harshly angular, but the inclusion of more surrounding space tends to give a little breathing room as compared with the original opening shot. The father exits in frame 1 and, as he walks to the garage, finds something in the grass. As he bends over to pick it up we cut to frame 2. What he's found is a sneaker. Shaking his head he walks a few steps towards camera into a medium shot and sighs. Cut to frame 3. The boy turns over in bed and his bare foot pops out from under the covers. We hear a door open o.s., and as the boy wriggles into a comfortable position, his father's hand enters the frame and puts the sneaker on the bed post.

1 **2** **3**

DAD FINDS SNEAKER. HE PICKS IT UP.

DAD EXITS FRONT DOOR AND STOPS HALFWAY DOWN WALK.

HOLD ON BOY AS HE SQUIRMS UNDER COVERS. DADS HAND ENTERS FRAME. HE PUTS SNEAKER ON BEDPOST.

VERSION THREE

1a

In this new version the film fades up to an opening shot of a bright orange space ship filling the screen in frame 1a. It flutters and shakes in the morning breeze. The camera pulls back and we realize that we are looking at a torn and rumpled kite impaled on the high branches of a tree brilliantly backlit by the sun. The wind dislodges the kite, which drops out of frame re-

FULL BACK AND PAN DOWN FROM C.U. KITE

SPACE RAIDER

KITE DROPS O.S.

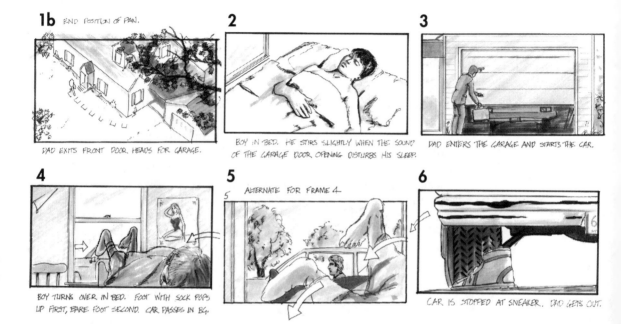

1b END POSITION OF PAN.

DAD EXITS FRONT DOOR. HEADS FOR GARAGE.

2

BOY IN BED. HE STIRS SLIGHTLY WHEN THE SOUND OF THE GARAGE DOOR OPENING DISTURBS HIS SLEEP.

3

DAD ENTERS THE GARAGE AND STARTS THE CAR.

4

BOY TURNS OVER IN BED. FOOT WITH SOCK POPS UP FIRST, BARE FOOT SECOND. CAR PASSES IN BG.

5 ALTERNATE FOR FRAME 4

6

CAR IS STOPPED AT SNEAKER. DAD GETS OUT.

vealing the house below in frame 1a. The father exits the house and goes to the garage in frame 1b. Cut to the boy in bed in frame 2. The sound of the garage door going up is heard in the background. Cut to the garage door in frame 3. The father goes to the car, and we cut back to the boy in bed in frame 4. The boy turns over and we see first one foot with a sock on it pass the window and then a second bare foot go past. Through the window we see the father backing the car out of the driveway.

The filmmaker immediately sees an improvement for frame 4 by framing tighter (frame 5). The moment after the car passes by the window the squeal of brakes is heard. Cut to a low-angle shot of the driveway and the car, which has stopped a few feet from the sneaker. The car door opens and the camera reframes slightly to include the father (feet only) getting out of the car in frame 6.

Again, the filmmaker stops at this point to rethink this latest version. He has generated some ideas he likes but can see that they need to be rearranged. First, he decides to keep the kite business but move to a lower viewpoint. In this way he can include some of the neighborhood before panning down to the house. Second, he feels the story focuses too much on the boy and his father. He would prefer to include more of the other members of the family in the hectic morning rush to start the day. This will require intercutting new characters, which will help break up the focus on the sneaker action.

VERSION FOUR

In this final version the filmmaker has combined the various elements to form a complete sequence.

PULL BACK FROM CU OF KITE. WIND BLOWS KITE DOWN. CAMERA PANS WITH KITE TO HOUSE. FATHER EXITS FRONT DOOR-GOES TO GARAGE AND STOPS. HE RETURNS TO HOUSE.

MOM ENTERS FRAME PICKS UP BRIEFCASE AND OPENS THE FRONT DOOR.

3

SHE'S WAITING FOR DAD WHEN HE
COMES UP STEPS.   HE TAKES THE
    BRIEFCASE.

4

DAD SMILES SHEEPISHLY GOING
DOWN STEPS. MOM EXITS TOWARDS
CAMERA.

5

BOY REARRANGES BED COVERS IN HIS SLEEP.

6

MOM IN KITCHEN - PUTS DISHES AWAY.
CALLS TO DAUGHTER "IS PETER UP?"

7

CAMERA ANGLE DOWN BED. LEFT FOOT WITH SOCK
APPEARS FROM UNDER COVERS. BARE FOOT APPEARS
NEXT. DAD BACKS CAR DOWN DRIVEWAY IN BG. —
(SFX) SQUEAL OF BRAKES O.S.

8

DAD GETS OUT OF CAR. SNEAKER IN BG.
BEHIND CAR.

9

MOM OPENS BATHROOM DOOR "IS PETER UP?"
DAUGHTER SAYS "HOW SHOULD I KNOW?"
(SFX) DOORBELL. MOM EXITS CROSSING FRAME.

10

MOM OPENS FRONT DOOR. SHE SEES DAD LEAVING
IN CAR. LOOK DOWN AND SEES SNEAKER ON
DOORSTEP.

PAN WITH CAR OUT OF DRIVEWAY. BUMPER
SNAGS KITE STRING HANGING FROM TREE
11 CAR PULLS AWAY DRAGGING KITE.

12

DAD'S CAR ENTERS FRAME. AFTER A FEW SECONDS
KITE APPEARS.   — END OF SEQUENCE —

The Filmmaker's Analysis

The filmmaker stops at this point because he has exhausted the possibilities for this latest approach to the opening. Many of the ideas could be improved and simplified if tracking and panning were permitted, but for now the filmmaker is more concerned with the overall tone and sense of the scene. There is no point in refining ideas pictorially if they will be rejected because they do not serve the narrative. The filmmaker feels that his solutions and story points are whimsical—the parallel forgetfulness of father and son and the gag with the kite—but the point of view of the boy has been lost in creating a plot-heavy opening. As a single lyrical element, the kite might still work, but after the opening shot, the point of view of the scene should move to the boy and remain with him. The filmmaker enters this in his notebook for a later version of the same scene.

Summary

A few words about this last storyboard sequence. A more fully worked out storyboard might show each stage of action by repeating the moving object in the frame. This is the case in panel 6 where the mother is pictured in the room twice. In panel 7, however, the appearance of the boy's left foot followed by his right foot is shown in a single panel, with an explanation in the caption. Since our filmmaker is familiar with cutting options and the details of the staging and is designing his own panels, there is no danger of confusion. However, when storyboarding the action for another director, it's important to include every significant movement so that there are no misunderstandings.

9 STAGING DIALOGUE SEQUENCES

When staging dialogue scenes for the camera, the director must fulfill two goals: the honest expression of human relationships and the presentation of these relationships to the viewer. The first goal is determined by the script and the actor's performance. The second goal is determined by staging, cinematography and editing. On the set, however, the director often finds that the actor's process and the practical and dramatic requirements of the camera are at odds. There is no right or wrong solution to this classical opposition, only what works best for the filmmaker in a given situation.

The visual challenge of staging is essentially a spatial problem—the ability to predict in three-dimensional space what will work on a two-dimensional screen. The spatial effect of a filmed sequence is particularly difficult to visualize because it is comprised of so many different fluid elements, such as the changing composition of the filmed image when the camera or the subject is in motion. Only a few dozen directors in the history of narrative film have exercised a recognizable staging style, and it remains a peculiarly elusive skill to acquire. The challenge is made more difficult by the lack of opportunities for practicing the craft.

A Method for Visualizing Staging

In the arts, technique is largely a matter of improved perception. In music, for example, this means learning to hear more accurately; in film it means learning to see more precisely. Specifically, cinematic "vision" relies on spatial memory and recognition, skills that can be learned and refined. This will be our goal in the next several chapters.

First, we will need a basic vocabulary of shots and actor placement. Any system of construction will suffice provided the filmmaker uses its elements consistently. For our purpose, the Hollywood continuity style offers a familiar set of solutions that can be broken down into a system of building blocks. This programmed approach, however, is not simply intended to offer stock solutions. By knowing the basic ways in which people position themselves in conversation and the accompanying camera setups used to record them, you will have a secure base from which to improvise, break rules and take creative risks, while fulfilling your basic responsibility to the actors, the script and your personal vision.

This spatial approach is made up of five basic areas:
Staging stationary actors
Staging moving actors

Using the depth of the frame
Staging camera movement
Staging camera movement and actor movement together

The first building blocks we'll look at are staging patterns for two subjects. In the photoboard examples camera angles, lenses and editing patterns will be compared so that you can see how slight adjustments alter our understanding of a scene. Once the staging patterns for two subjects are established, we can apply these same general principles to three- and four-subject situations in subsequent chapters.

Before getting to the actual examples, we should first look at some of the basic staging conventions found in narrative film with the understanding that they represent the starting point for new ideas rather than the limits of what is permissible.

Frontality

This is a basic convention of Western art. Frontality is just a way of saying that the subjects of a picture tend to face the viewer or, in the case of film, the camera. Many staging arrangements in the movies are basically frontal, meaning that subjects in conversation tend to face the camera rather than each other. This type of body positioning is not without precedence in real life, but in films it is often adjusted to the camera's needs.

A scene that stages actors in a frontal position can be recorded in a single master shot. If, however, one of the actors is turned away from the camera (partially or completely) more than one camera angle is necessary to see both actors' faces. This represents the two major editing approaches to staging: one in which the actors face a single camera setup and the other in which multiple camera viewpoints are edited together.

The Master Shot

The master shot is the one shot that is wide enough to include all the actors in the scene and that runs for the entire length of the action. When directors speak of the master, they usually mean that it is part of a plan of coverage that includes other camera setups in the triangle system that will eventually be edited together. But there are also times when the master shot is the only shot the director feels is necessary.

The Sequence Shot

Normally, the camera remains motionless in the master shot, particularly if cutting to other camera angles is anticipated. If the master is a moving shot, the camera is fluidly repositioned with a dolly throughout the course of the scene, essentially combining several camera angles that in an edited sequence would be obtained by individual shots. This approach to staging is also called the sequence shot and usually employs movement of the actors along with the traveling camera. Generally speaking, the sequence shot respects frontality more than an edited sequence. This is because editing permits, and routinely links, shots that are opposed by as much as 180 degrees. The equivalent change in a sequence shot is very nearly impossible to do quickly, let alone repeatedly. Therefore, the moving camera in a dialogue sequence shot tends to maintain a general viewing direction. We will look at this more closely in the chapter on mobile blocking.

Shot Size and Distance

One version of the master shot, the medium two-shot, was so characteristic of American films of the '30s and '40s that the French call it the "plan Americain" or the American shot. In the early '30s the two-shot was used to cover entire dialogue sequences without resorting to close-ups. This was due in part to the advent of sound in pictures and the long stretches of dialogue that accompanied them. The cumbersome blimped cameras were less mobile than the cameras used for silent films and the two-shot reduced the need to move the camera. This technical limitation was quickly overcome, but the two-shot remained in use for years because it was found to be a relaxed framing device for comedies and musicals.

Personally, I like the distance and objectivity that two-shot and full figure shots afford. The body can be wonderfully expressive, and people often use body language to indicate their relationship to others: for example, by where they stand in a room or by their different ways of approaching a rival, friend or lover. The way a person moves can be as distinctive as his or her voice, and most of us can identify a friend at a distance by some characteristic gesture long before we see his or her face. Expressive body movement falls within the range of the full shot and the medium shot. Entire scenes can be staged effectively at this distance without ever resorting to a close-up.

The Shot, Reverse Shot Pattern

When players are seen in alternating close-ups, the shot, reverse shot pattern is one of the most useful solutions. No cutting strategy better represents the Hollywood style than this one. The popularity of this setup is that it offers the widest range of cutting options and includes two important advantages that the two-shot lacks. The first advantage is that we get to see a subject's isolated reaction to dialogue; the second is that the point of view changes within the scene. In addition, the eye-line match between one character and another helps to establish a sense of spatial unity.

Sight Lines and Eye Contact

In any shot of one actor the closer the sight line is to the camera the more intimate our contact with the actor will be. In the most extreme case the actor can look directly into the lens and make eye contact with the viewer. This very confrontational relationship can be quite startling.

The most frequent use of direct eye contact is in subjective camera sequences in which the audience is made to see things through the eyes of one of the characters. This is relatively infrequent in narrative film and most of the time dialogue scenes are shot with the sight lines of the actors slightly to the left or right of the camera. In this case, it is common practice to maintain the same distance from the camera for sight lines in alternating

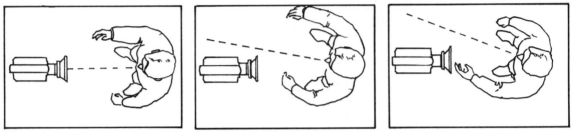

Figure 9.1

close-ups of two or more actors. Figure 9.1 is a comparison of setups for close-ups, each illustrating a different sight line relative to the camera.

Once you have acquired some feel for the psychological and dramatic implications of sight lines and eye contact, you will be able to make subtle shifts within a sequence for dramatic emphasis.

The Staging System

Unless a director spends a great deal of time training himself to see all the possibilities of setup and actor placement, he usually relies on a few all-purpose strategies for any scene. If he allows his actors greater freedom, interesting new options may arise, but unless he has a solid command of staging for the camera, the production process will ultimately undermine his experimentation. The director will find himself at odds with the cinematographer and producer, who won't understand why he keeps restaging a scene, with the consequent loss of time and, frequently, the spontaneity of his cast.

The skill this director lacks is the ability to visualize the actors and camera in space, and the composition that will result from any combination of these elements. This is where the pattern system of staging comes in.

Letter Patterns

The staging system we will be using from this point on identifies two categories of actor placement: pattern and position. We will discuss pattern first.

> Pattern: There are three basic *patterns* of figure deployment in a frame. We will call them the "A," "I" and "L" patterns. These are the letters that grouped players resemble when viewed from above.

The significance of the patterns is that *they are the simplest arrangement of actors according to the line of action.* Therefore, staging patterns relate to *camera placement.*

As you can see on the following page, the A and L patterns require three or more players to complete the letter shape. The only arrangement for two subjects is the I pattern. Figure 9.2 illustrates all three patterns.

Figure 9.2: Patterns.

Position: This refers to the direction the subjects are facing within a pattern. For any given pattern there can be many positions.

Most importantly, position relates to the composition of the frame. This means that once the camera has been placed for a given pattern, the more subtle arrangement of the actors (the direction they face in the frame) is determined by their positions. An experienced director will consider pattern and position simultaneously, but in the beginning they are more easily understood as separate concepts. Three typical positions in the I pattern are shown in Figure 9.3.

One last point: **The I pattern for two players is the basic building block in our system**. This is because the line of action can be established between only two people at a time. When there are more than two people in a conversation, the line of action moves as explained in Chapter 6. This is good news since we will only have to learn the positions for two subjects in order to apply them to larger groups. From the cameraman's point of view, the I pattern is found in the A and L patterns whenever a series of close-ups and singles are required.

Figure 9.3: Positions. All the positions are in the I pattern.

Staging Dialogue for Two Subjects

For the sake of clarity, most of the photoboards in this chapter are shot in simple surroundings staged for the static camera. Later, we'll see how camera movement or movement by the players can be substituted for cutting. For now, the camera is locked down and the photoboard sequences represent multiple camera angles that have been edited together.

POSITION ONE

Face-to-Face

The most basic positioning of two people in conversation is facing each other with their shoulders parallel. The first option is to frame the subjects in profile, as shown in the first six panels.

Compositionally, this staging allows for powerful subject oppositions. In this setup we do not get to see much of the players' expressions unless the composition is very tight (frame 6). If individual CUs are used the camera is usually repositioned for reverse OTS shots, although individual profile CUs are certainly possible.

POSITION ONE

OTS

This next series shows the classic shot, reverse shot pattern in over-the-shoulder framings. These might be the logical follow-up shots to the profile stagings on the previous page. Though OTS shots are usually shot as matched pairs maintaining consistent lens and framing choices, mixed pairs can be edited together. In a continuous exchange of dialogue, however, matched pairs are more commonplace.

In tight framings there are two major strategies for the OTS shots. Frames 3 and 4 include the foreground subject's entire head in the frame. In frames 5 and 6 virtually one third to one half of the frame is blocked off, strongly isolating the player facing us.

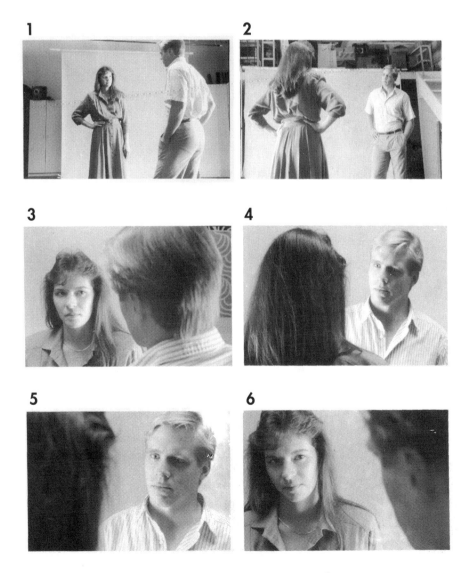

POSITION ONE

LONG LENS OTS

In the next series of OTS shots (frames 1–6), still using Position One staging, the focal length of the lens begins at 120mm and is increased to 200mm. The results are easy to see. Notice that for the first time the framing device of the face is a true over-the-shoulder shot since we see the shoulder and neck of the framing subject. This combination of lens and tight framing produces a more intimate feeling than would be obtained with a wider lens.

1

2

3

4

5

6

POSITION ONE

LOW-ANGLE REVERSE SHOTS

Another version of the shot, reverse shot pattern of Position One is seen in this next series, which can be described as over-the-hip shots. These are dynamic, low-angle positions that tend to put the subjects in an adversarial relationship. Frames 1 and 2 are only slightly low-angle and do not separate the subjects as much as do frames 3 and 4, which are shot from a camera height of 3 ft. In frames 5 and 6, the focal length of the lens is increased (100mm) to lose focus on the foreground framing subject, thus emphasizing the background figure.

POSITION TWO

Shoulder-to-Shoulder

This basically frontal positioning offers more options than most others because players can be seen full face or in profile in the same shot. In our example the subjects are faced forward, looking at a road map spread on the hood of the car, but when the couple speaks to one another they turn in profile to the camera.

Frames 1-3 are straightforward two-shots. Any of these could serve as a master shot, although frame 1 is somewhat wide for a conversation. Try to imagine a dialogue scene as you look at these frames. You will probably find that the size of the shot will affect what type of scene comes to mind. You can probably think of this as a reverse exercise since you will most often face the opposite situation: imagining a shot for a scene in a script.

1   **2**   **3**

Frames 4, 5 and 6 illustrate an actual sequence. We begin with the profile two-shot in frame 4 and move in to profile close-ups in frames 5 and 6. The camera would be moved in for the CUs, but it would still be directed along the same angle of view as for the open two-shot. (In my opinion, this use of CUs tends to break up the scene, though in the continuity style it's a perfectly legitimate cut.)

4   **5**   **6**

In frames 7-9 we open with the medium two-shot. This time we have replaced the CUs of the previous version with a profile two-shot by moving the camera around to the side and subsequently reversing to the OTS shot. Unfortunately, the framings don't fill the frame as much as I would like to see. If this were a storyboard I would know in advance that the shots should be tighter.

7   **8**   **9**

In this last series, frames 10-12, we begin with the master shot followed by two close-ups. This time we open with an angular two-shot. The camera is moved to the side for the shot, reverse shot CUs. Compare these with the two profile CU shots we used earlier in frames 5 and 6. Notice that these newer CUs give a stronger sense of presence. This happens because each subject in the CU is looking in our (the camera's) direction—in a sense, including us in the scene.

10

11

12

POSITION THREE

This basic staging deploys the figures at an angle of 90 degrees. This is a compromise between the parallel shoulder arrangement of Position One and the shoulder-to-shoulder arrangement of Position Two. It is a more casual pose, not one you would expect to see if the couple were arguing or having an intimate conversation. The looser relationship allows the couple to look away from one another and vary their head positions.

In the angular two-shot shown in frames 1 and 2 the player facing the camera is in the favored position. This type of setup is similar to the OTS shots, and we expect to see a reverse of the player in the secondary position.

The head-on two-shot in frames 3 and 4 puts the players on an equal basis and so is the logical choice for a master shot if no close-ups or reverses are used. The alternative is to have the player in the secondary position turn towards the camera to obtain the equivalent of a reverse shot. As with any of the "I" patterns, OTSs and CUs can be used, although this tends to force the subjects into the more direct relationship of Position Two. One way of maintaining the angular positioning is by composing the two-shot very tightly and closing the space between the subjects. A shot, reverse shot version of this is shown in frames 5 and 6.

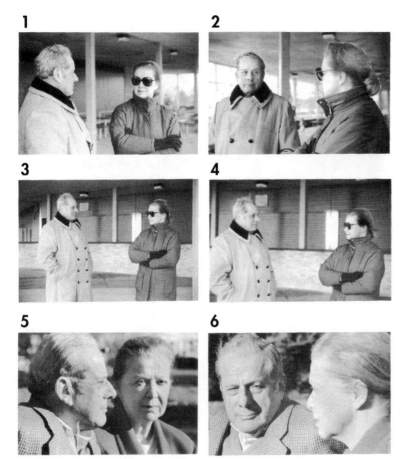

POSITION FOUR

Beginning with Position Four we will look at stagings that create tension. In all cases this is due to the absence of eye contact between the players. In this series, the woman has turned from her partner, and the sense of separation is clear. This type of framing puts the viewer in a privileged position because we can see what the man cannot: the woman's reactions to his words.

Staging in depth in this way clearly places us in a closer relationship with one of the players. This is a definite choice of point of view that depends on the basic frontality of the scene. A reverse shot in this staging would drastically alter the point of view. If a more neutral relationship with the players is desired, there are other, probably better, stagings that can be used. As you can see, I have not used any reverse shots with this staging, which is inherently frontal.

In frame 1 the two-shot is composed in depth with a 30mm lens. The result is that slight distortion can be seen in the foreground player and the player in the background seems far away even though the players are only separated by the length of a picnic table.

Frames 4, 5 and 6 present a slightly modified alternative. The opening two-shot is looser, allowing the viewer some breathing room. The close-up in frame 5 also has been made wider (almost a medium shot) to give the frame a more relaxed feeling. Frame 6 shows a lower angle close-up. Compare the feeling of this frame to frame 3 above. The result of these changes is that the sequence is less insistent.

POSITION FIVE

This is another staging that tends toward separation and tension. The body language of the woman's folded arms and the man's hands in his pockets or on his hips contributes to the interpretation of the scene. The framing can be used to emphasize the dramatic situation but is essentially neutral as to which actor is dominant. In the version shown, the woman refuses to look at the man. This, of course, is a type of control, and we can imagine that the man is placed in a position of weakness. We could just as easily propose a scene in which the man is confronting the woman with some lie she has told. In this case the man would be in the dominant role.

We begin with a high angle in frame 1. This view usually serves to create tension and isolation. The open surroundings contribute to this feeling. The cut to the two-shot in frame 2 is a legitimate edit, but I would prefer to show the players separated more. The next sequence (frames 3 and 4) shows a pair of reversed angular shots.

In frames 5 and 6 we see a pair of tighter reverse shots. In these shots the framing combines a CU framing and a medium shot. The obvious difference is that frame 6 features both players' faces, while frame 5 is really an OTS shot.

If it is necessary to withhold the woman's expression we could frame the scene from the opposite side of the action in the previous frames. In this case we will be crossing the line of action.

This staging would open with the high-angle shot in frame 7, cross the line to frame 8, and cross the line one last time to frame 9. This type of staging and shot sequence is not at all typical of the continuity style, but that is largely due to the unchallenged orthodoxy of the 180-degree convention. Do not automatically rule out a shot simply because it means crossing the line. If it works, use it.

5

6

7

8

9

POSITION SIX

This dramatic staging withholds eye contact for much of its effect. The value of this staging is its clarity, related in a sense to the shoulder-to-shoulder two-shot. The difference is that in-depth staging encourages us to identify with the foreground player. My feeling about this type of setup is that overcutting destroys the unity of the scene.

In frame 1 we see a wide shot of the setup, but frame 2 is probably the best distance for a master shot. In this type of staging the background player has room to move, pace, turn around or leave the frame momentarily, while the foreground player is restricted to a smaller space if both players are to remain within the frame. Frames 3 and 4 reveal the way in which identification can be controlled by placing us in an intimate relationship with the man. If cutting is used, the pair of close-ups in frames 5 and 6 retain the feeling of separation.

1

2

3

4

5

6

POSITION SEVEN

With this staging we continue the deployment of players who do not make eye contact. Because both players are looking offscreen in different directions, the viewer's attention is divided between the background and the foreground players. This produces an offhanded, relaxed dramatic situation. Notice that the background player is looking past the foreground player. This directs the viewer's attention to the foreground player and unifies the shot.

Consider this series a comparison of close-ups. The middle close-up of the man is a good example of how shot size contributes to the spatial unity of the sequence. Learn to move your eyes over the images without studying them. Reading a storyboard is a matter of editing with your eyes. This becomes easier when you have an actual scene to imagine.

POSITION EIGHT

This next version is a variation on the previous staging. As before, the players are in a right-angle relationship, but this time the background player is looking away from the other player. The three pairs of photos serve as a good example of the different ways in which the viewer's relationship to the players is determined. In frames 1 and 2 the woman facing us is favored slightly. As a general rule the player whose eyes are most clearly seen will dominate the shot. As we have seen before, in-depth staging encourages our indentification with the foreground player. Finally, the angular shots in frames 5 and 6 tend to balance the attention of the figures since both players are turned away from the camera.

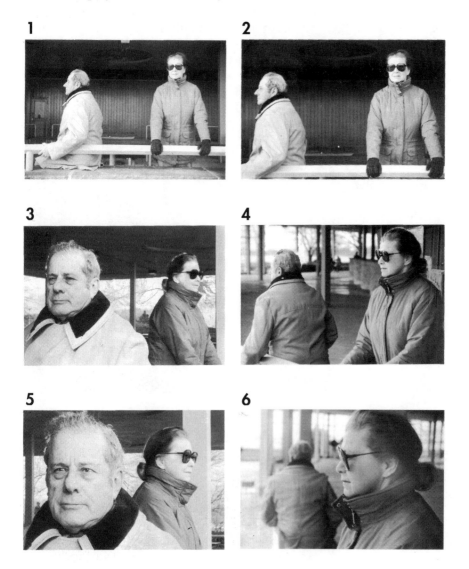

POSITION NINE

This series features a staging that has the players so completely opposed that it seems as though it belongs in a musical comedy. This is only true if we imagine that the players are aware of each other and have taken a defiant stance. We can change this very easily if we imagine that the scene is set on a railroad platform and that the man has been hired to follow the woman. The man moves into the crowd and stands with his back to her. In this case the staging would be suited to a thriller, not a comedy.

Comparing the stagings in frames 1 through 4 you will see that the somewhat stylized positioning in frames 1 and 2 is less artificial-looking as we move closer in frames 3 and 4.

1

2

3

4

Personally, I find frames 5-10 to be the most successful framings of this position. All six frames are evocative for the reason that the head turn indicates that the featured player is listening to something offscreen. In a sense this is an aural version of the cut on the look.

5   **6**

7   **8**

9   **10**

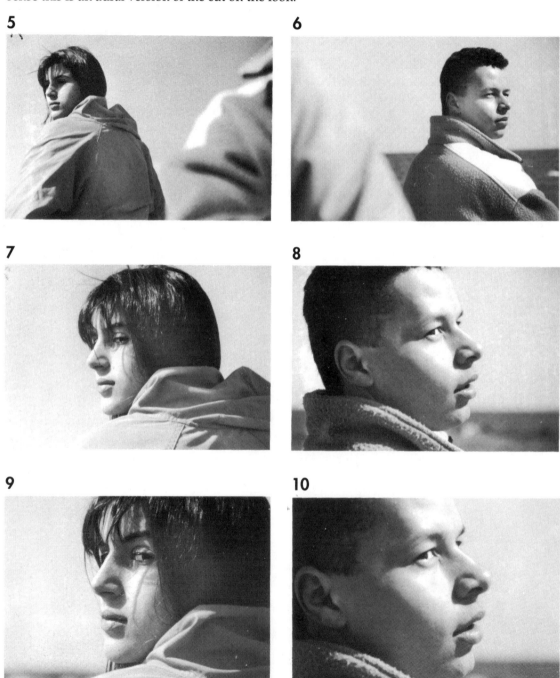

POSITION TEN

The following three sequences record a staging in which the players are positioned at different heights. This usually means that tight two-shots are framed as up or down angles, though in wider framings this is not necessary. No reverse shots are shown in this series, though that is certainly a workable variation.

Spend some time looking at the shot flow in these sequences. Try "reading" the frames from right to left or diagonally across to produce different combinations. Any of these shots works with any other, but each presents a slightly different feeling and spatial sense. Developing the skill to predict relationships between shots in a sequence will help you in composing individual shots.

There are innumerable variations on two-player stagings that we have not looked at, but nearly all the possibilities will share the essential physical and emotional qualities of at least one of the positions illustrated. The point is not to memorize every conceivable arrangement of player and camera, but rather to sharpen your awareness of the relationship of the elements from which the dramatic qualities of a shot are composed.

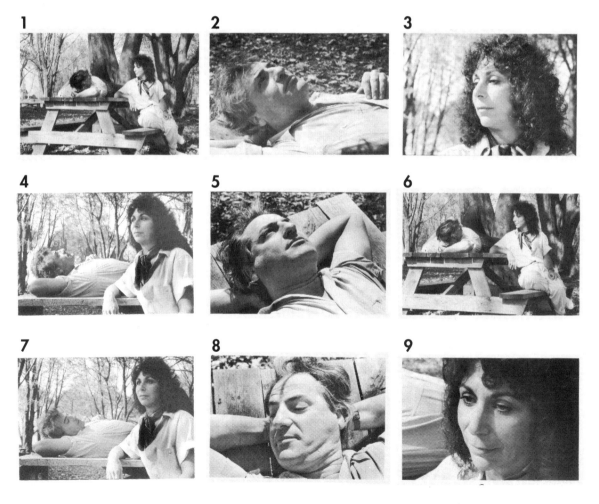

10 DIALOGUE STAGING WITH THREE SUBJECTS

N ow that we have looked at the 10 positions for the "I" pattern, we can add a third player to our stagings, which will make the "A" and "L" patterns possible. Remember, our system is based on three assumptions:

- The I pattern is the simplest building block. It is found in the A and L patterns.
- Patterns determine camera placement based on the line of action.
- Position determines the placement of players in the frame based on the basic staging pattern.

The Difference Between A and L Patterns

Because actors are not always arranged in precise A or L alignment, it is not always easy to decide which pattern to apply. In this case camera placement is the determining factor.

For example, when lining up players for a three-shot you may find that

two players are facing the third player. If the third player is framed between the other two, then the staging arrangement is the A pattern. If the third player is lined up outside the other two players, then the arrangement is the L pattern. This aspect of staging is called *opposition*. Figure 10.1 shows the various types of oppositions that can be obtained.

The Basic Patterns and Positions

In the two-player stagings of the previ-

Figure 10.1: Frames 1 and 2 show one subject opposed by two others. Since the lone figure in black is flanked by the other two, this is an A pattern. Frames 3 and 4 show the alternative setup for the three-shot in which the lone subject is isolated to one side. This is an L pattern. Frames 5 and 6 illustrate the type of opposition that can be obtained if we break down the three-shot into a two-shot opposed by a close-up. In frames 7–9 all the players are equally opposed in close-ups.

ous chapter, the models in the photoboards were arranged in open space. Having established the basic positions in those examples we can look at stagings that are less precisely aligned.

By adding the additional player we have increased the number of pattern and position combinations enormously. We do not need to look at all of them since we know that any combination can be reduced to the 10 positions in the I pattern that we have already seen. Conversely, we can reverse the process and construct dozens of three-player stagings from the 10 positions. This idea is shown in Figure 10.2.

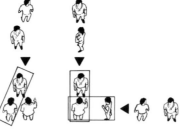

Figure 10.2: Here we see the boxed portion of the A and L patterns being replaced by the two alternate positions in the I pattern at the top of the figure. The box could just as easily be drawn horizontally or diagonally as long as two players are enclosed in the box.

Before looking at the photoboard examples, we can review the line of action as it pertains to three-player scenes. Figure 10.3 shows a typical staging situation in the A pattern.

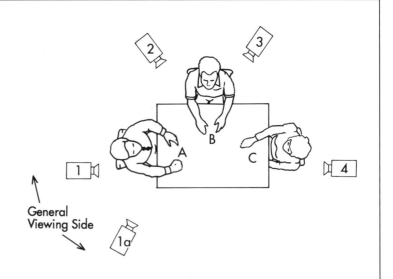

Figure 10.3: In this A pattern staging I first determined the general angle of view. Although the camera can move 360 degrees around the players, the scene should have a basic viewing orientation. The circumstances vary with the scene, but in this case the scene opens with a view from camera 1. The dialogue begins between players a and c. This establishes the line between them. Camera positions 1 and 2 for OTS shots are placed *outside* the line. Now player b speaks to player c, establishing a new line between them. On what side of the line do we place the camera? This is where the general view comes in. Rather than set up a new camera position *outside* of players a and b, as we did for players a and c, we stay on the same side of player a. Now when player b speaks to player c we stay on the same side of player b and use camera position 2. What about camera position 3? Do we actually need this angle? With the number of angles we already have, it may be unnecessary. This example can be handled in other ways, but the general idea is to reuse positions when possible rather than constantly creating new ones whenever a new line is established.

In the following examples we will consider some common and some not so common staging situations with three players.

A Pattern (Version One)

Here is the same staging situation we just looked at in Figure 10.3. Frame 1 is the only combination of setup and staging for this pattern that permits us to see all the subjects clearly. This makes it the obvious choice for a master shot.

In the first series of frames (2-5), single shots (medium shots and a close-up) are used after the opening master shot. This produces two results. First, it tends to fragment space, and secondly, it prevents us from seeing the player speaking and the players who are listening in one shot. Compare this with the next sequence.

1

2

3

4

5

In this next series of six frames (6-11), OTS shots have been used to unify space. After the establishing shot, an entire conversation can be comfortably handled in OTS shots and an occasional three-shot or two-shot to vary the rhythm. As you can see, the OTS shots are framed in the same way we would handle the staging if there were only two players. The several OTS variations in the I pattern introduced in the last chapter all apply to the staging we are looking at here.

A Pattern (Version Two)

This "A" pattern staging is a direct positioning of opposed figures as might be expected in an interview or meeting in which the parties are on a formal basis. Again this is a very common staging position whether the players are standing or sitting. Notice that the man's sight line in frame 1 is very close to the camera, placing him in a direct relationship with the viewer. In frame

2 we see the women in profile, and their relationship to the viewer is deferential. It looks as though the women are the listeners and the man is in a position of authority. Frame 3 preserves this relationship even though we do not see the man's face. This is because a down shot of this type is not the type of framing we would expect if either woman had anything important to say.

1   **2**   **3**

Compare frames 4-6 with the last series. Frame 4 places the man in a very direct relationship with the viewer. Personally, I do not like the rendition of space in frames 4 and 5. Frame 5 was shot with a 40mm lens, but it looks too wide to me. What do you think about frame 6? Now look at both sequences and compare the experience of "reading" them. Which sequence do you find the most successful in terms of shot flow? If you could substitute shots from one sequence for some in the other which ones would you choose?

4   **5**   **6**

In this next series you can see how the man's presence is diminished when he is not in a frontal position. Before he was in command; now he is in a reactive position. If we started with a picture of the woman facing the camera followed by the profile shot of the man in frame 7, the woman would be in the position of authority.

7   **8**

A Pattern (Version Two)

The two series of frames below are a good comparison of overlapped space and discontinuous space within a frame. Frame 10 in the top row is an OTS shot and includes some of the man from the previous shot. This is what is meant by *overlapping* space. The reverse CU shot in frame 11 does not include space from the previous shot and is therefore *discontinuous*. Overlapping ties together the scene space. At the same time, close-ups like the ones in frames 12 and 14 isolate a subject in a way that might be justified dramatically.

Notice how frames 11 and 13 serve as pivot shots directing our attention to the appropriate CU, frame 12 or 14. The direction of the man's look is the determining factor. Cutting on his head turn is a powerful editing cue.

One last point to be made is the importance of lens choice. These shots were all photographed in the 50 to 90mm range. The three shots, frames 9 and 13, were the widest at 50mm, and it might have been possible to bring the women in the foreground into a closer relationship with the man with a longer lens. Manipulating scene space with the lens is a powerful technique, but if used carelessly it can cause spatial inconsistencies.

9   10   11

12   13   14

L Pattern (Version One)

Here we see a typical use of the L pattern. An angular view in frame 1 moves to a low-angle OTS shot in frame 2. Actually we are seeing a portion of the man's arm, not his shoulder, and it preserves the spatial unity of the opening shot. We then move to two close-ups. Notice the rhythm created in four frames by the change in shot size and camera angle. We become progressively tighter for three frames and then back out to a slightly wider CU in frame 4. Compare this with the next series.

Frames 5-7 show how the sequence would look if we only used OTS three-shots. An entire conversation could be shot this way, though frame 6 could be a little tighter. Generally speaking this sequence has a more relaxed, stable feel than the previous version.

L Pattern (Version Two)

Here's another version of the L pattern. This time the opening shot of the scene is a two-shot. Not until frame 3 do we see an overview of the scene space. This is an interesting strategy for opening a scene—deliberately withholding the full context of the scene. We also see a typical use of the two-shot in frame 1. It is typical because the L pattern generally groups the two players on the long top of the L together. Almost always, the L seating or standing arrangement occurs when a single player is addressing two others.

1 **2** **3**

We can compare the use of the three-shot in this last series with the two-shot in the previous series. Both three-shots are OTS framings. An alternative three-shot is shown in the bottom row. One last point: The frames in all these series are necessarily small for presentation purposes. In a theater the subjects in these shots would appear considerably closer and more intimate.

4 **5** **6**

7

I Pattern

This is a simple version of a common staging. Once again we can see that the options for cutting tend toward shot, reverse shot patterns. If cutting is not used, we can employ more complex staging in depth, but quite often OTS shots, two-shots and close-ups are the best way to frame the action. In this series we find this strategy working effectively. By adding a dolly move and by repositioning the players, we have obtained many of the same angles seen in multiple shots using only the master shot. Later we'll look at staging techniques that use a master shot for an entire scene.

A Pattern (In-Depth Staging One)

This next series is an unusual staging of a dialogue sequence. I have included it as a study of in-depth staging and the use of lenses.

Frames 1-4 are straightforward stagings of the players. A line of action is established between the man and the two women. Respecting the line we can move to the low angle two-shot (frame 3) or the subsequent OTS shots of the women (frame 4), which establish a new line.

If we want to explore more fully the relationship between the man and the women we can use a pair of reverse shots. Here's how we might cross the line: We could open the scene with a medium shot of the man in frame 5. This could be followed by the man's head turn as he looks at the women in the foreground in frame 6. After several seconds the man will turn away, and we can cut to frame 7. Now we can cut to the two-shots or the OTS shots from the previous series. We also have the option of cutting to OTS shots on the *opposite* side of the women after frame 7.

A Pattern (In-Depth Staging Two)

This staging in depth is a good example of the use of frontality. It has been designed to work without reverses or shots taken from the side. The camera is able to move all the way to the background to feature the women coming through the gate. After the establishing shot a scene staged this way might only use frames 2 and 3 for an entire conversation.

Frames 4-6 represent an alternative establishment of scene space. In this version the scene opens with the woman in the background. We are intrigued by her look and cut to the wider frame of the other two players in frame 5. This is a cut on the look, but it is not a POV shot. That would require a reverse angle. Finally, we widen all the way out in a wide establishing shot. This might serve as a dramatic pause in the middle of the scene or as the final shot.

A Pattern (Experimenting With the Line of Action)

This A arrangement stages the players at different heights to obtain interesting angles. This is also an example of the unorthodox use of the line of action. Frames 1 and 2 establish the line in an unconventional manner by not basing it on the sight lines of the players. Frame 3 is a radical shift to a low-angle shot. But the scene geography was so clear in frame 1 that we remember where the boy on the railing was seated. Also the gun stock was deliberately included in the shot as a spatial signpost.

Frame 4 observes the new line established between the two boys on the railing, but in frame 5 we violate that line to get the shot of the boy standing on the ground. Frame 6 is a reestablishing shot and frame 7 again crosses the line. It is likely that an actual sequence would use head turns and other spatial cues that would make the editing pattern more cohesive. However, whether or not this rule-breaking approach works for you is your decision.

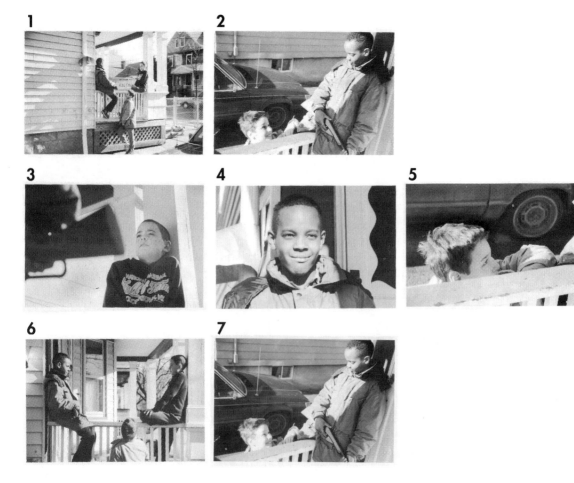

L Pattern (Version Three)

Here's an alternative treatment of the previous scene. In this version the cut on the look motivates many of the shots. We open with the three-shot in frame 1 (the third boy is hidden behind the railing). In frame 2 we cut to a reverse on the boy's head turn and look. We reverse again and move to the CU of the boy behind the railing looking back. In frame 4 the boy seated on the railing throws a pebble at the boy behind the railing who looks up in frame 5. We open up to a wide shot in frame 6 as the boy in the foreground calls to his two friends. This motivates the head turn of the boy in CU in frame 7. Throughout this sequence cutting has been motivated by either action or the cut on the look.

11 FOUR OR MORE PLAYER DIALOGUE STAGINGS

Staging dialogue scenes with four or more subjects utilizes the same A, I and L patterns that we used for three-player dialogue scenes. However, as the number of subjects grows, so do the possibilities for individual shots or group shots. For instance, for a scene with five subjects, there are 5 possible CUs, 9 two-shots, 6 three-shots, 6 four-shots and 1 five-person master shot, or approximately 27 shots. Obviously, this is an overwhelming number of choices for any scene, and while some setups are clearly impractical, photographing groupings with more than three subjects is a matter of consolidation and simplification.

In nearly all cases, dramatic structure in fiction does this for us by representing a generalized view of the human situation through the actions of individuals. In practical terms this is found in any scene involving large numbers of people when we focus on the key experiences of the main characters within a compressed time frame. While these are dramatic conventions, they are similar to how we experience any large gathering of people in real life. At a dinner party, for example, people arrange themselves into small groups because it's simply too difficult to converse with more than five or six people simultaneously. Even when one person gains the attention of the other guests, it's basically a two-person arrangement: the speaker and his audience. When filming a large group where several players speak, close-ups are often used in favor of three- and four-player group shots, since this helps differentiate the players.

If we look at Figure 11.1 we see one man surrounded by seven other people. It would be unusual for each of these players to have significant speaking parts. Even if

Figure 11.1

that were the case, one or two players would almost certainly emerge as the central players. The key to camera positioning is identifying which players are the central players in the scene.

Figure 11.2 shows the line of action established between the principal two players in the scene. CUs of all the other players might be used, but the basic staging preserves the line of action as established by these players.

Figure 11.3 shows what happens if three players share the dialogue equally. In this case the A pattern applies and the camera can be positioned accordingly. As we learned

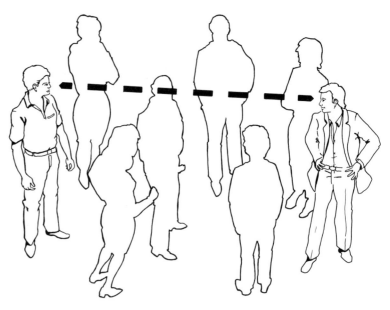

Figure 11.2

in the previous chapter, even the A pattern is ultimately reduced to the two-subject I position when determining the line of action. The players who do not have dialogue may be included in the shot, but the camera position is restricted to the 180-degree working area on one side of the line of action.

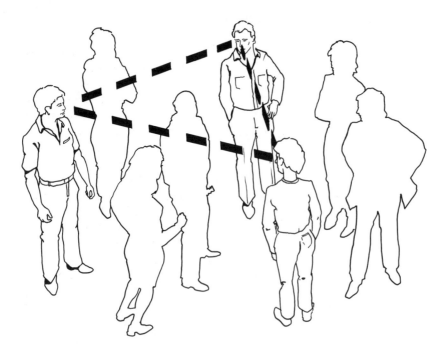

Figure 11.3

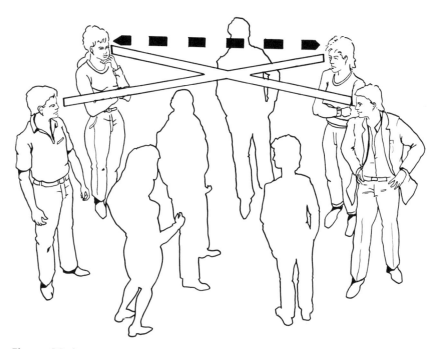

Figure 11.4

In Figure 11.4 the same logic applies to four key players. In this situation we have multiple lines of sight or potential lines of action. While it is possible to puzzle out camera placement for each pair of players, there is a simpler way to work out the staging. Limit yourself to a few key setups. If you are establishing more than four sightlines to move around space in a large group, you are creating unnecessary problems. The dotted line in Figure 11.4 represents a basic line of action that permits close-ups, singles, two-shots and a group shot. This means that we are establishing a general viewing direction.

It should be mentioned at this point that all this attention to the line of action and camera setup implies an active cutting style. In any of the previous examples of large group stagings, a single camera setup could be used, and this of course would eliminate continuity problems.

While it is easy to visualize this in illustrations from an uncluttered high-angle view, it can be anything but simple to visualize a scene when you're on the set with a large cast. But no matter how complex the staging becomes, the camera geography of any scene is easily determined by keeping the line of action in mind. This is true whether you choose to violate the line or not. The Japanese director Yasujiro Ozu, whose staging style required him to cross the line, was as consistent in his rejection of the traditional rules of continuity as any Hollywood director is in observing them. The purpose of describing staging in terms of the line of action is to help a director make clearheaded choices. The line and the patterns based on the line should be thought of as a system of organization, not as an aesthetic choice. If it helps you to break through to some new way of working, so much the better.

A Pattern (Version One)

This time 5 players are seated in a circular arrangement. In this case it's possible to interpret the staging as an I, A or L arrangement depending on which players are being emphasized. The determination of the line of action, general viewing angle and staging pattern is your choice.

In this situation, the predominant viewing angle is over the shoulder of the grandmother shown in Figure 3. All the other players can be viewed from this position. Only one reverse is required to see the grandmother.

In this situation the line of action is extremely flexible. The reason is that the line of action is generally determined by the sight line of the players featured in the scene. As you can see, there are so many possible sight lines in this circular staging that we could easily establish a new line anywhere in the scene space.

Frames 2, 3 and 4 show an editing pattern in which subjects on the sides of the table are seen in angular shots, essentially from the point of view of the grandmother in frame 3. An unorthodox alternative is the side-by-side OTS shots of the grandmother in frames 5 and 6.

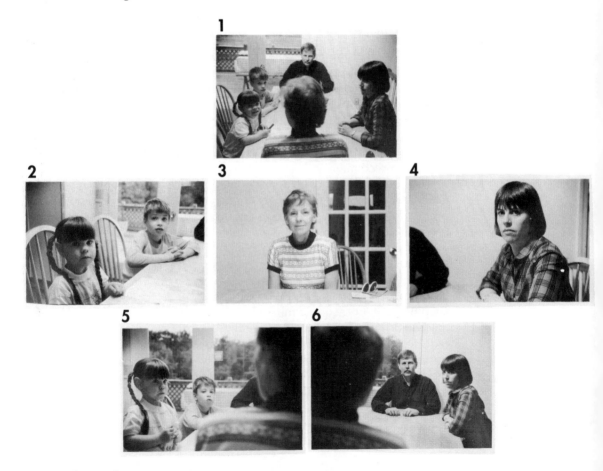

L Pattern

This is a good example of how a group of four players is treated in CUs, two-shots and three-shots. In this arrangement the two girls seated side-by-side clearly work as a two-shot and form the center of the scene. We can frame them as though they were one player opposite the boy, which means we are essentially working with the I pattern.

In frame 1 we set up the full group and move into a wide OTS three-shot in frame 2 (the fourth figure is partially visible). The OTS two-shot in frame 3, the two-shot in frame 4 and the medium single shot in frame 5 make up one simplified treatment of the scene, assuming that editing is called for.

To show how easy it would be to stage the scene for a single master shot, consider frame 2. If the camera were shifted a few feet to the right and tilted up, all four figures would be framed. In this arrangement the seated figures would be in profile and the standing figure would be in a frontal position.

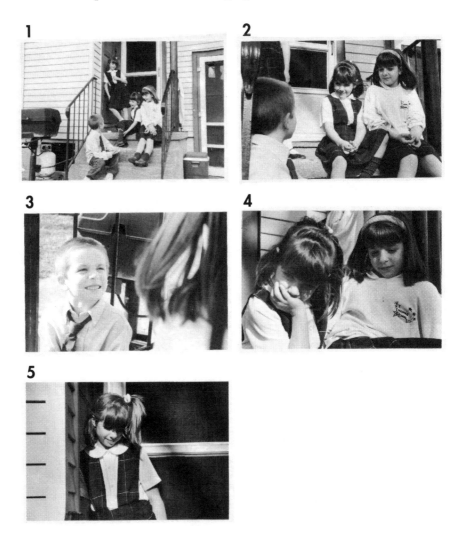

A Pattern (Version Two)

This next series of nine panels shows three staging possibilities comparing I, L and A pattern stagings. In the first example we have a classic three angle treatment of the I pattern. Panel 1 shows the head-on center position. From a closer position, but still located midpoint between the subjects, the camera is pivoted left and right to obtain panels 2 and 3.

In the second sequence we open up with the girl who is standing lined up to one side of the seated figures. This makes it the L pattern. At the same time the camera has been moved to a position almost along the line of action and outside the scene space. Two angular shots give us a single and a three-shot.

In this next sequence we have an A pattern interpretation of the same scene. In this case the girl standing is lined up so that she is flanked by the subjects in frames 7 and 8. In these two shots the line of action practically runs through the camera position.

Patterns can also be mixed. If you read the frames vertically, for instance, panels 1,4 and 7 shots from the I, L, and A patterns work together quite comfortably. The choice is essentially between symmetrical or asymmetrical framings. This is most obvious in the shot, reverse shot pattern.

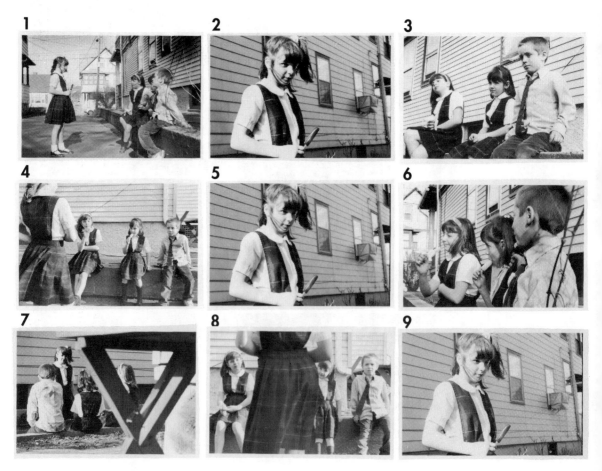

Frontal Positions for Single Setups

By now the various possibilities for staging two-, three- and four-or-more-subject dialogue sequences should be familiar as recognizable framing and editing patterns. In midsized groups where each subject is dramatically significant, master shot stagings are often desirable. The three examples that follow show asymmetrical stagings and the use of depth in figure placement.

1

In a group master shot in which the action is staged for one viewpoint, the screen too easily becomes the theatrical proscenium. Rather than have a scene staged across the frame, players can be staged along the lens axis, as with the group of boys in the hallway in frames 1 and 2. Here the players are seen in profile. Foreground players may turn from the camera occasionally to react to background players, but they can be directed to speak or respond to players across from them as well.

2

In-Depth Frontal Positions

In this next series of frames, an in-depth composition is used with a foreground player close to the camera. The overly composed theatrical positioning in frame 3 is modified in frame 4 so that the background players form a looser group arrangement.

The evolution of the compositions in frames 1-6 is representative of the staging process carried out on the set by the director, the actors and the cinematographer. Frames 1 through 6 are all ways of dealing with the same scene, with frame 5 coming closest to an acceptable solution. However, I would probably bring the seated figure on the right forward slightly.

When staging groups, filmmakers are sometimes fearful that their players are not seen clearly within the frame. The result of overcomposed figures is staginess, and the only cure is a disregard for ordered framing. In the following examples figures are overlapped or cut off by the frame, and this freedom permits many more options for staging action. This style of composition is known as open framing and will be discussed further in a later chapter.

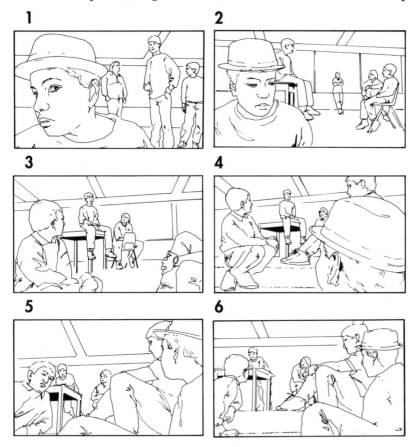

Crowds and Large Groups

In concluding the dialogue staging section we come to the treatment of individual players when they are in crowds or other large gatherings of people.

When staging a dialogue scene in a crowd, the subjects in conversation are still placed in accordance with the concepts we applied to 2, 3, and 4 players. However, there are some additional camera techniques available that solve some of the spatial problems that arise when the scene space is densely packed with people.

There are two basic approaches to shooting dialogue in or around a crowd: The camera is either in the crowd looking out or outside the crowd looking in. The execution of each approach is largely dependent on the focal length of the lens that you use. Shots framed from within the action are normally taken with a wide or normal lens, while shots taken from outside the action are shot with a telephoto lens.

Telephoto Lenses

Apart from the specific visual appeal of a telephoto shot, long lenses have become popular in the shooting of large crowds for logistical reasons. For instance, it is possible to simulate large masses of people with a limited number of extras strategically placed in depth for the telephoto lens. In addition, due to the shallow depth of field, the telephoto lens can isolate principal subjects from foreground and background elements whether the crowd is staged or real.

At the same time, the camera can be placed at a distance from the crowd, making it easier for the cameraman to work. Spatial relationships within shots and between shots are indefinite due to the shallow depth of field, and the specific location of action is difficult to identify. The telephoto lens permits cameramen to work in crowds discretely, allowing them to photograph actors in real situations (as in the photos accompanying this section.)

The use of the telephoto requires keeping the camera outside the action. If the camera were in the midst of the crowd, it would have to be a great distance from the players in order to frame them, thereby allowing too many extras to come between the camera and the subjects. The result would be that the crowd would obscure the players. Therefore, telephoto shots of subjects within a crowd must be carefully staged so that just the right number of people move between the camera and players. Since this turns out to be only a few people, 10 to 15 extras can be made to seem like a big crowd.

Wide Lenses

Staging action for the wide lens is far more difficult. Generally, the camera is in the action, close to the subject of the shot. As with the telephoto shot, extras must be carefully arranged between camera and subject, but the greater depth of field and clarity of the normal lens is less forgiving in terms of framing. The positioning of figures is much more critical, and a slight variation of any element can wreck the shot. If the camera and subject move, many more extras are necessary, and because the camera is within the action, a quarter turn takes in 90 degrees of space. This is space that might require dozens or hundreds of extras to fill. At the same time, the camera and crew have to work in close quarters and moving dolly track or lights requires clearing the area.

For all this, the normal lens has decided advantages for creating understandable geography, as well as for its particular graphic qualities. It is usually necessary to stage physical action with the wider lenses, while dialogue stagings can be shot with a telephoto. We can now look at some examples of actual shots.

Lens Comparisons for Crowd Scenes

The arrow indicates the subjects of our shots. Frame 1 is a moderate wide-angle shot (35mm) outside the action. Frame 2 is shot through the parade and views our subjects from within the action using a 40mm lens.

In frame 3 we are again on the same side of the street as our subjects, this time with a longer lens to bring the background closer. One slightly unorthodox effect is that the subjects are in soft focus due to the shallow depth of field. While some filmmakers object to allowing principal subjects to go soft even while they remain the center of attention, I find that the subjects can be recognized if their clothes or appearance has been estab-

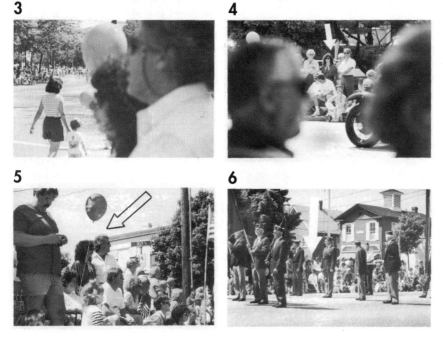

lished in previous shots. Frame 4, taken with a 500mm lens was shot from across the street using two foreground spectators as a framing device. Finally, frames 5 and 6 are on the perimeter of the action, very nearly in the thick of things, shot with a 50mm lens.

We conclude with a comparison of lenses. First is a 40mm lens with figures in the middle ground, second is a 50mm lens with the figures in the foreground and last is a 300mm lens shot with the figures in the background.

40mm lens

50mm lens

300mm lens

12 MOBILE STAGING

When Fred Astaire left Broadway for the studios of RKO he summed up his thoughts about motion pictures and dance this way: "Either the camera will dance or I will." This is pretty good advice for a choreographer to follow, but it also happens to be a succinct way of describing the two basic methods of staging mobile action: move the camera or move the subject.

In the previous three chapters on staging dialogue we built sequences by using multiple camera viewpoints to direct the viewer's attention—the camera moved around players who remained in a fixed position. There is an alternative to this way of staging action: directing the viewer's attention from one subject to another by having the subjects move within the space framed by the camera. In practice, both approaches are frequently combined to present a varied and fluid dramatic sequence. In addition to cutting multiple viewpoints together and moving the subject in the frame, we can also move the camera in a tracking or crane shot. These three methods of photographing action in sequence represent the entire range of camera and subject staging techniques.

In Figure 12.1, frames 1 and 2 illustrate a simple shot, reverse shot editing pattern using OTS framings. This is a straightforward way to treat

Figure 12.1

Frames 1 and 2 show the shot, reverse shot cutting pattern. Frames 3 and 4 represent a continuous shot in which the man turns around to face the camera. This strategy uses mobile staging to achieve the same results as cutting.

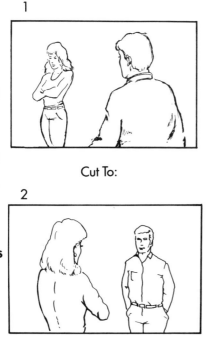

Cut To:

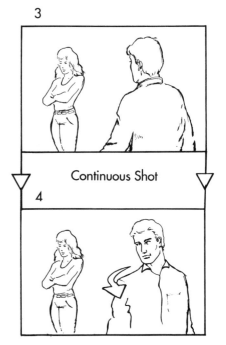

Continuous Shot

a dialogue scene if the subjects are stationary. The alternative is to allow the players to reposition themselves as part of the action in a single shot, as shown in frames 3 and 4. By having the man turn around in frame 4 we obtain the frontal view that previously required a new shot.

A variation on this same idea of substituting the actor's movement for editing is shown in Figure 12.2 This time the girl in the background of the shot comes forward until she is seen in close-up. The man with his back to the camera in frame 1 turns with her so that they are both facing the camera. In a sense we have obtained the equivalent of a medium OTS shot, a close-up and two-shot without resorting to cutting.

These two examples of mobile staging will give you the basic idea. The only criterion the actor's movement should meet is whether it is motivated or not. This type of staging falls under the category of "stage business." This can mean anything from lighting a cigarette (the classic piece of stage business in the '40s) to moving around a bedroom while getting dressed in the morning. You should never really have to invent artificial business just to add action to a scene. If the story, actors and the directing process are working together, ideas will emerge from this collaboration that are accurate observations of human behavior.

Building Blocks

Think of the longest, most involved sequence shot you can remember from a film. Now imagine how you might draw that sequence in a storyboard. Since you cannot depict continuous movement in a single panel, you would

Figure 12.2

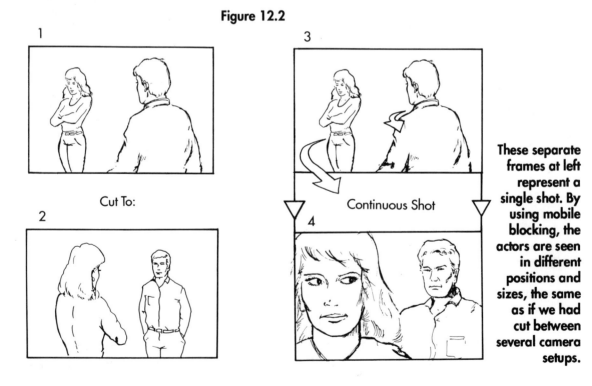

1

Cut To:

2

3

Continuous Shot

4

These separate frames at left represent a single shot. By using mobile blocking, the actors are seen in different positions and sizes, the same as if we had cut between several camera setups.

have to choose key moments in the action and draw them in a series of panels. As it turns out, this is fairly easy because most action staged for a long interrupted shot is composed of these very same moments choreographed into a smooth continuity. We can also reverse the process and devise a continuous shot built from the same individual key events in the action.

We've already looked at the building blocks for this approach in the patterns and positions catalogued in the previous chapters on staging. Working out choreographed movement with the actors is merely a matter of connecting different patterns and positions so that all the separate views of a scene are linked into a single shot.

Mobile Staging (Example One)

Let's try building a simple two-position sequence using camera movement and a subject who is repositioned in the shot. This strategy is shown in figure 12.3. The movement of the camera and the actor represents a single

Figure 12.3

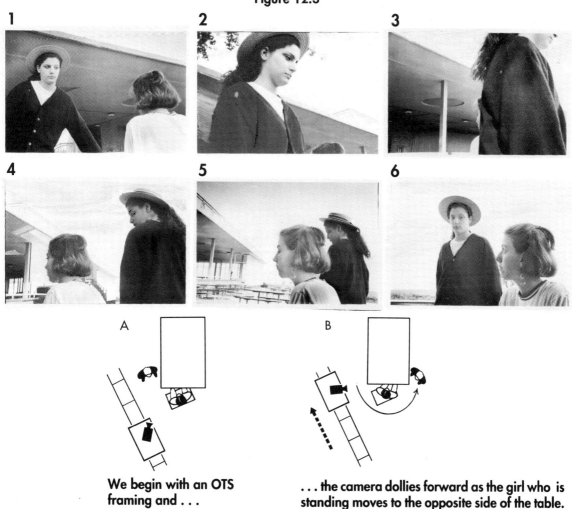

A

We begin with an OTS framing and . . .

B

. . . the camera dollies forward as the girl who is standing moves to the opposite side of the table.

unbroken shot. The accompanying diagrams show an aerial view of the choreography.

Imagine that the two girls in the photographs have been speaking for several moments in the wide OTS shot in frame 1. Rather than cut to a new shot of the seated girl as she begins to speak, we dolly the camera forward 4 ft. while the girl in the hat walks to the other side of the seated girl. In this version both camera and player move simultaneously, and the final staging in frame 6 permits us to see both players. You might recognize this arrangement; it is position five from the two-player stagings in Chapter 9. This particular type of move, in which a subject moves in the opposite direction of the camera, is called a *counter move*. In this version the girl who walks past camera is absent from the frame for a moment, but the whole action is very short and only a few seconds elapse from frame 1 to frame 6. Of course, the variables in timing and positioning are considerable and have a great deal of impact on the dramatic emphasis within the scene.

Now we're ready to try a considerably more ambitious sequence shot using staging patterns and positions we learned in the previous three chapters. We can begin with position four, version #8, from the two-subject dialogue stagings (chapter 9) and combine it with another position at the picnic table. The following pages illustrate how a series of separate shots can be combined into a single shot by moving the actors and the camera.

Mobile Staging (Example Two)

In frame 1 the girl refuses to acknowledge her boyfriend. He moves forward and takes a seat at the opposite end of the table in frame 2. The schematic drawings show the movement of the camera to accommodate the new staging.

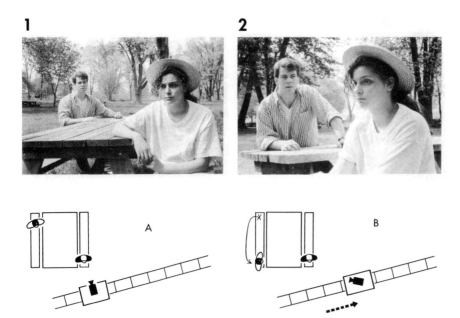

Frustrated, the boy stands up and walks a few steps away, still speaking to the girl (frame 3). After a few moments he returns to the table (frame 4) and angrily tries to provoke some kind of response from the girl. The camera has not dollied during this action.

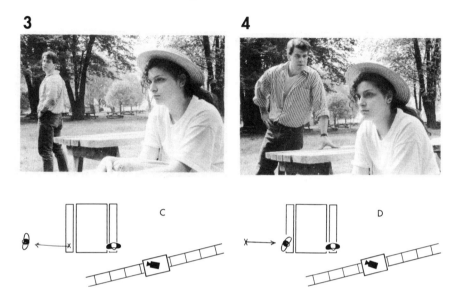

Now the boy walks towards the camera and the camera dollies ahead of him a few feet until he turns to face the girl in frame 5. As the boy speaks the girl turns toward him to listen (frame 6). As this happens the camera retracks towards her, leaving the boy out of frame. Once she is framed in a medium shot the camera comes to rest for a few moments.

The camera slowly moves in front of the girl in frame 7 as the boy re-enters the shot, sitting down behind her in frame 8. The camera comes to rest in this framing for a few moments, but when the boy leans left across the table the camera moves with him and pushes in to a closer shot as he makes his final appeal to the girl in frame 9.

7 **8** **9**

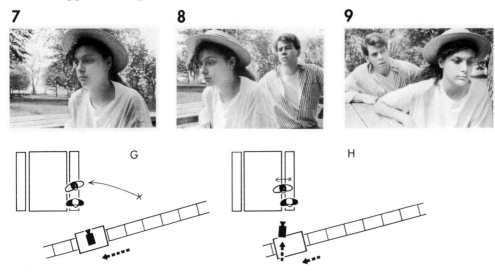

Finally, the boy gives up, and making his parting comments he stands up in frame 10. The camera backs up a few feet to a wider shot as the boy walks away. The final framing of the shot is seen in frame 11.

In this example of mobile staging in a sequence shot we used several different techniques to get the maximum use of a 15-ft. piece of track. This included staging in depth to vary the framing, panning from a stationary

10 **11**

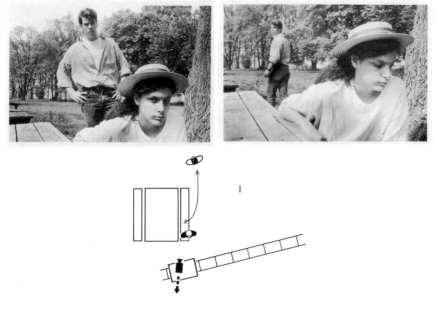

position to reframe, retracking over the same space by reversing the direction of the camera, following one subject (the boy) and then another (the girl) and pushing in towards a subject and then backing away.

Visualizing the staging of a scene requires collaboration on the set by the director, the cast, the cinematographer, the weather, happenstance and any crew member who has a good suggestion at the time. Particularly important is the camera operator: The speed and timing of a camera move and the transfer of attention from one actor to another are ultimately his responsibilities. These subtleties cannot be anticipated in a storyboard and must be worked out on the set during rehearsal. The communication between the cinematographer and the director must be very precise if the director is to get what he wants.

Loosening Up Your Staging Style

While the director is helping the actors to shape their performances and interpret the script, he is evaluating the visual and technical consequences of whatever staging improvisation takes place on the set. The restrictions placed by the camera on an actor's movement are usually a distraction to the actor, and complex staging only increases the problem. On the one hand, the director wants to make the actor's job easier, but he also has a visual plan that must be accommodated. There is no magic solution to this opposition of goals except for the director to have a broad knowledge of the creative options. The following suggestions are intended to overcome some staging conventions that hold directors back from taking chances.

Action and Reaction

First, there are only two types of shots in a conversation, the action and the reaction. Filmmakers are frequently over-concerned about the action. The truth is, we learn as much from the reaction as we do from the action. Knowing this will loosen up your staging because it means the person speaking need not be the center of attention. One version of this is shown at left.

The choreography in Figure 12.4 shows the man in the background circling our main subject. As you can see from the two frames, most of the background player's action is offscreen. The camera actually pushes in to a CU of the foreground figure so we can see his reaction to a long speech made by the background player as he walks out of frame.

The reaction doesn't have to be a CU of the man's face. It could also be a CU of his hands as he nervously fingers his car keys or a shot of his foot tapping impa-

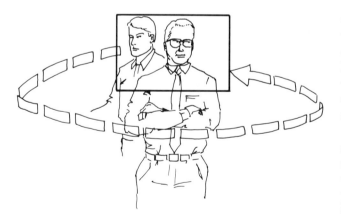

Figure 12.4: The arrow indicates the path of the background player. He passes the camera once before entering the frame on camera right. Our only indication of the background player's location is the movement of the foreground player's head or eyes, which might follow the other man as he walks.

tiently, or any other visual or physical index to the person's feelings. If the person who is reacting is looking into a fireplace we might see the flames for an extended period or just a shot of ashes. Sharing his point of view can help shape our understanding of his reaction.

Moving the Center of Interest

The camera following a subject who is the center of interest can move around other players so that the subject directs us to the reactions of the other players. This can be done in a single shot. The subject who is the center of interest need not be emotionally dominant but may have special knowledge that is of interest to the other players. From a practical standpoint the advantage of this staging is that one player moves while the other players are stationary.

An extreme example of the moving center of interest strategy is the Marine Corps sergeant drilling new recruits, a scene we have watched in many movies. If the camera pans to follow the sergeant in a long continuous shot as he moves in and around a small formation of men, the background will include the faces of the recruits while featuring the sergeant. Carefully executed, this staging technique can provide many opportunities to include action and reactions simultaneously in a variety of compositions.

Indirection

Not every story point and line of dialogue in a scene needs to be emphasized. Film is such a direct medium that holding back its expressive power from time to time is a way of emphasizing all the other moments. In staging actors and choosing camera setups this could mean relegating some action to the background even if it is central to the narrative.

Similarly, the notion that an important line of dialogue requires a close-up is simply not true. People are often most attentive to the person who speaks most softly. What this means for the filmmaker is that he or she is freed from trying to compose every dramatic point full screen. Sometimes the smallest gesture is the most telling.

13 DEPTH OF THE FRAME

So far we have concentrated on the placement of the subject in front of the camera. First, we looked at a system of patterns and positions to organize the staging of actors. Second, we looked at ways of moving the actors so that several staging patterns and positions could be combined into a single choreographed shot. This approach emphasizes points in space rather than the space itself. While this gives us considerable control over compositional elements within the frame, we will not have explored the subject of staging fully until we examine the scene space in which the actors move.

It's not unusual today to hear about mainstream feature directors who shoot dialogue sequences with five and six setups for just one actor. This is clearly a symptom of indecision and a failure to commit to a directorial point of view. Admittedly, if shots were judged by pictorial quality alone, there are dozens, perhaps hundreds, of interesting compositions that a director and cameraman could devise. We can cut the problem down to size by organizing the possibilities according to a few basic conceptions of space.

The Dramatic Circle of Action

No matter what you are shooting, the space before the camera has limits within which the action of the scene is confined. As a way of organizing the scene space, we will divide this action area into three segments using the traditional terms for depth in the graphic arts: the foreground immediately in front of the lens, the middleground and at the farthest reaches of the location, the background. In staging action for the camera, these terms have a particular meaning. Simply put, the dramatic circle of action for any scene is determined by the size and shape of the space that the action covers.

In the Action/Out of the Action

At a football stadium, space is clearly defined: The players are confined to the field and the fans to the seats. Assuming that the game is the center of attention, there are only two ways of looking at the action: from the outside looking in as a spectator, or from the inside looking out at the action surrounding you as a player on the field.

These are the two basic ways that the camera can record action and space. The variable here is the "shape" of the action. A parade, for example, may appear in a long line as it approaches the camera, stretching into the distance through foreground, middleground and background, but if it crosses our path horizontally, the marching figures occupy a small portion of the middleground like a curtain drawn across our field of vision. If we are in the playground of an elementary school, a game of tag can be far more shapeless than a parade or a football game, with kids running every which way, disappearing around the corners of the school or behind us. In this situation it's the filmmaker's job to evaluate what portion of the whole event he or she wants to feature and from what vantage point to view the action. In most cases the physical action of a scene has dramatic high points that are more significant than others. By deciding where and how the significant action should be staged for the camera, the filmmaker controls the point of view, level of viewer identification and emotional direction of any scene.

Staging in Depth

For our first example illustrating the circle of dramatic action we will concentrate on camera placement rather than blocking. Here's the scene: A man walks from a pay phone to his car. A profile illustration shows us the location in Figure 13.1

Figure 13.1: Ext. phone booth—suburban neighborhood.

Let's first assume that we won't be able to cut multiple views together and that the action will be photographed in a single shot. The aerial view in Figure 13.2 illustrates camera positions in and out of the circle of dramatic

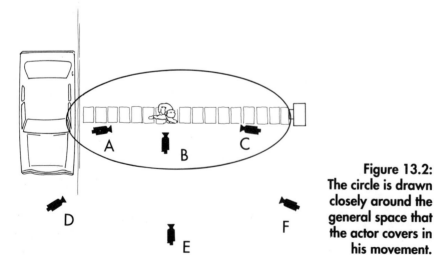

Figure 13.2: The circle is drawn closely around the general space that the actor covers in his movement.

action. The shape of the circle is determined by the space covered by the actor walking to his car. If he were to make a side trip off the flagstone walk for any reason, the circle of action would include this additional space.

Camera positions A, B and C are all *in the action*. In order for any one camera to cover the actor's entire movement from the pay phone to the car, the camera would have to pan until aimed out of the circle. Also, the man's prominence increases or decreases depending on whether he is walking towards or away from the camera. In a sense, the action has a beginning, middle and end, like a self-contained drama. Being in the action also affects point of view: Positions A, B and C accentuate our identification with the salesman, while positions D, E and F produce shots that tend toward distanced and more neutral observation.

Camera positions *outside the action* can cover the actor's entire movement with little or no panning if a sufficiently wide-angle lens is used. A camera outside the action maintains a stationary, narrow view of the man's entire movement, while a camera inside the action might pan as much as 180 degrees to photograph the same action. Also, when photographed from outside the action the actor remains about the same size throughout the shot. If photographed by a camera inside the action his or her size in the frame would vary considerably.

When there is more than one player in a scene, the circle of dramatic action is determined by the placement of the players. If the actors remain in the A, I or L pattern without movement, the circle of dramatic action is drawn tightly around the pattern.

The Purpose of the Dramatic Circle of Action

Like the A, I and L patterns, the circle of action is a way of looking at staging situations to discover familiar arrangements of camera and subject. The immediate benefit of analyzing action this way is that a filmmaker may discover new ways of setting up a scene. It is particularly useful when it helps a director to gain an overview of a complex staging.

To help familiarize yourself with the circle of action, learn to watch television and movie sequences in terms of space rather than shots. This means visualizing the geography of the location and the placement of the camera within that space. One good exercise is to keep track of where the camera is stationed for any scene staged in an interior location. Pay particular attention to how each new scene is introduced in the opening shots. You will soon begin to recognize basic strategies for establishing scene space and learn how each approach affects the narrative.

For instance, cinematographer Gordon Willis often places the camera deep in the circle of action and permits the players to flow around the camera as if the camera were an intimate witness. This results in framings and compositions in which a player passes within inches of the lens, momentarily obscuring the background. Using the opposite approach, director Jim Jarmusch prefers to keep his distance from the action, often using deadpan graphic framings that are like comic strip panels. Jarmusch often likes to stay outside the circle of action for entire scenes. Looking at the work of a random selection of filmmakers, such as Bernardo Bertolucci,

Otto Preminger, David Lynch, Spike Lee and Francois Truffaut, will provide examples of the various ways that space can be presented.

Interior Depth

Looking at the way a wide selection of directors set up a scene in a room will confirm that there are only three places to put the camera: the foreground, the middleground or the background. Shown in Figure 13.3 is an aerial view of a room with one camera placed adjacent to the door, a second in the center of the room and a third at the wall farthest from the door. If a player enters the room and takes a seat at the table, the choice of camera position

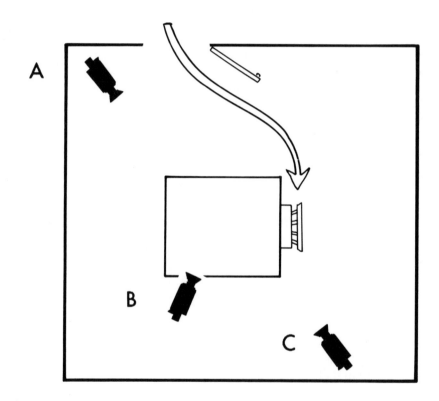

Figure 13.3

determines whether or not the player approaches the camera (B or C) or walks away from the camera (A). Because the room is relatively small, all three positions are in the circle of action.

Once we have established the location with one of the three basic camera positions, the staging of actors is the next decision. Figure 13.4 includes three diagrams of rooms, each showing one of the three basic uses of the circle of action. It doesn't matter which of the staging patterns (A, I or L) we're using. What we are interested in is whether or not the camera is in or out of the action. For instance, we could have a tightly staged A pattern with actors standing close together or an A pattern in which they are

Figure 13.4

A. Placing the camera outside the action and locating a cluster of actors in some part of a room is the most common staging technique. Cutting is usually required for differentiation, since all the players are approximately the same distance from the camera and are therefore seen in similar shot sizes.

B. Deep staging of this type is typical of Orson Welles and William Wyler. It permits the use of a single setup so that cutting, if used at all, is kept to a minimum.

C. This is an exaggerated version of a type of staging in which the camera is at the center of the circle of action. It is virtually the antithesis of frontality. The camera can point anywhere from this central location, but the deployment of the actors on the perimeter of the room forces cutting, since no single composition can include more than two players.

A.

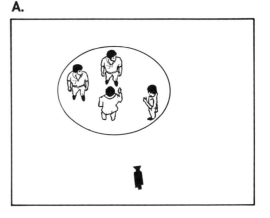

B.

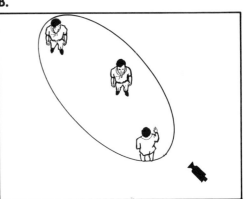

C.

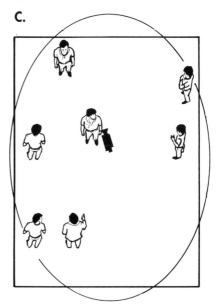

spread out across a room. For any given pattern the camera can be inside or outside the action.

Staging In Depth

Using extensive depth in the staging of shots serves two purposes: One, it can eliminate cutting by allowing the filmmaker to compose subjects within a single shot, and two, it enables the director to selectively emphasize dramatic elements. Graphically, staging in depth depends on the use of scale. This creates oppositions within the frame that can be substituted for the differentiation between players that is normally established by editing. We saw this in several of the patterns and positions illustrated in earlier chapters. Though it might seem axiomatic that near players are stronger in the frame than far players, attention can be shifted to the far player by the use of lighting, depth of field and narrative context. Mobile staging can further extend the range of emphasis so that near and far players can exchange positions or meet in the middleground on equal terms.

This is the fundamental staging difference between Jean Renoir's and Orson Welles' use of deep space. In *The Rules of the Game* Renoir moved his actors from the foreground to the background in a single setup using them to lead the attention of the viewer from one location to the next in order to introduce the next stage of the story. Welles, on the other hand, was inclined to separate his players in foreground and background spaces. This was frequently done in *Citizen Kane* to isolate Kane emotionally from those around him. Near the end of the film Kane and Susan Alexander are staged in depth at opposite ends of a huge room, each imprisoned spatially by the camera. Welles' space is used for separating his characters; Renoir uses space so that his characters will intersect.

Another more conceptual use of the depth of the frame is the linking of ideas through space. For instance, a clock in the extreme foreground of a shot may remind us that the old man in the background hasn't long to live. There is no reason to limit the frame to only two levels of meaning, and the depth of the frame can be divided into as many distinct areas as can be clearly defined by the filmmaker.

Deep Focus Cinematography

In depth staging is often confused with deep-focus cinematography. Though they are frequently used together, the connection is not automatic. There are times when staging in depth permits the foreground or background to be slightly out of focus for pictorial reasons, or attention may be shifted by moving the area of focus from a far to a near subject. The type of deep focus associated with Orson Welles, William Wyler and cinematographer Gregg Tolland used short focal length lenses stopped down to small apertures to keep foreground and background in focus. When this appeared as a staging style in the '40s, deep-focus photography was at the cutting edge of technology. Today, faster films (and the resulting smaller apertures and increased depth of field) have extended the range of the area in focus, making deep-focus work considerably easier. But since there are still limitations to the available depth of field in any lens, special techniques for deep-focus photography have been developed.

Special Effects To Achieve Depth

There are several alternatives to wide-angle lenses for deep-focus photography. In *Citizen Kane* some of the most striking deep-focus compositions were accomplished with in-camera effects that could not be achieved at that time with just a wide-angle lens. These were accomplished by exposing the film twice with the camera locked down. For instance, on the first exposure, one side of the frame was masked while the unmasked side was focused on a foreground element very close to the camera. For the next exposure, the film was rewound to the same starting point and the opposite side of the frame was covered so that the foreground side would be unaffected by the second exposure. During the second camera pass the lens was refocused at a background element and recorded on the previously masked side of the frame. In this way two areas of focus were combined onto one strip of film, permitting extreme deep-focus effects.

In the end shot of Hitchcock's *Spellbound*, we share the POV of a man about to commit suicide. We see his hand in the extreme foreground as he turns the gun towards the camera (himself) and fires. This type of dynamic framing was standard practice in the adventure comics of the time, but Hitchcock found he was unable to hold focus on the foreground gun and the background at the same time. Hitchcock's solution was to have the prop department build an oversized gun and hand. The prop could be placed farther from the lens within the depth of field and still fill the frame as though it were in the extreme foreground.

Split-Field Lenses

One of the simplest solutions to the problem of filming extreme foreground and background space is to use a split-field diopter lens. A full (or unsplit) diopter lens is simply a lens that is attached to the main optic already on the camera to permit close-up photography. Technically, a diopter is a unit of measurement for the negative focal length of a diverging lens, but over the years it has come to mean a close-up lens attachment. Diopter lenses are attached to the end of the main lens like a filter. Since a diopter permits a lens to focus closer to the subject, a split-diopter does the same thing, but only affects one side of the lens. The uncovered side retains the normal focal length, while the covered side has a shortened focal length. Therefore, the lens can be focused on far objects and near subjects simultaneously. The effect isn't perfect though. Since the diopter covers only part of the lens, a slight blurring is visible along the line where the effect begins. This line must be concealed through artful composition of all the elements in the shot. Furthermore, split-diopters can only be used with the camera locked off with foreground and background elements restricted to one half of the frame, so that no person or object moves across the line.

Frames 1 and 2 of Figure 13.5 show the effect of a split-field lens on a conventional OTS framing. In this case, a 40mm lens set at f8 fails to hold

1

2

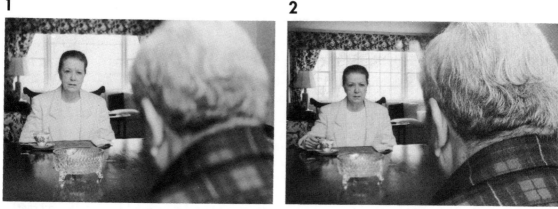

3

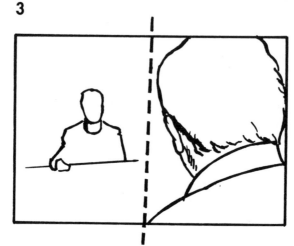

In frame 1 the man's head is beyond the depth of field. By using the split diopter in frame 2 the foreground and background are in focus. Diopter lenses can be rotated and positioned so that the split line (frame 3) can be located at the most advantageous place in the shot.

both subjects in focus in frame 1. As you can see the man is out of focus. Using the split-diopter the back of the man's head is sharply defined even though he is only approximately 14-18 in. in front of the lens. The location of the split line is shown in frame 3. You can detect a small degree of blurring along this line in the photo.

Compressed Depth

Where Welles and Renoir utilized deep-focus photography, filmmakers such as Robert Altman and Akira Kurosawa turned to documentary films for inspiration, appropriating telephoto lens documentary techniques. For Kurosawa the shallow-focus effect characteristic of telephoto lenses was added to his already personal and wide-ranging style, which was rooted fundamentally in Hollywood technique. Altman, however, developed a style that relied far more on long lenses, creating a muted and dreamy *mise-en-scène* in which his characters are seen in overlapping images and sounds. He did this by using telephoto lenses in the familiar documentary fashion to move in close, but also in a new way by shooting his wide and medium shots in the wide-screen format, thereby compressing his master shots.

The Staging Patterns and Telephoto Lenses

By eliminating depth in the frame telephoto lenses emphasize the width of the scene space. Differentiation between staging patterns becomes more difficult unless the separation of players is lateral. This is particularly true when subjects overlap in the frame. Mobile staging is equally problematic with telephoto lenses since only lateral movement effectively emphasizes key moments in a scene. Subjects repositioning themselves in depth will appear to move without arriving at a new space. For the same reason camera movement in depth will appear to be negligible.

Conversely, lateral camera movement with a telephoto lens will exaggerate planes of depth. For instance, a lateral tracking move will create powerful graphic tensions between two subjects standing a few feet apart. The background, brought up close by the characteristic spatial compression, will be emphasized moving across the frame like a huge cyclorama.

The trend towards the use of longer lenses in narrative film continues. Much of the telephoto's appeal is graphic, but it is also popular because it eliminates many of the continuity challenges of staging action. As a result, the general sophistication and variety of continuity blocking has declined in the last decade.

14 CAMERA ANGLES

I n narrative film there are many reasons for varying the viewing angle: You might change the angle in order to follow the subject, reveal or withhold story information, change point of view, provide graphic variety, establish a location or develop mood. Of all these, following the subject is the goal that many filmmakers consider primary. This approach tends to overlook the importance of the space in which the action takes place, when in fact it supplies the context that defines the subject.

In part, this division of the subject and space is a holdover from the studio system of the '30s and '40s. In order to cut down on expensive location shooting, dialogue scenes were photographed in studio sets and later integrated with stock location footage, creating the illusion of a spatially continuous world. The unconvincing process shots with cars driving in front of projected backgrounds never fooled anyone, but the story and the stars were held to be the only really important elements anyway. The audience paid to see the stars, and if the stars pleased them, the unconvincing effects were overlooked. By establishing a scene space in a wide shot and moving to medium shots to photograph the subject the studios were able to save money frequently by sacrificing the full expression of the spatial/dramatic context of a scene.

Today, the separation of subject and environment continues, and though location shooting has replaced the studio, many directors still consider photography of the actors to be the main storytelling imagery with the location the equivalent of stage scenery, appropriate only for establishing shots.

The truth is that the subject is never separate from the location in either the narrative or the pictorial sense. The subject of a shot is often the subject *and* the location taken together, each informing the other and creatively inseparable. Together they can contribute to the mood and atmosphere, shape psychological and dramatic elements and interact to produce new meaning in any shot. To a large extent the spatial relationship of subject and environment is determined by the camera angle.

By themselves camera angles have no meaning. The (by now) reductive analysis that claims that low-angle views of a subject place the subject in a dominant position while high-angle views place the subject in a diminutive position is only valid in certain situations. The value of a shot really depends on the narrative.

For example, in *Citizen Kane* low-angle shots are used throughout the entire movie, but their significance depends on the context. In the early scenes of Kane as a young man, when he seems to be a brash crusader, we may have ambivalent feelings about his use of power, but we probably envy the way he is able to snub the powerful forces of the status quo as represented by his stodgy guardian Thatcher. In most of these scenes the ceilings are low, and Welles, who actually was tall, seems to dominate his surroundings. By the end of the film, Kane, an old man who has lost much of his influence, is still photographed from low angles, but now the huge spaces of the rooms and halls of Xanadu dominate him and he seems small by comparison. The narrative undercuts the conventional understanding of low-angle perspectives.

Viewer Placement

In film the viewer identifies with the camera. When the camera moves either in a tracking shot or through cutting, the viewer experiences the sensation of movement as well and frequently finds the images on screen

Figure 14.1

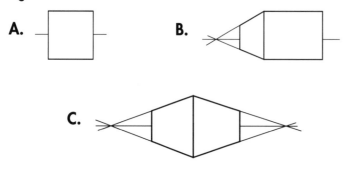

Linear Perspective

Whether we're looking at a room, a building or a densely wooded forest certain viewpoints will emphasize depth and volume more than others.

The five cubes in Figure 14.1 illustrate how linear perspective is used to create the illusion of depth. Cube A is viewed head on. This type of rendering is called the orthographic view and does not attempt to show perspective. Cube B is turned slightly so that an additional surface is exposed. This surface is foreshortened and the top and bottom lines converge at the horizon. This is called one-point perspective. Cube C is shown in two-point perspective. Cube D is turned so that now there are two foreshortened sides. This makes the perception of depth even more pronounced. Cube E is drawn in three-point perspective. This picture reveals the greatest sense of depth.

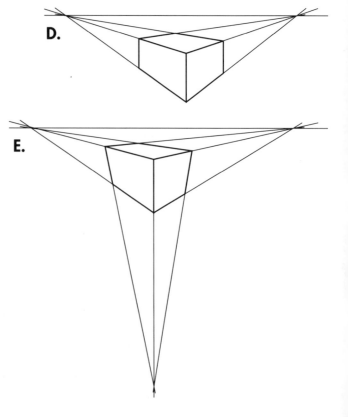

more real than the space in the movie theater. Psychologists call this illusion transference. Though it's not often acknowledged, one reason for varying the viewing angle is for the physical excitement of transference, a viewing experience common in film. Viewer placement doesn't necessarily require elaborate camera moves and wide vistas to produce an effect; a sequence in a cramped diner can be as evocative as one set in a vast forest if the camera angles are chosen judiciously. Since transference implicates the viewer in any camera movement or change of angles in an edited sequence, the viewer becomes part of the choreography. Complex sequences may very well provide an experience as rhythmically and spatially inventive as a dance, dependent to a great extent on the arrangement of camera angles and perspective.

One way to learn how the change in perspective works from shot to shot in a sequence is to reduce perspective to simple forms. Once the basic forms are understood you will be able to recognize them more easily when you are devising sequences.

Perspective

Every storyboard artist and production designer has a solid grasp of the principles of perspective and uses them frequently to visualize sets and camera angles. When composing a storyboard, a knowledge of perspective frees the artist to imagine different viewpoints in a real location or to create a location that is entirely imaginary. This type of representation is called linear perspective and is just one of many drawing systems, no more valid than any other, though it conforms fairly closely to our way of seeing the world. Linear perspective has been the predominant way of creating the illusion of space in representational drawings since the Renaissance.

But when a filmmaker places two shots side by side the interaction between the images produces an entirely new type of spatial experience that can best be described as sequential perspective. This is how he creates the type of cinematic choreography that includes the viewer in the space on the screen, a major factor in the design of shot flow.

To better understand the effect of a series of camera angles we can look at the subject in traditional terms, as the study of perspective. The cube illustrations in Figure 14.1 show the basic forms.

Now let's take the various views of the cube and use them as the basis of a location in a storyboard. A convenience store can be modeled on the cube, with a big sign on a tall post separate from the building. Figure 14.2 shows the store in one- two- and three-point perspective.

Now let's look at four versions of sequential perspective in storyboard form. The action is simple: A man drives up to the convenience store to find a phone. He goes to the door but then sees that there is a phone booth alongside the building. He walks to the booth and makes a phone call.

The purpose of the following examples is to illustrate shot flow as a rhythmic variation of angles. In the continuity style this means establishing the volume of a given space by moving through that space. Where there is motion, there is acceleration, velocity and inertia, and continuity editing can establish its own physical laws. This type of "shot ballistics" is most pronounced in the kind of dynamic views that follow.

Figure 14.2

One-point perspective.

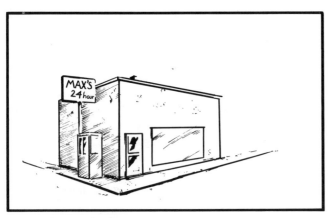

Two-point perspective.

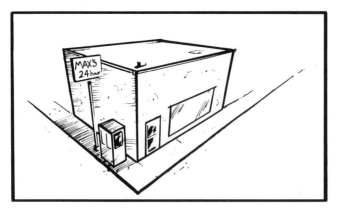

Three-point perspective.

1

2

Eye-Level View

In this first version I've used straight-on eye-level views. Opening frame 1 uses the flatness of the buildings to reinforce the effect of the road reaching into the distance. Eye-level views tend to be stable and can serve as a contrast to dynamic compositions. Compare these eye-level views with the more angular compositions in the next series.

3

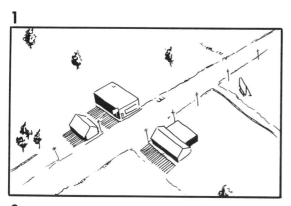

1

2

High-Angle View 1

Notice that these three shots proceed in a generally smooth movement. First, the degree of perspective increases in each frame: Frame 1 has one foreshortened plane, frame 2 has two foreshortened planes and frame 3 shows all three planes receding so that the depth of the shot increases as we go along. Second, the shots become tighter as we move to the phone booth. This creates a sense of forward motion. This type of shot flow is progressive.

3

High-Angle View 2

This next series is nonprogressive. This means that the angular view in one frame conflicts with the view in the following frame. The degree and direction of the conflict is varied but is most pronounced between the last two frames.

Low-Angle View

This is another example of conflicting frames. The contrast here is slight until the last two frames. Compare this with the eye-level views, which keep the same general distance from the subject as this series but are far less dynamic.

Space vs. Subject

One way of looking at camera angles and how they depict the scene space is to create the storyboard without the subject and just concentrate on the background. This was my approach in the convenience store storyboards. In visualizing that sequence, I drew many sketches and cut them out so that they could be rearranged easily on my drafting table. Each time the drawings were put in a new order I could imagine a different version of the scene. Any change in viewpoint suggested subtle changes in mood, pacing and even the narrative events of the scene.

This is worth remembering when you are devising sequences. In the same way that we substituted the spatial concept of the circle of action for the subject-oriented patterns for staging, we can frame shots based on the location rather than the subject. Ultimately, the subject will become the determining factor, but by that time many new ideas may have been discovered.

Recent Trends in Perspective Rendering

The way interiors are shot has changed over the last 25 years. Location shooting has slowly replaced studio sets not only for economic reasons but also because of the strong trend toward realism that studio sets have difficulty matching. Without the removable walls and ceilings of a studio set, wide-angle lenses must be used in the often cramped quarters of a real interior so that full-figure shots can be framed. Often, filmmakers choose lenses to solve these practical problems, and pictorial considerations become secondary.

If you find yourself in an interior where the perspective of the wide-angle shot is determined by the size of the room rather than by design, try using a longer lens. Shooting through doorways and windows and past foreground objects instead of trying to find a clear frame in a room are some of the ways of utilizing a longer lens. The wide-angle interior shot is a staple of television, and since it reflects a budget choice rather than an artistic decision, new ideas might arise from bucking the cliché.

We can now look at a narrative situation that permits a wide combination of angles and lenses: the action sequence.

Narrative Problem (Camera Angles in Action)

The following action sequence features a back-lot baseball game. The treatment is humorous and somewhat stylized, which for our purposes encourages the use of vigorous camera angles.

The storyboard begins on a blustery late afternoon with broken clouds and a bright sun. A batter is at the plate. The count is 3 balls and 2 strikes. The sunlight shines into the batter's eyes, and he has difficulty seeing. Fortunately, a few patchy clouds move in, blocking the sun momentarily and giving the batter a break, but the pitcher stalls by adjusting the laces on his sneaker until the sun reemerges.

1. The count is 3 balls and 2 strikes.

2. The sun makes the batter squint as he checks to see where the outfielders are standing.

3. Batter's POV of the bright sun.

4. The pitcher starts his windup . . .

5. The pitcher is ready to throw when the field darkens.

6. Clouds block the sun.

7. Not wanting to give the batter a break, the pitcher stalls by adjusting the laces on his sneaker.

8. The pitcher stands when the sun returns. The team at bat jeers as the pitcher winds up and—

9. We go to slow motion for the pitch.

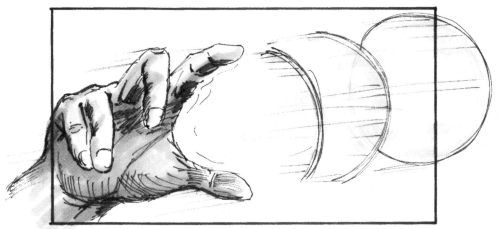

10. We stay in slow motion as the ball is released.

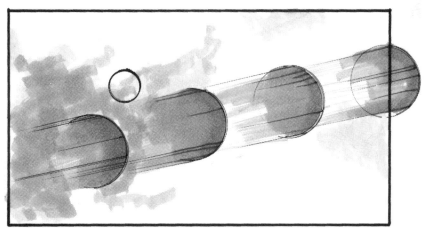

11. Camera points straight up as ball passes sun in slow motion and clouds move in to block light.

12. Shadows fade in slow motion.

13. Batter smiles because of this lucky break. He sets himself for the swing.

14. Crack! We return to normal camera speed as the batter connects with the ball.

15. It's a perfect hit.

16. A kid seated on the hill jumps up to watch the ball climb into the sky. "Damn!"

17. Camera pans through panels A, B and C.

18. Continue pan shot following the ball.

19. Pan ends as ball nears telephone pole.

20. Ball bounces off the pole . . .

21. And right into the window of a nearby house.

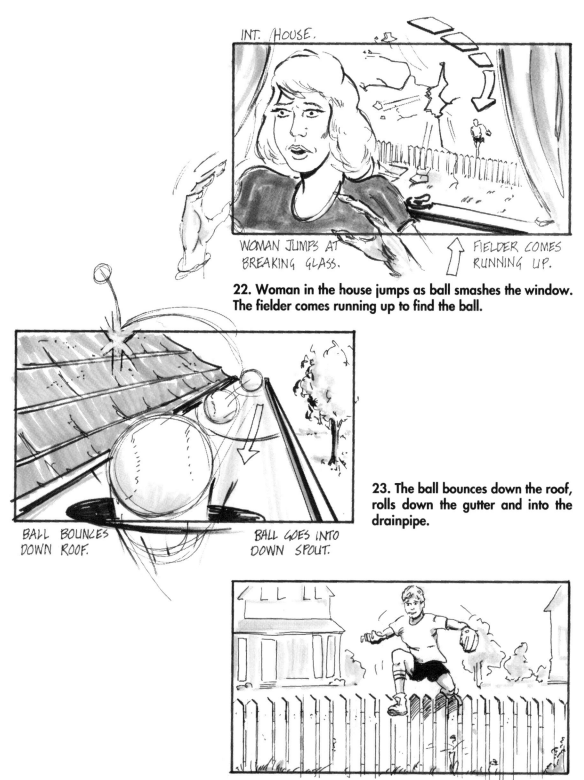

INT. HOUSE.

WOMAN JUMPS AT
BREAKING GLASS.

FIELDER COMES
RUNNING UP.

22. Woman in the house jumps as ball smashes the window. The fielder comes running up to find the ball.

BALL BOUNCES
DOWN ROOF.

BALL GOES INTO
DOWN SPOUT.

23. The ball bounces down the roof, rolls down the gutter and into the drainpipe.

24. The fielder hurdles the front fence.

25. The fielder snags his foot on the fence.

26. The fielder falls, landing with a thud.

27. The ball shoots out of the drainpipe. . .

28. . . . and rolls right by the fielder.

29. Back at the infield, the batter heads for third. The fielder appears in the background with the ball and throws it in.

30. The second baseman and centerfielder botch the catch.

31. The batter rounds third.

32. The pitcher screams "You idiots!" at the infield.

33. The batter heads for home.

34. The shortstop scoops up the ball and throws home as the batter runs by in the foreground.

35. Extreme down shot. Slow motion. The camera pans with the shadow of the running batter. The ball slowly enters the shot. It's a race of shadows.

36. Slow motion continues. Camera points down the baseline to home as the catcher gets ready.

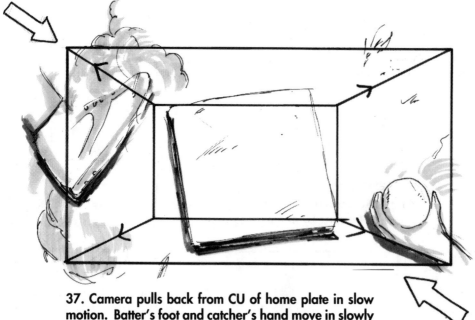

37. Camera pulls back from CU of home plate in slow motion. Batter's foot and catcher's hand move in slowly towards the plate. Dust covers the frame.

Summary

As you can see from this brief story, camera angles are strongly dependent on narrative as well as other graphic and staging strategies. In this case, slow motion and the use of shadows motivated some of the camera angles, as well as the use of "graphic staging," since the ball traveled high above the scene while the shadows were on the ground as if they were actors in the scene. Naturally, forcing the camera to follow action that is low and high will have a lot to do with the camera angles needed to record a scene. Of course, slight variations in camera angle are as important as the more extreme angles of view and help to establish a rhythm of movement.

I should add that this storyboard is a first draft based on thumbnail drawings, which were used to plan out the basic idea. The first 20 rough sketches took a little more than an hour to draw in pencil. More than half of the panels did not change significantly from these first compositions, while the rest of the panels were redrawn. In practice there might be 2 or 20 drafts of a storyboard until the ideas are worked out satisfactorily. For example, the initial idea was just to have a pitcher come to the plate and hit a home run. The business with the sun and the clouds and the slow motion developed from the rough sketches. When I went to ink the panels I decided to add the fanciful gutter pipe gag, which would probably not survive another draft.

15 OPEN AND CLOSED FRAMINGS

T he terms open and closed compositions are used to describe the types of framing techniques and strategies devised to include or exclude the viewer from the picture space. In film, open framings are compositions of the type usually found in documentaries, where many of the elements in the frame are beyond the filmmaker's control. In such stagings, several subjects may be partially cut off by the edge of the frame or partially obscured by foreground elements. Closed framings are compositions with subjects carefully positioned for maximum clarity and graphic balance. This way of composing pictures is likely to be found when the camera is placed outside the circle of action. Open forms seem more realistic, while closed forms seem staged.

This distinction is not without contradictions. The truth, of course, is that all compositions are arranged by the photographer to some degree whether it is obvious to the viewer or not. Television commercials have borrowed the pictorial look of documentary film, carefully arranging compositions to look unarranged. This kind of studied off-handedness trades on the public's general association between documentary style images and objective reporting. Alternately, many documentarians produce highly stylized compositions by waiting weeks or months for the exact conditions of weather and season to produce an image for heightened effect. In our image-saturated culture it is becoming increasingly difficult to differentiate between open and closed forms since image makers of all types are fully aware of their popular meanings, often using them to deceive the viewer.

It's probably best to think of open and closed framing as general descriptions, remembering that techniques derive their significance from the contexts in which they are placed. For the narrative filmmaker, the most interesting aspect of open and closed framings is the way in which they are used to offer the viewer varying degrees of involvement and intimacy with the subjects on the screen. How the filmmaker uses this relationship raises the issue of aesthetic distance.

Aesthetic Distance

Aesthetic distance is a phrase used to describe the degree to which a work of art manipulates the viewer. All communications are in some way manipulative, but some works allow the viewer greater opportunity for reflection and participation at the moment of viewing than others. In filmmaking, aesthetic distance is aptly named, because unlike the novelist or poet, a filmmaker actually creates the illusion of physical depth and distance in the frame and, ultimately, in the movie theater. The size of a shot, from an extreme close-up to a long shot, places the audience in a physical relationship with the subject that has psychological and, ultimately, moral implications.

Levels of Intimacy

In this next section of examples we'll look at the ways that framing, choice of camera angle and lens affect the degree of involvement the viewer has with the scene space and the individuals in the scene.

Our narrative follows a man and woman in bed. The man has spent the night with the woman after having just met her the night before. He knows that she regrets inviting him to her apartment, and now, as morning light enters the room, they are both reluctant to face the expectations each of them has for the other. The filmmaker would like to bring the viewer into the dramatic circle of action, so that he can feel the intimacy of the relationship. Since the scene is written from the man's point of view, the filmmaker feels he must maintain this view in the composition of shots.

Open Framing

Version One

The filmmaker decides to open the scene with a wide shot of the bedroom. He shoots three test shots, frames 1, 2 and 3, and places them side by side. Because the scene is written from the man's point of view, he selects a view shot from the man's side of the bed. He places the camera at a low angle so that the man is easier to see than the woman, thereby encouraging our identification with the man. The filmmaker considers his choices and realizes that frames 2 and 3 may be too close to the subject. Since he expects to move in to CU framings later in the sequence he would like there to be a significant change in shot size from the opening shot to the anticipated CUs. Therefore he chooses frame 1 to open the scene.

1   **2**   **3**

Open Framing

Version Two

The filmmaker decides to move in for a shot of the woman and photographs three OTS shots to choose from. In each the man is clearly looking at the woman.   Notice how frames 2 and 3 use depth of field to selectively emphasize one of the subjects. Though it is generally thought that the focused player is the one that is emphasized, this is not always the case. By choosing just the right framing and action, the unfocused player can be made the key subject. The filmmaker selects frame 1 because he wants to move in to the scene slowly and feels that frames 2 and 3 are too intimate at this stage in the action.

Open Framing

Version Three

The filmmaker compares two new shots, this time from a reverse angle that will be used after the previous shot. Having maintained emotional distance in the last shot, the filmmaker decides to move in somewhat closer this time. He chooses frame 2. This is done to involve the viewer in a more intimate way and for the graphic contrast that the change in size produces.

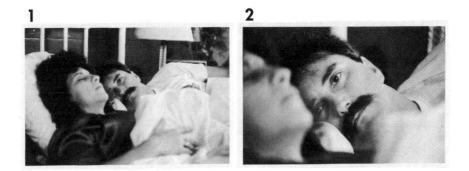

Open Framing

Version Four

The filmmaker reviews the sequence and is bothered by his last choice. He likes moving in to a closer shot for the reverse, but feels that the clarity of the CU of the man in the reverse is too bold. He also feels that he would like to see more of the woman. He now realizes that frame 2 is too much of a

summation of the man's position—too egocentric.   He tests two new
compositions, frames 3 and 4.

3   **4**

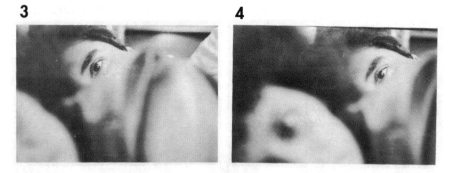

These two frames are extremely open. In both of them, the woman has
been repositioned so that she is turned away from the man. The shots are
nearly identical except that frame 4 permits us to see the woman's face even
though it is beyond the depth of field. Most important, we can see that she
is awake with her eyes open.   Each shot strongly affects the dramatic
emphasis of the scene. Frame 3 expresses the man's inability to understand
the woman. She masks our view of him, and yet she also is withheld from
our view. In a sense we are placed in the same position as the man. Frame
4 is almost painfully revealing. We now see that the woman is awake but
unable to face the man. The sense of separation is acute. This is the shot the
filmmaker chooses.

The open framing creates a context in which we share the man's
psychological point of view through the use of framing and story elements.
If the filmmaker had wanted to allow the viewer to watch the scene from a
neutral perspective, he might have created the scene using closed framings.
This distancing is not absolute but, like open-framed strategies, can be
created in varying degrees. It is rare to find a film that uses open or closed
framings exclusively. The filmmaker decides that he will reconceive the
bedroom scene using closed framing, permitting the viewer to watch the
scene unfold with less physical and emotional involvement.

Closed Framing

Version One

The filmmaker tests three different camera angles for the opening shot,
frames 1, 2 and 3. Frame 1 is symmetrical, with little dynamic tension to
motivate the next shot. This permits the viewer to access the frame and the
action without the pull of shot flow. The action is so far away, however, that
the move to a closer shot is required if more detail is to be seen.   The
filmmaker may opt to hold this shot throughout the scene and move the
action towards the camera by having the couple leave the bed rather than
change viewpoints through cutting. Frame 2 permits a better view of the
couple and limits the degree of intimacy the viewer feels by placing the

couple in a viewpoint that is not on the human scale. In this case, we are not only outside the circle of dramatic action, we are high above it. Finally, frame 3 is the least closed shot, but it still maintains a neutral and distanced stance. Notice that the angularity tends to make the shot less closed.

The filmmaker likes frame 1 and considers staging the scene so that the players must sit up in bed to play out the action. Before doing this he tries one other series of shots.

1 **2** **3**

Closed Framing

Version Two

The three frames in this last closed composition series are a sequence, not individual versions of a master shot. The filmmaker decides that if he is not going to use CUs or medium shots of the couple he can maintain emotional distance while cutting from the appropriate side of the bed when we hear the thoughts of the man or the woman. This entire approach is highly stylized and avoids the psychological identification with character that is fundamental to the continuity style. Neither approach insures balanced treatment of the subject, though open-framing devices and other distancing strategies have been lauded by radical filmmakers as less manipulative. Ultimately, the viewer is manipulated no matter what technique is employed, and a film can have no more integrity than the intentions and perspicacity of the filmmaker permit, regardless of technique.

1 **2** **3**

Framing Devices

As we have just seen, open framings utilize foreground elements to enclose a subject for emphasis or as a way of placing a subject within a new context or including the viewer in the scene space. Framing devices are also used for purely compositional reasons to increase the sense of depth in the frame. Several framing devices are shown below.

In Figure 15.1 doorways become frames within the frame, distancing us from the action. We are placed in the position of eavesdropping on a conversation.

Figure 15.1

Different levels of action can be isolated, as in the next shot in Figure 15.2. In this case architecture is used to frame the action.

Figure 15.2

In Figure 15.3 (page 265), telephoto lenses, because they compress action in depth, crowd many foreground elements (that may actually be very far away) in front of the camera. This use of framing devices tends to withhold information by revealing only portions of the principal subject. This is the opposite of a window or doorway frame, which directs our attention more emphatically to the subject within the square.

Figure 15.3

Mirrors have always fascinated filmmakers and can become a way of combining the "shot, reverse shot" cutting pattern in a single shot. A shot of this type is shown in Figure 15.4.

Figure 15.4

We now can move on to point of view, the subject of the next chapter, which is intimately connected to the type of framing devices we have just looked at.

16 POINT OF VIEW

In the last chapter on open and closed framings, we considered the ways in which graphic and editorial techniques determine *the level of involvement* the viewer has with the characters on the screen. Point of view, on the other hand, determines *who* the viewer identifies with. The two concepts are closely related and nearly always work together in any sequence.

Each shot in a film expresses a point of view, and in narrative film the point of view changes often, sometimes with each new shot. For the most part, point of view—what is often called narrative stance—is largely invisible to the audience, though the accumulated effect of the changes profoundly affects the way the audience interprets any scene. Apart from the familiar subjective techniques of the kind used by Alfred Hitchcock, the ways in which camera placement, editing and composition shape the narrative stance of any scene generally is overlooked. This probably accounts for the fact that point of view, which may be the most important aspect of a director's contribution, is handled indifferently in so many films. Frequently, narrative stance is the accidental result of technical or pictorial concerns, or worse, relentless manipulation.

To better understand how the filmmaker can use the camera to determine point of view, let's begin by looking at the three types of narration used in films, borrowing the terminology used to denote point of view in literature.

First-Person Point of View

First-person narratives are exemplified by the subjective techniques of Hitchcock in which we see events through the eyes of a character—the "I" of the story. Extensive use of the subjective viewpoint has always been awkward in narrative film largely because we are only given the visual point of view of a character and are deprived of seeing his or her reactions through facial or other gestures.

Third-Person Restricted Point of View

Third-person restricted, which presents the action as seen by an ideal observer, is the style of narrative most common in Hollywood movies, but rarely is it used as the sole viewpoint. Most of the time it is combined with limited use of omniscient and subjective passages.

Omniscient Point of View

For film to present the omniscient point of view we have to know what the characters are thinking. This requires some type of narration, voice-over or graphics. Overt narration is thought by many to be uncinematic and is rarely used. Actually, narration has been explored only tentatively, and so far no mainstream narrative director has evolved a style that combines words and images in a particularly inventive way. The field is open for new ideas.

Levels of Identification

In a novel or short story there is no question whose point of view we are reading at any moment. In film, the point of view can be less definite, and in some instances a shot can convey a narrative stance somewhere between a third-person and a fully subjective shot.

In editing, the most powerful cuing device is the sight line of an actor in CU. Figure 16.1 illustrates a typical setup for a POV shot: the cut on the look. Below this first shot are three possible reverse CUs.

In frame 1 a man looks at a woman seated next to him in a car. In frame 2 we cut to his POV, a CU of the woman looking back at him. Since it is a subjective camera shot, she looks directly into the camera. Used in this way the CU is clearly seen from the man's POV. Compare this with the CU in frame 3, shot at about 45 degrees from the woman's sight line. This is clearly a third-person restricted view. The shot does not elicit our identification with either the man or the woman. But what happens if we move the camera a few degrees outside of the woman's sight line as shown in frame 4? In this case we are placed in a closer relationship to the man, provided the narrative sets up the CU as the man's look. In a sense, this is a modified subjective shot.

This is a valuable concept: *There are degrees of subjectivity, or to put it more accurately, degrees of identification for any shot*. For this reason, OTS shots and

Figure 16.1   **1**

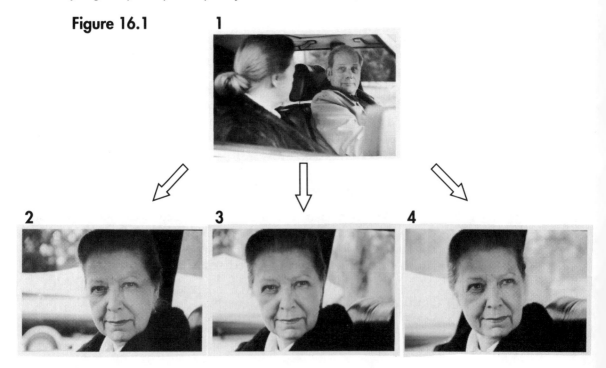

two-shots can favor the point of view of one of the players in a scene, depending on the line of sight of the actors and the narrative context. Generally speaking, *the closer the sight line of a player in CU is to the camera, the greater the degree of viewer identification.*

Viewer Involvement and Identification

There are two ways to determine viewer identification: by graphic control or by narrative control. Graphic control elicits our identification with a player using composition and staging. The modified subjective shot we considered on the previous page is an example of graphic control determined by how a player is composed in the frame.

Narrative control directs our identification using several strategies, but these are largely dependent on editing. For instance, in a detective story, the plot usually follows the private eye. Scenes begin when the private eye arrives at a location and end when he exits a scene. Even when this kind of story is covered in third-person restricted camera setups in closed framings, the narrative context implies that we are learning of events from the private eye's point of view.

Shaping Point of View

There are no hard and fast rules for the graphic and narrative control of point of view. Both factors are dependent on one another for their full meaning. One of the most important skills a filmmaker develops with experience is a greater awareness, largely intuitive, of the predominant point of view in any shot and sequence.

In the following examples we join the filmmaker as he returns to the scene of the man and woman in bed from the previous chapter. This first series of photoboards stages a subjective sequence using the cut on the look to set up shots. However, the basic principles shown here also are applicable to dramatic situations that are not purely subjective.

Point of View (Version One)

The filmmaker begins frame 1 by fading up from black as a subjective equivalent to the man opening his eyes as he awakens in the morning. Frame 1a is the CU shot of the woman from the man's POV after the fade up is completed. Frame 2 is a reverse CU shot of the man partly obscured by

1 **1a** **2**

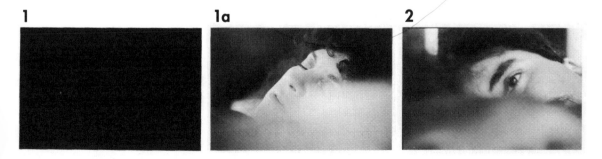

the bed covers. This is a reversal of the usual editing pattern of the cut on the look. In this version the POV shot comes first and the "look" second.

The filmmaker decides to revise the sequence with a new opening shot of the woman in frame 3. This time we see only the back of her head and her fingers in her hair. She turns towards the camera in frame 3 completing the movement in frame 3a. Frame 4 serves as the cut to the look, though we do not see the man's eyes in this tight OTS shot. Compare this frame with frame 2 in the previous series. Both frames serve the purpose of identifying the CU of the woman as a POV shot.

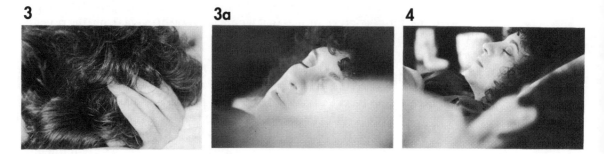

3 **3a** **4**

Point of View (Version Two)

The filmmaker decides to open the scene in a traditional POV editing pattern beginning with the ECU of the eye. This is followed by the obligatory reverse to the POV shot and an OTS two-shot. Now go back and look at the previous version. These might be the choices offered to you by an editor in a rough cut based on these few shots. If the footage was photographed with a stationary camera you could easily change the order of the shots. If, however, the shots involved zoom movement or camera movement, your options would be reduced, assuming you followed traditional continuity practice.

1 **2** **3**

Point of View (Version Three)

This time the filmmaker will devise an aural/subjective sequence. The viewer will see and *hear* things from the man's point of view. This extended sequence begins below and continues on the following page. Frame 1 opens in darkness. Sounds of soft breathing are heard, and the picture fades up slowly to frames 2-4, which are CUs of the bed covers moving with the woman's steady breathing. In frame 5 we see a CU of the man, very nearly a CU of his ear. This is the aural equivalent to a cut on the look beginning with a shot of the eyes. We cut to frame 6, a CU of the woman's face with her breathing emphasized on the soundtrack. In frame 7 we return to the man, who is awake and watching the woman. Frame 8 is a visual subjective shot of the woman's shoulder from the man's POV as she turns away from him. In frame 9 we return to an ECU of the man's eye watching the woman. In frame 10 the filmmaker abruptly *changes to the woman's point of view*. We stay with this shot for several seconds until the woman moves out of frame as she sits up.

In frame 11 the woman sits on the edge of the bed and then turns to the man in frame 12. The filmmaker cuts on the look to an OTS shot. Because frame 13 is so tight over the woman's shoulder and is clearly lined up along her line of sight, we share her general viewpoint and identify with her. The filmmaker doesn't take the scene any further than this moment but makes one last change to limit the number of shots by replacing shots 12 and 13 with a single reverse two-shot in frame 14. In this case the framing includes the woman's look and the object of her look in a single shot. Interestingly, while the action is seen from the position of a third person, the staging encourages us to identify with her. On a visual level, the subject of the shot is the woman looking at the man. This, however, is merely a way of provoking our interest in knowing her reaction to what she sees. The secondary subject of the shot is the woman's thoughts since her reaction is not externalized in dialogue or other behavior. By asking the viewer to consider the woman's feelings this setup shares many of the qualities of a subjective shot.

1 **2** **3**

4

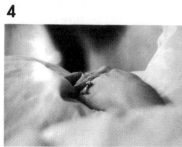

5

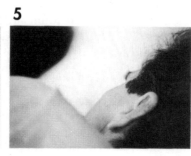

6

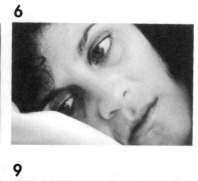

7

8

9

10

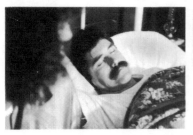

11

12

13

14

Narrative Control of Point of View

In this next situation a woman looks for her husband on the beach and finds him sitting alone by the shore. Our purpose here is to discover ways of achieving viewer's identification with one of the characters in a scene.

Narrative Control (Version One)

This first sequence uses the classic subjective setup: In frame 1, a woman looks at something offscreen; in frame 2 we see the object of her attention. In frame 3 the geographical relationship is established in a two-shot. In this sequence we identify with the woman for two reasons: First, she is the person who escorts us, the viewers, into the scene. Second, in frame 3 the two-shot favors her line of sight. This is undercut slightly because we are outside the circle of dramatic action, tending toward the view of a neutral observer.

Compare this with the next series, frames 4-6, which ends with a new shot at the end. In this case we have remained within the woman's line of sight in the final shot, but from a reverse angle. These two graphic strategies develop our identification with the woman differently. Interestingly, being closer to the man in frame 6 does not significantly diminish our identification with the woman. This is because the narrative context of the sequence, beginning with the woman, shapes the way we read the following shots.

Narrative Control (Version Two)

In this next series we can see what happens if we begin the previous sequence with the man. The question is whether or not this establishes our identification with him instead of the woman. The answer, I think, is that the point of view is divided between the woman and the man, depending on the editing. To test this point, look at this sequence as you might expect it to appear on screen. First, time the shots as you read them so that the shots of the man are longer than the shots of the woman. Now read the scene and make the woman's shots (frames 2-3) longer. Identification usually will side with the subject given the most screen time. Also, the woman is clearly looking at the man, while the man's attention is not focused on any activity that we can easily share.

Part of the strategy that sets this up is the right-angle shot of the man, which is in contrast to the woman's line of sight. This introduces another factor in determining point of view related to the eye-line. Any aspect of a shot that suggests thought on the part of a subject sets up conditions that are favorable to identification. Shots of the eyes, and CUs in general, fall into this category. This is why the over-the-hip shot of the woman in frame 3 does not greatly enhance the cut on the look in frame 2. If an OTS shot were substituted showing the woman's head, our identification with her might be stronger.

1

2

3

4

Narrative Control (Version Three)

In this final series we combine the strategies of versions one and two to see how subtly identification can be controlled. In frame 1 we begin with the man and cut directly to the woman looking at him. If we stop right here our identification is with the woman. The cut to the woman's point of view clinches our identification with her as does the final frame along her sight line. But now look over the shots again: As you can see, the man has the

strongest CU graphically and is in three shots, while the woman is in only two.

It's clear that the type of shot and the cooperation between shots is more important in developing a consistent point of view than the number of shots given to a particular character. Finally, it is important that the subject we identify with be seen consistently. In this last series, two shots of the woman from the same angle build identification more strongly than the three shots of the man, each from a different angle.

Part IV

The Moving Camera

17 THE PAN

I n the next four chapters we'll be looking at techniques for using the moving camera. Generally speaking, a moving shot is more difficult and time-consuming to execute than a static shot, but it also offers graphic and dramatic opportunities unique to film. Camera movement replaces a series of edited shots used to follow a subject, to make connections between ideas, to create graphic and rhythmic variation or to simulate the movement of a subject in a subjective sequence.

Of the three types of camera movement, panning, tracking and craning, only panning is accomplished without moving the camera from one position to another. When the camera moves through space on a crane or a dolly it is said to be travelling. The different types of camera movement are frequently combined in a single shot, and a crane or dolly shot usually requires some panning to hold the subject in the frame. In a sequence shot, a tracking shot may combine a crane move with lateral tracking movement while panning and zooming to frame choreographed action.

The pan is the simplest of moving shots, comparatively easy to execute with modest equipment. Like all moving shots it provides multiple views within a single shot as an alternative to editing.

Panning and Tilting

The pan shot is extremely versatile and is one of the easiest moves to execute, requiring none of the preparation or heavy equipment that tracking and craning do. In the horizontal panoramic shot the camera rotates on its vertical axis as much as 360 degrees, taking in the entire visible horizon. The camera also can be angled up or down in a vertical pan or tilt. What distinguishes the pan from other types of camera movement is that the camera rotates on an axis in one location rather than actually being displaced. Consequently the pan shot does not offer the dramatic shift in perspective that tracking, crane and hand-held shots do. In this respect it is similar to the static shot. At the same time, the pan can cover space faster than tracking and crane shots, in which the camera must be physically moved over the ground, usually with an operator and his or her assistant. The pan can easily frame one goalpost on a football field and move to the opposite goalpost in a second. Even a fast-moving tracking shot would take 15 seconds or more to cover the same distance.

A pan can be used to:
- Include space greater than can be viewed through a fixed frame.
- Follow action as it moves.

- Connect two or more points of interest graphically.
- Connect or imply a logical connection between two or more subjects.

Panoramic Shot

The most familiar use of the pan is a slow move over a landscape—a staple of home movies and outdoor pictures where wide open spaces are featured. The scenic pan is usually used as an establishing shot. Typical uses are the vertical pan up or down a skyscraper to convey a feeling of height and the horizontal pan to convey the immensity of a location like a desert or ocean that spreads well beyond the borders of a fixed frame.

A 180-degree pan of this type was used in a well-known shot by Howard Hawks in the western, *Red River*. Early on the morning of the first day of the massive cattle drive that serves as the center of the film, Hawks wanted to illustrate the immensity of the undertaking and the huge herd of cattle. He placed the camera in the middle of the herd near several of the principal characters who were seated on horses. A slow pan begins, taking in the nervous anticipation of the cowboys and the thousands of cattle that extend as far as the eye can see in all directions. The camera rotates in a semicircle until it reaches the dominant figure of John Wayne 30 seconds later. As the leader of the group of men who have staked their ranches on the success of the cattle drive, Wayne has the responsibility for their families and their futures. The pan allows us to share the moment when he considers the enormity of what he is about to do. The shot tells us that men are small and the undertaking is great. In the context of the western this relationship also defines the men's courage.

Panning to Reframe

The least noticeable use of the pan is to follow action as it moves within a restricted area or over a much greater field of view than that of the frame. In the first instance the pan is used to reframe a subject so it remains in a desired portion of the frame. For example, reframing might be used to follow a police detective as he moves back and forth behind a suspect who's being interrogated. The detective may never leave an area larger than the field of view of the frame, but the moving camera simulates the human inclination to move our head and eyes to keep areas of interest centered in our cone of vision. The slight movement required to follow the detective is less distracting than a locked-off camera would be, since the movement of the detective within the fixed frame would create compositional imbalances. The choice of reframing or locking the camera in position depends on the dramatic intent of the scene.

Panning to Cover Action

When the field of view is great and the camera movement necessary to follow the action is extensive, the pan can cover wide spaces more quickly than any other type of camera movement.

Camera placement is the key to panning with the action. As with any staging consideration the type of panning required depends on whether or not the camera is in or out of the dramatic circle of action. Accentuating the sense of motion and space usually is done by placing the camera within the action. If the subject is moving, the camera will be forced to pan more extensively than if the camera is viewing the action from a distance.

Panning and Lenses

The sense of motion and space of a shot is not entirely dependent on the range of the panning move. In any given situation the perception of motion and space can also be manipulated by the choice of lens. Longer focal length lenses, for example, increase the perceived speed of objects moving across the field of view. Because the longer lens frames only a small part of the background compared with a wide-angle lens, a panning movement over a short lateral distance can be made to seem longer than that achieved with a wide-angle lens.

When making a panning move, a long lens also can be used to create a greater sense of motion. Director Akira Kurosawa frequently uses the telephoto pan for action employing foreground, middleground and background elements to achieve different levels of motion and depth. The small depth of field apparent with the telephoto lens is used to isolate the subject as well as increase the sense of motion when the camera moves. In his Samurai films Kurosawa often followed running figures or galloping horses through woods, allowing the background to become a blur of light and dark shapes, while foreground elements like trees interrupt the frame rhythmically for a stroboscopic effect.

The use of the telephoto lens for this type of shot requires adroit camera operation; high-speed panning can be difficult, particularly in low-light conditions. Even so, extreme telephoto lenses can be used to great effect

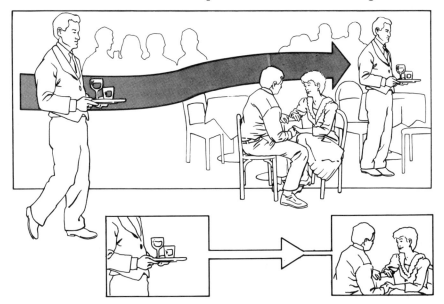

Figure 17.1

in demanding situations. While covering the fast white-water rafting action in John Boorman's *Deliverance*, cinematographer Vilmos Zsigmond used a 1000mm lens to follow the erratic and unpredictable path of the main characters on the river. The 1000mm lens is very nearly the longest camera optic available, requiring extremely precise framing and focusing. Although Zsigmond was advised that he might have trouble following the action with this lens, he reports that the sequence was fairly easy to shoot.

Panning for Graphic or Kinetic Effect

The pan is highly manipulative and easily leads the eye from one point to another. A passing car or the motion of leaves blowing along the ground can motivate a pan to an area of narrative significance. The car or leaves may have no specific relationship to the action of the story, but the pan is such a compelling move that we usually do not question the effect, accepting it as a pictorial device. An attention-leading device of this type is shown in Figure 17.1 on page 281.

A slightly more complex version of this technique is the cross pan, in which a moving subject leads to another moving subject. This requires that the two subjects cross paths. Cross pans of this type have a choreographic quality: Attention skips from subject to subject motivated largely by kinetic force. Movement is not restricted to one direction only (as in the examples of the car and the leaves). In fact, the direction of the pan can change completely, going first in one direction and then in the opposite direction without pause. If the action is sustained—for example, a dance in a ballroom—cross pans can work like a perpetual motion, moving from couple to couple indefinitely. Figure 17.2 illustrates the basic crossing pattern.

Figure 17.2

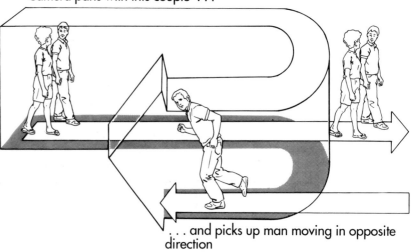

Camera pans with this couple . . .

. . . and picks up man moving in opposite direction

Panning to Emphasize Depth

Though the pan generally moves our attention horizontally or vertically across the frame it can also be used to lead our attention to near and far elements staged in depth. Figure 17.3 illustrates a pan shot that begins with a boy in the background running down a street towards the camera. The camera pans with the runner as he turns a corner and moves left to right

Figure 17.3: Depth shifts from background to foreground.

until he goes behind the woman seated in the car in the extreme foreground.

Panning for Logical Connection

In addition to its use in following action, the pan also can serve as a device to connect elements in the frame, automatically suggesting a logical relationship. When the pan moves from one point of interest to another it poses the question: "What is the connection between these two objects?" Depending on the narrative strategy the connection may be immediately clear or the filmmaker might create narrative motion by withholding the answer until later. Either way, the pan juxtaposes elements in a way that clearly makes the connection worthy of our interest.

Summary

The pan is an extremely versatile tool that seems to have fallen out of favor. Many contemporary filmmakers prefer the cut as a way to connect space and story elements so that they will have greater freedom when editing. As a result their use of space is restricted and may have a choppy look.

The next time you are at a place where there is activity—the grocery store, the parking lot of a shopping center or on line at a movie theater—imagine a scene including many of the images that surround you. Now imagine connecting these images by means of a continuous pan. You will probably be surprised at how the action around you overlaps and intersects. Inevitably, certain images will connect logically, but in some instances you will use the pan to connect images based solely on their graphic compatibility and later realize that this has suggested logical connections that you hadn't thought of before.

NARRATIVE EXAMPLES

We now return to the narrative problem we last saw in Chapter 8. This was the sequence in which a boy is waking up in his bedroom while his sister gets ready for school, his mother fixes breakfast and his father leaves the house for work. In the version storyboarded at the end of Chapter 8 only static shots were used. In this new version the filmmaker decides to try a different storytelling style by using extensive pan shots.

Version One

The filmmaker utilizes two shorthand storytelling devices, which he will intercut. The film will open on a CU of the refrigerator and the many notes, letters and cards attatched to it with magnets. The camera will pan over these notes capturing fragments of messages and images. This will be intercut with a similar panning style framing specific articles on the floor of the boy's bedroom shown in Figure 17.4.

The storyboard begins in frame 1 with an overview of the refrigerator door with halftone lines describing the path of the camera. In the actual pan shot the camera would only partially frame the messages:

1. A reminder of an appointment at the dentist's.

2. A note from school to the boy's parents: "Dear Mr. and Mrs. Dreyfuss, Mark has been late to school six times in the last month. He failed to hand in several assignments and is already quite far behind in math. He explained his lateness was due to a nervous disorder. I asked him to bring a note from the doctor. . . ."

3. A postcard from Mr. Dreyfuss from a hotel in Chicago.

4. A second postcard from Mr. Dreyfuss still on a business trip.

5. A third postcard from Mr. Dreyfuss. We learn that he travels a great deal.

6. A one-panel cartoon torn from a page of *Good Housekeeping*.

7. A second note from school inquiring about the first note and requesting a meeting with Mr. and Mrs. Dreyfuss.

Figure 17.4: The camera opens in ECU on a refrigerator magnet—one of those "Have a nice day" faces. The camera pulls back until it covers a field of about the size of a postcard. The camera begins to pan over all the notes and cards attached to the refrigerator door. All the while we hear kitchen sounds and Mrs. Dreyfuss and her teenaged daughter speaking.

Under the refrigerator shot in frame 1 we hear Mrs. Dreyfuss in the kitchen asking her daughter if Mark is up yet. We learn from this simple pan that Mark has trouble in school and that his father is often away on business.

Version Two

The filmmaker thinks that this first opening has merit as a visual idea, but unless this strategy is used under the titles at the opening of the movie it is too stylized for the opening, which is meant to carry a great deal of exposition.

A new idea is planned in which the extended pan over "storytelling" objects is moved to the boy's bedroom. In this setup the camera is placed in a central location in the action so that it will cover nearly 180 degrees of space.

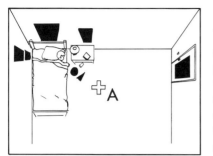

The aerial diagram illustrates the position of the separate elements in the storyboard. The camera is at position A. It begins pointing down at the triangle of the paper airplane on the floor, moves up the boy's arm to the posters behind him on the wall, moves across the wall left to right until it reaches the door and then pans back to the boy in bed. The specific action is described in the following storyboards.

1

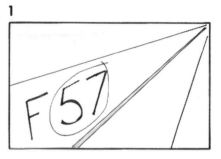

The movie opens on a big red F 57. The camera pulls back to reveal that this is written on the wing of a paper airplane to look like the markings on a fighter plane.

2

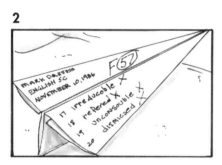

As the camera backs out we realize that the paper airplane is actually the paper from a spelling test and that the F 57 is not the boy's idea of aeronautic identification but the failing grade given by his teacher. We see the boy's name.

3

The camera pans over a nearby sandwich on a plate, an overturned drinking glass and the boy's hand hanging down alongside the bed.

4

The camera pans up the boy's arm but does not frame the boy's face, continuing up and over the bed to several posters on the wall. In each poster the boy has placed a photo of himself over the original photograph. This way he appears with the rock bands U2 and Pink Floyd and on the cover of *Time*.

5

The camera continues to pan to the right over more posters, including one of the first man on the moon, but the face of Neil Armstrong has been covered by a photo of Mark Dreyfuss.

6

The camera continues to the bedroom door where Mark has placed another of his photos on the body of a body builder.

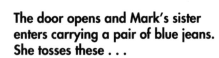

7

The door opens and Mark's sister enters carrying a pair of blue jeans. She tosses these . . .

8

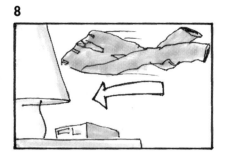

. . . and the camera follows the blue jeans through the air . . .

9

. . . until they land on Mark in bed. This is the first time we actually see him, but we recognize him from his photographs.

18 THE CRANE SHOT

T he crane shot is usually thought of as a strictly vertical movement, but actually the crane is capable of moves in many directions, though the distinguishing factor is its vertical capability. Used in this way the crane shot is perhaps the least naturalistic move in the moving camera repertoire. It is not analogous to any perception in normal experience, since we rarely see the world from the privileged position that a towering crane move allows.

Crane shots are inherently majestic and hold our interest regardless of the subject because of the sheer physical pleasure of the move: The power of the exotic viewing angle and the seductive change of perspective draw us in. Used at the beginning of a sequence the crane shot emphasizes the sense of presence and establishes the geography of an environment at the same time. The crane move that enters a location is a "once upon a time" shot directing our attention from the general to the specific. Where the establishing pan shot moves across a wide expanse of space surveying a fictional world, the crane shot permits us to "feel" the dimensions of that world by penetrating space, further endorsing its reality through the illusion of depth.

The crane shot has many other uses besides the epic grandeur of the establishing shot. In Alfred Hitchcock's *Notorious* the crane is used at a party to descend two stories from the ceiling of an enormous hall to a set of keys in Ingrid Bergman's hand. Here the purpose is to underscore the psychological tension that the keys represent in the story.

Another move of this type used to dramatize a character's anguish is the opening shot in Bernardo Bertolucci's *Last Tango in Paris*. Marlon Brando is walking on a sidewalk under an elevated train after the suicide of his wife. The camera reveals his torment by making a sudden rapid descent to a close-up of his upturned face as he screams at the sky.

Besides being used to move the camera within a shot, the crane can serve as a mobile tripod. The crane can rapidly deploy the camera within a scene for static shots that would normally require scaffolding or a tripod. During the studio production era in Hollywood, studio sets were the ideal location for a crane because even in small interiors, walls and ceilings were "wild," meaning that they could be easily removed to access lights or clear the viewpoint of the camera. The bulky Mitchell cameras could be rapidly repositioned within a set, and the director was able to make fairly rapid adjustments in the position of the camera. Today, when most films are shot on real locations, this freedom of movement with a big crane is only possible outdoors, but the smart filmmaker who understands the varied uses of the crane will make use of it for more than just a few impressive moving shots.

The Range of Motion

The crane's range of motion depends on the type of crane, but generally the camera can move up and down in an arc around its base. Included as a member of the crane family are jib arms and booms, which are added as accessories for many dollies. Because the dolly can move laterally during a shot, the range of motion is greatly increased by adding the vertical capability of the boom. Figure 18.1 shows the full range of motion for a remote-control type crane operating from a fixed point. When the terrain permits, a crane can also drop below the base, very nearly doubling its vertical range.

When the base is in motion the crane can continue to move vertically, thereby greatly increasing the area covered. A crane or boom arm can be attached to a camera car or any other stable moving platform to allow for vertical movement alongside a moving subject. Figure 18.2 shows a remote-control crane moving on track while simultaneously making a vertical move. Actually, following a subject's every move is not always advisable even though the newer camera support equipment is highly mobile. Up until recently, the limitations of heavier cameras and crane rigs forced cameramen to overcome technical problems by devising blocking solutions

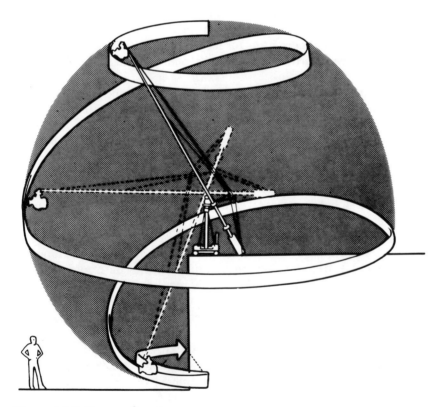

Figure 18.1: Range of motion.

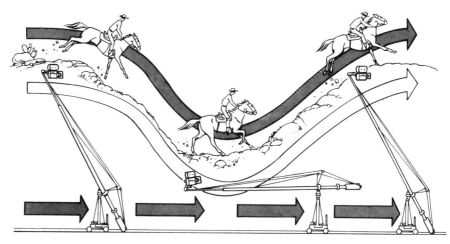

Figure 18.2: Simultaneous vertical and horizontal movement.

in which the subject and the camera cooperate. With these limitations removed the tendency is to have the camera slavishly follow the subject. This often means following a difficult path merely to hold the subject in a medium or full shot for the length of the action. While this may demonstrate technical ingenuity it lacks the perspective and compositional variety that a simpler camera move provides when the shot size changes as a player moves towards or away from the camera.

The crane can also be an inquisitive observer. Not only can it rise to get the overview of a scene, but it can go from the overview to the details of a scene and then return to the wide shot. A crane can move over an obstacle like a fence or a wall. Figure 18.3 shows the kind of gymnastic movement that can be accomplished with newer remote-control cranes.

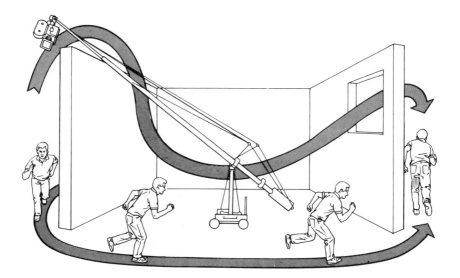

Figure 18.3: The inquisitive observer.

Point of View

A crane move can reinforce the subjective feel of a shot by imitating the general path of a subject, as shown in Figure 18.4. As the subject goes up a hill to look over the crest, the camera follows from behind. Since information is revealed to us as it is revealed to the subject, we see things from his general viewpoint.

Figure 18.4: Point of view.

Following a subject's line of sight doesn't have to cover a great distance. A boom arm on a dolly, which is still essentially a crane shot, can imitate a person dropping to a crouching position. Figure 18.5 shows a fairly simple move that would encourage the viewer to interpret the shot as the view seen by the man looking under the garage door. The camera would frame the crouching subject, using him as a framing device, or continue to move past him toward the object of interest.

Like all long moving shots the crane shot can be used as a sequence shot moving from one point of interest to another. This can be done to make comparisons. For example, for a film set in South Africa the crane can move from a close-up of a cross atop a beautiful church steeple and then slowly

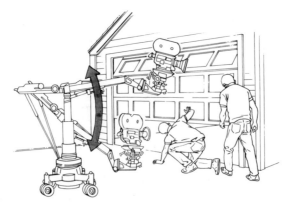

Figure 18.5: Point of view.

descend past this symbol of Christianity to the all-white congregation of Afrikaners below as they turn a black couple away from the doors of the church. This is only the most obvious type of symbolism, but it illustrates the cinematic relationship between the conceptual use of imagery and technique. Naturally, more subtle comparisons can be made, permitting the viewer greater freedom to interpret, but the point is that the crane shot is more than a tool for pictorial invention.

Equipment

In recent years, remote-control devices and cameras with video taps (remote video monitoring through the camera lens) have led to the development of variations of the traditional jib arm and crane devices. This new equipment allows the cameraman to control the framing and focus of the camera from a distance (rather than riding on the crane with the camera), permitting greater mobility of the camera itself. Two of the better known devices, the Louma crane and the Skycam system, are camera movement devices that rely solely on remote-control operation. The Louma crane uses a boom supported by a dolly in an arrangement similar to a conventional dolly and jib arm, but because the camera and the specialized controls weigh considerably less than a manually operated rig, the light boom arm and dolly have an enormous range of motion. The camera is suspended under the boom arm and can travel in spaces that would be impossible with any other device, allowing complex moves in, out and around tight spaces, such as crowds or street traffic.

The Skycam is a remote-controlled device that operates on a cable system. Four cables are suspended above the ground on post supports, or from a ceiling in a square configuration. The four cables are anchored to a special camera harness that is suspended between the four anchored corners. Each of the four cables is wound around a computer-controlled drum. By controlling the amount of cable paid-out or rewound on the drums, the position of the camera can be controlled.

A subsequent, though related, development is the use of the type of motion-control systems developed for special effects work, resulting in "smart dollies" that can be programmed on a computer to make complex moves to exacting specifications. As with the remote-control system, motion control operates all the functions of the camera normally controlled manually—focus, aperture, vertical and horizontal displacement, pan, tilt and roll—and stores the commands in a computer. Once it is captured in memory the most difficult movement can be infinitely repeated for multiple exposure of the film for special effects.

Visualization for Crane Moves

There is no getting around it: Executing a crane move eats up time on the set. Therefore, careful planning and preparation is vital. Because a crane moves through space in three dimensions, models are an excellent way to plan the coordination of the various production departments. Contrary to what is generally believed, models are not necessarily a major expense. For instance, photos of the actual location can be blown up as inexpensive photocopies for a backdrop. Photographs of buildings can be cut out, pasted to foam core and positioned in scale in front of the backdrop. This is as useful for choreographing action as it is for planning the movement of the camera, particularly if many people are involved in the shot.

The most exciting new tools for planning crane moves or sequence shots are the various computer-aided design (CAD) programs used for visualization. This type of software, now affordable for personal computers, lets the filmmaker preview a camera move in full motion for any lens. Complex locations can be designed on the computer within several hours. Once the architectural or location plan is entered, camera moves can be animated in a few minutes so that several versions can be compared side-by-side and stored for reference. Key frames from two computer-rendered crane shots are shown in Figures 18.6 and 18.7. Unlike the frame excerpts seen here, the computer can play back the actual move in full motion on the screen. These examples were created in Virtus WalkThrough, which operates in real time, permitting the filmmaker to move through the three-dimensional space onscreen as if he were really on location. Any camera move can be recorded in the program and saved for comparison with any other camera move. The speed, timing, focal length and the direction of the move can all be varied easily and minute corrections can be made and viewed instantly.

Learning the Moves

Beyond the obvious advantage CAD programs offer for planning difficult shots, this type of visualization is a tremendous tool for learning the subtleties of camera movement. Like any skill that involves movement and perception, such as dance or gymnastics, the control of camera choreography improves with practice. Unfortunately, without a crane or dolly to work with on a regular basis a filmmaker has little chance of refining his kinesthetic perception and skills. The new CAD programs go a long ways towards solving this problem by providing a very credible substitute for any type of camera move. At present, Virtus WalkThrough offers the best learning environment for camera movement since you are able to walk or fly through a location in real time once it has been created. This allows the filmmaker to repeat a camera move until it has the precise framing and ballistics he's looking for. Every move has a unique feel and a crane shot with a steep ascent frames a narrative differently from a crane shot that moves laterally while ascending. Using CAD programs as a workshop, a filmmaker can acquire skills that previously took years to learn.

Figure 18.6: CAD model, example one.

1
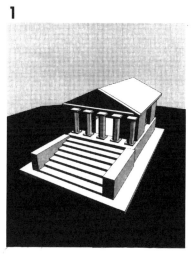

2
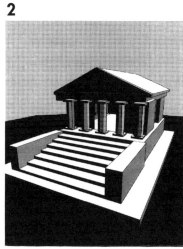

3
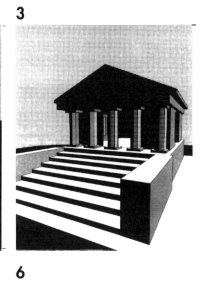

4

5

6

7

8

9

Figure 18.7: CAD model, example two.

1

2

3

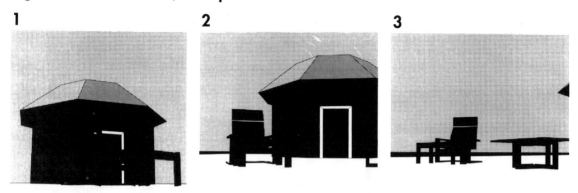

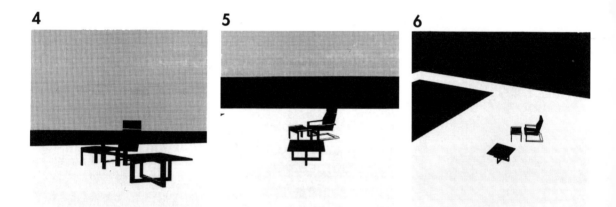

4

5

6

7

8

9

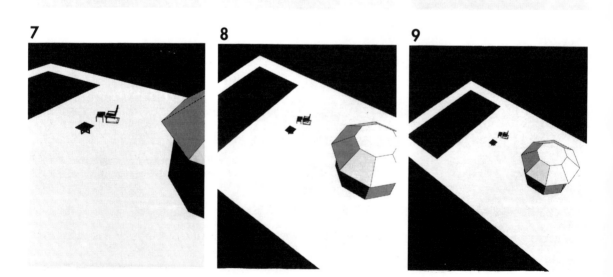

19 THE TRACKING SHOT

The tracking shot is used to follow a subject or explore space. This can be a simple shot framing one subject or a complex sequence shot that connects multiple story elements varying the staging and composition in a single flowing movement. However, even the most intricate tracking shots can be understood more easily if we look at the narrative and pictorial building blocks on which they are based.

The Circle of Action and the Moving Camera

The circle of dramatic action is almost the same for the moving camera as it is for the stationary camera we looked at in Chapter 13. For instance, if there is a ballroom dance and the camera is on the floor surrounded by dancers, it is *in the action*. If the camera dollies along a balcony to cover the action of the couples dancing some distance away, it is *outside the action*. This would also be the case if the camera were stationary. The difference between the stationary and the traveling camera is that the traveling camera can move into or out of the action within a single shot. In story terms this means moving from the general to the specific view of things or vice versa. This change between the interior and the exterior of the circle of action is one of the most useful features of the moving camera; it enables the filmmaker to structure story elements visually.

The Subject To Camera Distance

In addition to entering or exiting the circle of action the camera can travel towards or away from a subject to shape our identification with that subject. Moreover, a moving shot develops in time so that the degree of emphasis is variable within a shot.

By comparison, a stationary close-up has only one graphic value for the length of the shot, but a moving close-up shot can include a range of values from a wide close-up to an extreme close-up. Depending on whether the move is towards or away from the subject, the general increase or decrease in intimacy (or any other effect of the framing) evolves during the shot.

Planning for the Tracking Shot

We can identify the various ways a tracking shot can be planned if we think in terms of first, the traveling camera's relationship to the circle of action and second, the subject-to-camera distance. These two factors determine the type of spatial relationship that exists between the camera and the subject of any shot. Regardless of whether the camera is inside or outside the circle of action, the subject-to-camera distance may increase or decrease or remain the same.

As discussed in Chapter 5, one of the ways a scene in a script can be broken down into shots is by asking what is the point of view of the scene and what is the appropriate emotional distance between the viewer and the subject. Of course, before analyzing a scene you may have a moving shot in mind that came to you while reading the script. Even so, it might be helpful to make a list of the elements that are to be emphasized in the shot you imagine. If you draw a schematic of the tracking shot you can write the key moments along the path of the camera. This could include important lines of dialogue or specific choreography for the actor. While this type of planning can be used to organize a specific shot, thinking in terms of the dramatic circle of action is useful when trying to find a shot to record complex action. In the remainder of this chapter we will look at the basic traveling camera strategies to help build a vocabulary of moves.

Tracking to Introduce a Subject or Location

A tracking shot can inspect a location or subject, revealing it to us slowly by focusing on individual details of the overall location. This can be done from inside or outside the circle of action. In one version the camera begins in close-up, pulling back to a wide view so that we move from the specific detail to the general outline. For example, the camera moves down a sidewalk on a deserted street of shops. At first the view is in CU so that we see only peeling paint, broken glass and other signs of decay at a bake shop. Details of this first store reveal the signs of a failed family business. The camera pulls back, tracking past dilapidated storefronts and vacant businesses. "Closed" or "Out of Business" signs are in many of the windows. A homeless person sleeps in the door of an empty store. The signs of economic disaster are revealed slowly until an entire street is in view. In this way, camera movement relates the citywide economic depression to the individual level by first showing us the bake shop.

Often a tracking shot follows a lateral path along subjects deployed over a large area, such as at a state fair or cars in traffic—for example, Godard's long traveling shot past car after car in *Weekend*. While it may be convenient and appropriate to move along a straight path, a tracking shot is not restricted to a straight line. The camera can also turn corners, move forward and backward, come to a halt and begin to move again, change speeds, cross its own path, frame subjects in close-up or wide shot or move through windows or doors or any other visual scheme the filmmaker can conceive and the crew can execute.

Tracking at the Same Speed as the Subject

The most familiar use of the tracking shot is to follow two or more people in conversation. When the subject and the camera are moving at the same speed and the subject-to-camera distance does not change, the moving shot is the compositional equivalent of a static shot. The camera can track directly ahead of or behind the subjects, it can track on a parallel path in line with the subjects or it can parallel their path from a position slightly ahead or slightly behind them. Basic tracking angles are shown in Figure 19.1 The subjects can also be framed in full figure, medium shot or close-up, placing the

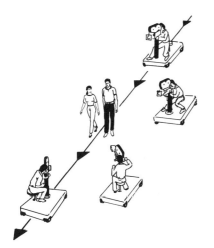

Figure 19.1

camera inside or outside the action. This same parallel tracking shot is used frequently to record conversations in cars, on horseback or boats or any other conveyance. The shot is also useful in action sequences in which car-mounted cameras are often used to move alongside fast-moving subjects.

Tracking Faster or Slower Than the Subject

This is really a variation on the parallel tracking shot. The only difference is that the camera is moving at a different speed from that of the subject. In this way the subject will approach the camera as it moves or be left behind when the camera moves faster (Figure 19.2). This gives the filmmaker the ability to let the subject enter or exit the circle of action as the camera is moving.

If we use a tracking shot to show that a runner is losing a race, the camera can move slightly faster than the runner, passing him during the course of

Figure 19.2

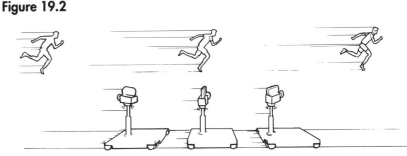

The camera moves slower than the subject.

The camera moves faster than the subject.

the shot. If we want to show the runner winning, obviously we would have the runner going faster than the camera. In an action sequence this is a more dynamic shot than the conventional parallel tracking shot because it develops while it's on the screen as the subject travels across the frame. This holds our interest more than a shot in which the camera and subject move at the same speed. Also, when the camera is moving at a different speed from that of the subject the perspective is accentuated by three planes of motion—background, subject and foreground—rather than two planes of motion, which is the case when the camera and subject move at the same speed. Using three planes of motion increases the sense of depth.

Not only can the subject and camera move at different speeds, but they can change speeds within a shot. When recording conversations, the camera can keep pace with the subjects and then slow down as the subjects move ahead of the camera, leaving it behind. Another variation is to have the subjects overtake the moving camera and then move along at the same speed. Still another version might have the camera at rest as the couple approaches, then begin to move along with them at the same speed throughout their conversation and have them leave the camera behind at the end of the scene. All these variations have the same purpose: to create the sense that we have eavesdropped on a real conversation that continues after the subjects move on.

Moving Towards or Away From a Subject

So far we have been interested in parallel tracking. The camera can also move directly towards or away from a subject or object, increasing or diminishing its importance within the context of a story. The basic move is illustrated in Figure 19.3.

A dolly move towards a subject's face can be used to emphasize a character's moment of realization. This familiar convention is often set up as a cut on the look. For instance, a woman arrives at a bar and finds her husband embracing another woman. There are three possible camera moves: 1) The camera dollies in to a CU of the woman looking at her husband, 2) the camera dollies towards the husband and 3) both dolly shots are used sequentially.

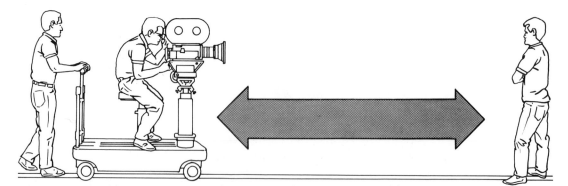

Figure 19.3: The push-in or the pull-back.

A dolly shot can also deemphasize a subject by pulling back. This tends to isolate the subject as well. For example, a woman is standing on a railroad platform as the train pulls away with her only child, a daughter, onboard. Mounted on a train the camera might back away from the woman on the platform, indicating her sense of loss as her daughter departs.

Perhaps the most familiar use of the backtracking shot or pullback is as an introductory shot at the beginning of a scene. This familiar technique draws a relationship between the object at the beginning of the shot and the location in which it is set. In a typically commentative use the camera might pull back from a worn but expensive topcoat to reveal that it is on a chair in a squalid one-room apartment. This ironic setup tells us that the owner of the coat, formerly a wealthy businessman, has lost everything except this last possession from better days.

Varying the Camera Angle Within the Shot

Figure 19.4 illustrates a typical tracking setup for a dialogue scene. In this parallel tracking arrangement the camera is moving alongside the couple. The height of the camera is slightly below eye level, but because the camera is several feet away, the angle of view is indistinguishable from an eye-level shot, as shown in storyboard frame A. If the scene builds to an angry exchange between the players, the director might want to cut to a lower angle framing for a more dynamic composition. Normally this would mean cutting to a new angle. An alternative solution would be to move the actors closer to the camera, forcing it to tilt up to include the actors' heads in a medium shot. Storyboard frame B shows the result of moving the couple to within a few feet of the lens. The same effect is produced if the camera dollies to the couple.

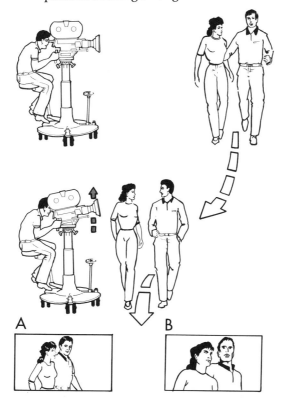

A   B

Figure 19.4: To combine low and high angles in a single tracking shot, change the camera-to-subject distance. As the subjects get closer to the dolly, the camera must be tilted up to include them in the frame. The change in angle is shown in storyboard frames A and B.

Tracking Around a Subject

The camera can surround the dramatic circle of action by completing a full circle with the subject at the center, as shown in Figure 19.5. Extreme examples of this appear in similar ways in two films, Woody Allen's *Hannah and Her Sisters* and Brian DePalma's *The Untouchables*. In both films a completely circular track surrounds people seated at a table. Even when the camera movement is slow, the shot is designed to

Figure 19.5

draw attention away from the characters as individuals so that we will evaluate the situation as a whole. In *The Untouchables* the circular tracking shot symbolizes that the four crime fighters, individuals from diverse backgrounds, have finally become a team. The camera surrounds them, unifying them in space.

Allen's use of a similar circular tracking shot is parenthetical. Here, the camera circles the sisters seated at a table so rapidly that it overpowers their conversation. The shot dismisses their observations and opinions, putting them on display for our inspection. The viewer is put in a superior position, knowing that what the sisters are saying reveals what they don't know about themselves.

Still another use of the circular tracking shot is seen in Martin Scorsese's *The Color of Money* (1986), the follow-up (25 years later) to Robert Rossen's study of a pool hustler in *The Hustler* (1961). In this case the camera is used to convey the character's state of mind. The camera circles the character, Fast Eddie, in CU framing as he enters the first world-class competition since his retirement 20 years before. He is momentarily overcome by the rush of excitement, and the movement of the camera conveys Eddie's feelings in a single move.

Combining Interior and Exterior Spaces

The change from adjacent interior and exterior locations is usually handled by a cut between shots of each space. This eliminates the problem of matching interior and exterior lighting, which can vary greatly. Photographed separately the two locations need not actually be near each other, so a studio interior can be combined with a real outdoor location halfway around the world. This is a decided advantage from the production manager's point of view, but artistically the separation of exteriors and interiors diminishes spatial unity.

The alternative is to move the camera from interior to exterior or vice versa in a continuous move. Here are some of the possibilities:

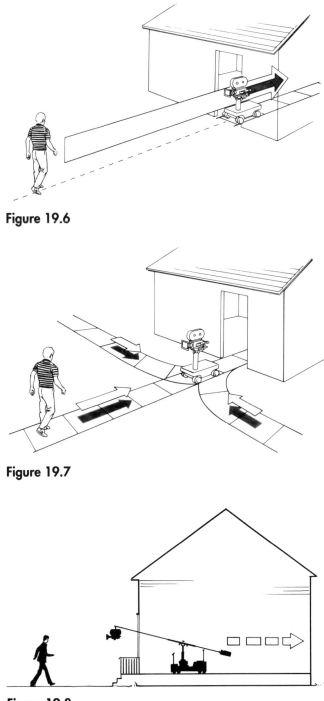

Figure 19.6

Figure 19.7

Figure 19.8

Entering an Interior

The dolly is set up so that the camera tracks in front of the subject as shown in Figure 19.6. The camera is stationary as the subject approaches. When the subject is within a few feet of the camera the dolly is pulled backward into the room followed by the subject.

The camera can also precede the subject from any angle or path using curved track or a temporary platform of boards or plywood. Typical angles of entry are shown in Figure 19.7 If the move is small, another variation could add a jib arm to the dolly. The dolly would remain inside the house on the level floor of the interior space and the jib arm and camera would be extended out the door. As the subject approaches the door the dolly is pulled back until the jib arm is inside the doorway waiting for the subject to follow. One advantage of this setup is shown in Figure 19.8. Because there are steps up to the front door, a dolly would have to be placed on a ramp with a gentle slope. Apart from the time it would take to build the ramp, it would be a difficult shot to execute smoothly. The jib arm solves the problem and offers considerable flexibility if there is a need to change the staging.

Even without the jib arm, the camera and dolly can be placed indoors and still connect exterior and interior space using a dolly move. If the camera is close to the door frame it can be aimed outside to frame what looks like an exterior shot, since the door frame is not seen. As the subject approaches the door from outside the camera pulls back deeper into the room until the door frame and the room are included in the shot. An additional alternative is to use a zoom lens to cover the subject's approach, gradually widening out to frame the subject. Eventually, the shot will include part of the door frame and part of the room.

Shooting an Interior From the Exterior Position

It is also possible to move from an exterior to an interior space by allowing the subject to pass a moving camera, as shown in Figure 19.9. In this case the camera pans with the subject to the edge of the doorway but remains outside. The subject enters the interior, and the camera photographs the scene inside while remaining outside. With the right choice of lens and staging, the results will appear as though the camera had entered the location.

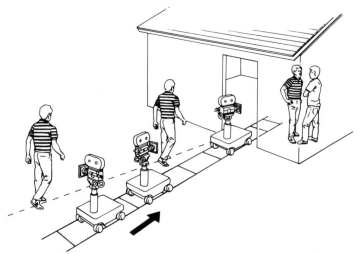

Figure 19.9: Shooting an interior from an exterior position. The camera dollies and pans with the subject, but remains outside to shoot the interior.

Shooting Through Windows to Combine Interiors and Exteriors

In this last setup the traveling camera is placed in an interior location. The camera frames a subject through a window as he approaches the house

Figure 19.10: Shooting through windows to combine interiors and exteriors.

(Figure 19.10). The camera is placed close enough to the window glass so that the window frame is not visible and the viewer is unaware that the camera is inside the room. As the camera pans to follow the subject entering through a doorway, the camera quickly pans past the wall and door frame, following the subject into the house. At this moment the viewer realizes that he's been watching the subject from inside a room. With this arrangement, track can be laid inside the room so that the moving shot can continue in the interior space.

Obviously the positioning of the camera is dependent on the room and the action of the subject, but the principle in the last three shots is the same: The selective view of the camera can make it seem as though the camera has crossed from an interior to an exterior (or the reverse) while following a subject.

Editing Tracking Shots

Directors are often unsure of the cutting rules for tracking shots and are reluctant to use them in many situations. This fear of potential editing problems is unfounded, and apart from the line of action, which is observed for both moving and static shots, tracking shots do not pose any special continuity problems except for the difficulty of executing prolonged action. As mentioned in the chapter on editing, a tracking shot can be time-consuming and the director may be put in the position of having to gamble the success of a scene on a single, long, moving shot. Time constraints may force coverage and backup footage to be sacrificed, and this accounts for the general belief that tracking shots are difficult to cut. Naturally, if a tracking shot is the only version of a particular action in a scene, there will be no way of altering the footage except by removing the shot—along with the action it contains.

This brings us to the one legitimate cutting problem that tracking shots pose: A static shot cannot be inserted easily into a tracking shot of the same action. This single case has led to the exaggerated view that moving and static shots can be difficult to join smoothly. The belief persists that there is some encompassing rule, serving the same function as the line of action, that determines the dos and don'ts of continuity for the tracking shot. No such rule exists.

Apart from interrupting a moving shot with a brief static shot of the same action, there are no special editing rules for traveling shots that don't apply equally to static shots. Static shots can be easily joined to traveling shots, and traveling shots can be joined to other traveling shots, or joined in an extended series of traveling shots. In fact, in certain situations a series of traveling shots blends motion more successfully than a similar series of static shots. For instance, a series of short tracking shots moving past rows of soldiers in formation can be cut together so that each shot leads to the next. A similar series of static shots would appear to be overcut.

A traveling shot tends to prepare the viewer for graphic complexity and change in the following shot in a sequence. In many situations the traveling shot can smooth graphic transitions similar to the way that a dissolve smoothes temporal transitions. For instance, a graphic jump cut (one in which the camera is moved less than 20 degrees, but in which time is continuous) is less harsh when made between traveling shots.

While the traveling camera can set up a change in angle or movement in the following shot, continuity is still dependent on the same types of compositional and editing strategies that promote smooth shot flow in a series of static shots.

Traveling Shots and Camera Angles

The traveling camera increases the effect of all other perspective cues that help us judge distance. Since we identify camera angles by the way in which they render perspective, it stands to reason that the traveling camera will intensify our perception of space for any angle. In the chapter on camera angles it was established that three-point perspective provided the greatest amount of information about the spatial relations for any of the possible views of an object in space. Similarly, the traveling camera can move through one, two or three planes of movement. To move in three planes simultaneously the camera must move forward or backward while moving vertically and horizontally. If the camera is performing this type of movement while framing an object in three-point perspective, the maximum degree of depth will be achieved for any given scene. The use of any foreground elements or other pictorial or compositional devices that help the viewer understand spatial relationships will further increase the sense of depth.

Viewer Placement and the Moving Camera

Placement, as described in Chapter 14, is the movement of the viewer to different viewing positions in a scene through changes in camera angle. This was compared to choreography, because the viewer experiences a whole range of kinetic and physical effects as carefully arranged as a dance performance. Shot-flow choreography is present in any sequence of shots, but it is most palpable when the camera is in motion.

A moving shot may pass through several angles of view or present only one angle of view during the length of a shot. When following a subject at a fixed distance the angle of the shot does not change. But if the camera approaches or retreats from the subject the angle of view may change. Directors interested in exploiting the "pull" of this type of perspective shift will learn to stage action to force the camera to move along more than one axis or move around objects to include a range of views.

We can represent the perspective shifts of camera movement in drawings I call "perspective tunnels." This type of diagram is really an extension of the "Quatraccento Cube," the term used to describe the conception of the picture space in a painting or drawing that began with the development of linear perspective in the Renaissance.

Two well-known traveling shots are illustrated in Figure 19.11 First is the long descending crane shot in Alfred Hitchcock's *Notorious*. The camera descends two stories to end in CU on a set of keys in Ingrid Bergman's hand. A more complex move is shown in the long crane move into the El Rancho cabaret in *Citizen Kane*. The actual shot was done using a miniature for the exterior and a full-scale set for the interior completion of the move, but the extended perspective cube or tunnel would be the same in any case.

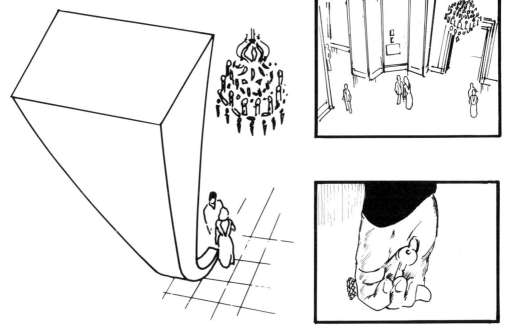

Figure 19.11: The long crane shot from *Notorious*.

The crane shot that passes through the skylight in *Citizen Kane*.

20 TRACKING SHOT CHOREOGRAPHY

Now that the basic types of moving camera shots have been described, we can look at how actors staged in depth and multiple centers of interest can be combined using the traveling camera. The variations possible with a simple track setup can range from a stylish move alongside two players in conversation to the multicharacter sequence shot that connects several story elements and locations.

Moving Camera and Mobile Staging

There are two staging options available with the moving camera: First, you can move the camera around a fixed subject, as demonstrated in the previous chapter, or second, you can move the subject and the camera simultaneously.

In the same way that there are basic staging patterns for dialogue in static shots, there are also basic camera moves for staged action. These moves are governed by two practical considerations: 1) the camera's range of motion when moving on dolly track or other equipment and 2) the fact that it is easier to move the actors than to move the camera.

The basic camera moves outlined in this chapter represent a flexible system that will give you an understanding of how the choreography of camera and actors can be integrated. The ultimate goal of this system is to encourage and facilitate a varied use of space, camera angle and composition, thereby stretching the limits of the frame.

There are two parts to our staging system for the traveling camera:

- Tracking Choreography: This refers to the path followed by a moving subject relative to the path of the moving camera.

- Patterns and Positions: This is the same staging system for actors we used for static shots in Chapters 9, 10 and 11.

The basic idea in our staging system for the moving camera is that *any number of individual shots can be connected to form a single, uninterrupted shot.* This approach analyzes a moving shot as represented in a storyboard. Each frame in a storyboard represents a static staging pattern that can be connected to other frames to form a single shot using the moving camera and mobile staging.

We can begin by looking at the simplest use of a straight track dolly move.

Tracking Choreography One

In figure 20.1 we see three separate versions of the basic tracking shot presented side by side. Below each dolly is the frame as the camera views the subject. In each of the three camera moves, the subject-to-camera distance remains the same and represents a basic unit or building block.

This type of staging is used all the time in dialogue sequences, though almost always as a medium shot or full shot. In its simplest form the shot opens with the camera and subject in motion and ends without any change in the subject-to-camera distance. In this sense the subject is seen very much as he would be in a static shot with only a small amount of background movement visible.

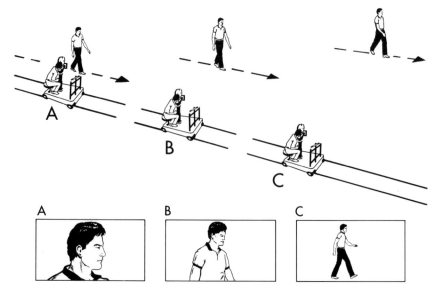

Figure 20.1

It's possible to cut between any of these moving shots to vary the shot size, but a more fluid way to change the framing is to have the subject move closer to or farther away from the camera during the course of the shot. This is usually done at the beginning or the end of the shot. In the aerial view of straight track shown in Figure 20.2, the gray areas at either end of the track represent the possible areas of approach or departure for any subject that moves parallel to the track. The filmmaker should consider the wide range of options the gray areas provide, since the approach can be used to include any area in the location that is of interest. Depending on the angle of approach or departure, the camera must pan to follow the subject. This becomes an opportunity to include a great deal of the action in the vicinity of the camera even before it begins to move.

The long track between

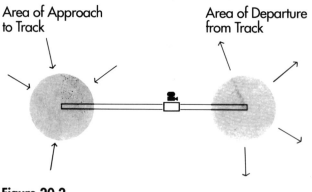

Area of Approach to Track

Area of Departure from Track

Figure 20.2

the circles could be used to record the subject in any of the framings shown in figure 20.1, only the subject would approach the camera from a distance in the beginning of the shot and exit into the distance towards the end of the shot.

With this type of staging the camera may be motionless at the beginning of the shot while the subject approaches and then slowly begin to move as the desired framing is obtained. This framing is held for most of the shot. As the tracking move nears completion, the procedure is reversed and the camera slows down, possibly to a complete stop, as the subject moves away from the camera through the departure area. The approach may start very far away from the camera so that the subject is first seen in a roomy full shot and may depart framed in the same way.

Tracking Choreography Two

Figure 20.3 is a variation in which the area of approach is not merely an introduction, but part of the main dramatic action of the shot. In this case the approach is directly towards the camera. If this were a dialogue scene, the subjects would be speaking during their approach to the track before the camera began to move. It has become a familiar convention to allow the audience to hear the subjects' conversation clearly even when they are very far from the camera.

As you can see, this choreography combines two storyboard building blocks—a full front shot and a profile medium shot. The illustration shows the subjects walking side by side throughout the tracking move, but of course the director is free to place the actors in any of the staging patterns and positions outlined in Chapter 9.

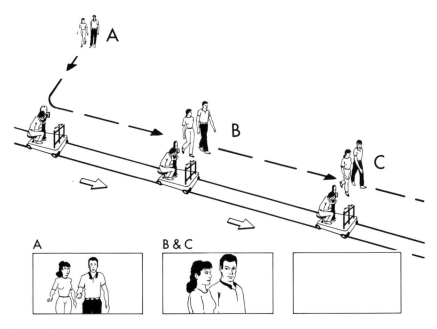

Figure 20.3

Tracking Choreography Three

Figure 20.4 demonstrates how three shots can be combined: a full figure profile, a full front shot and a medium profile shot. To combine these views the camera moves at the beginning of the shot at the same pace as the subjects, coming to rest as the subjects turn to approach the camera. When the subjects turn a second time to walk parallel to the track the camera begins to move again. Other variations might include staging the action so that it takes place at different heights. For example, the track might be laid on a dock alongside a cruise ship. The first portion of the camera move would follow a subject on board the

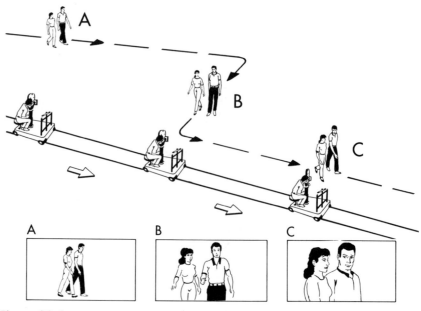

Figure 20.4

ship as he walks along the railing 20 ft. above the camera, which is moving parallel to the track. As shown in Figure 20.5, the player could then approach the camera when exiting the boarding ramp and complete the third leg of the tracking shot on the dock walking alongside the camera.

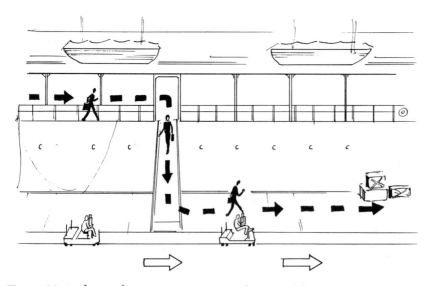

Figure 20.5: The tracking move covers a subject at different heights.

Tracking Choreography Four

Figure 20.6 is almost the same as the previous S bend setup, with one important difference: The players cross the track. Again, a long or full shot is combined with a full front shot and a medium shot, but with a change in direction as shown in frame C of the storyboard. If this change in direction looks disconcerting, it is perfectly understandable in the actual shot, since the change of direction is gradual. The pivot point for the camera can be on either side of the players' path when they cross the track. Refinements of this type are determined by the location and the specific needs of the scene.

Crossing the track will work for any tracking layout in this section. Moving the action around the camera and forcing it to include 180 degrees of space places the camera in the center of the circle of action.

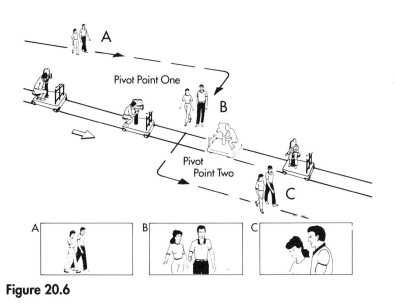

Figure 20.6

Tracking Choreography Five

Figure 20.7 reverses the framing of the two previous S bend patterns so that the players begin close to the camera and then move away. As with the other S bend moves, three framings are combined.

Applying this or any of the other choreographed moves to a real staging problem is of course dependent on the location, but the basic principles will work for any subject whether it's two people in conversation, a car or a speedboat.

Even the track is dispensable, used here as a convenient way of indicating the path of the camera. The camera could just as easily be mounted on a crane, remote-control boom, camera car or Steadicam rig, each adding its particular personality and range of motion to the process of designing the shot.

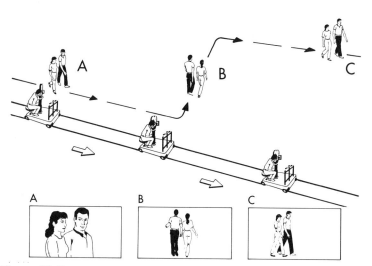

Figure 20.7

Tracking Choreography Six (Revealing Space)

Figure 20.8 begins with the subject in close-up. The subject moves angularly away as more of the background is revealed. In this case, the tracking move can be seen as combining two shots frequently paired together: the close-up shot of a subject and a cut on his look. For example, Figure 20.7 might show the subject approaching the camera for a close-up at the beginning of a scene. We hold on his look and his reaction to surroundings that are not included in the frame. This forces us to experience the location through the experience of the subject. As he moves away from the camera the background is revealed slowly, and we learn that the man is moving through the smoking ruins of a factory that has burned

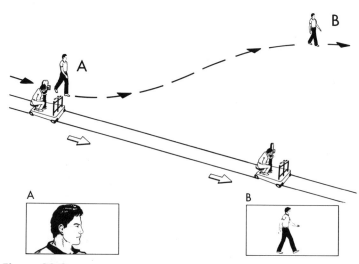

Figure 20.8

down. As the shot continues to widen, we see the victims of the fire being helped by police and emergency medical technicians.

Tracking Choreography Seven

Figure 20.9 illustrates a reverse of the strategy shown in Tracking Choreography Six. This time we begin with a wide shot showing us what the location looks like. Instead of being introduced to the scene by studying the reaction of a particular player to his surroundings, we evaluate the location first and the player approaching us second. If this staging were used in the factory scenario from Tracking Choreography Six we would form our own opinion of the locale and the action. When the player is finally seen in CU at the end of the shot, we are interested in finding out if he will react to the damage as we have. This is another instance of spatial control used to determine a question and answer strategy.

Figure 20.9

Tracking Choreography Six and Seven are shots that encourage comparisons between the subject and the location.

Extended Choreography

Now that we have looked at several possibilities for camera and subject choreography we can make more complex arrangements by combining the seven tracking patterns. For instance, we can string patterns Three, Seven and Five together for a tracking shot in the park location (Figure 20.10). Furthermore, all of the shots we have looked at can be joined together and combined with additional camera movement. Figure 20.10 shows a simple track setup, but a crane could easily be substituted to add vertical motion.

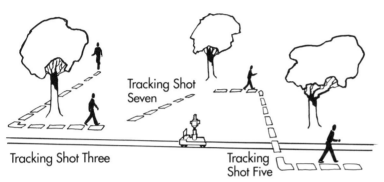

Figure 20.10: Three tracking patterns are combined to create a complex choreography.

Controlling the Camera Path Instead of the Subject Path

So far we have only considered tracking shots where the subject was choreographed around straight track. However, there are many times when this is not possible—for example, when the action must follow a road, a path in the woods or any other fixed route, or when the terrain restricts the movement of the subjects. In this case, the graphic variation within the shot—namely, shot size and camera angle—is determined entirely by camera placement and the choice of lens. In the next three examples we will return to the extended choreography we looked at in Figure 20.10, only this time the camera paths have been chosen to illustrate the value of retracking and countering.

In Figure 20.11 the camera tracks angularly through the scene in the opposite direction of the subject. This is a countermove that begins with the subject facing the camera until it passes the center of the shot, at which point the sub-

Figure 20.11: Extended counter move. In this setup the camera and the subject move in opposite directions. The arrows indicate the panning action of the camera.

ject is facing away from the camera. As with any move in which the subject crosses the camera path, there is a reverse of screen direction. Because the change is gradual, crossing the line is unobtrusive.

In Figure 20.12 the camera tracks towards the subject to the center of the shot and then reverses direction and moves back in the same general direction as the subject. The reversal of the camera is usually a distracting maneuver unless the camera comes to a stop before changing direction. This would be justified if the subject stopped for a moment to perform some action—for instance, taking off his jacket on a hot day. Here is how it might be set up: The camera and subject are approaching each other and meet at about one third of the distance illustrated. The subject and camera stop at this point and the subject takes off his jacket and wipes

Figure 20.12: The camera approaches the subject (gray arrows) and then reverses direction remaining ahead of the subject (black arrow).

his brow with a handkerchief. After a moment the subject continues on his way and the camera moves back along the path it just covered. The viewer will be unaware that the camera is retracking along familiar ground because the camera is pointed in a new direction.

In Figure 20.13 we see a side view of the pattern we've been studying. The camera path is parallel to and in the same direction as the path of the subject in three areas. When the subject approaches the camera directly it pauses until the subject makes the turn to the next parallel course. This is a case where stopping the camera is necessary to keep the subject in the frame.

The arrow in the diagram at right indicates the direction of the track illustrated below.

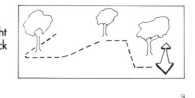

Figure 20.13: The direction of the camera move is indicated by the solid diagrammatic line. The camera parallels the subject during the lateral movement, pausing when the subject approaches the camera.

Tracking Around an Obstacle

If there is one lesson to be learned about designing movement for the traveling camera it is that it's always better to work with, rather than against, the location. All too often directors rely on the sheer technical virtuosity (and forbearance) of their crews to move the camera over difficult territory. The Louma crane, Skycam, Steadicam and other camera supports intended to extend the camera's range of motion have their place, but resourceful staging is by far the most useful asset a director can call upon. In Figure 20.14 the camera is unable to follow the subject closely and include the background desired by the director because the swimming pool is in the way. A jib arm or remote-control crane might be able to put the camera above the water in the middle of the pool, but there is an equally good solution that is easier to execute. The action could be staged so that the camera frames the subject and pool area in wide shot, arriving in the middleground at the same time as the subject.

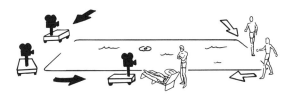

Figure 20.14

We could carry the idea further by continuing the movement of subject and camera in a countering move that circles the woman on the lounge chair, as shown in Figure 20.15.

Figure 20.15

Permitting obstacles to remain between the subject and the camera can actually be of value since they may serve as framing devices. In the action illustrated in Figure 20.16 a

Figure 20.16: The camera tracks parallel to the driver as he walks to the office. As seen in the storyboard the moving line of trucks is used as a framing device. When the driver enters the office the camera frames him through the window in panel 4.

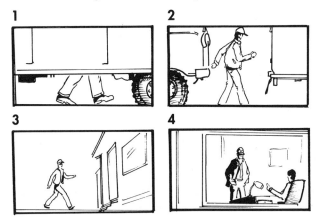

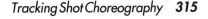

truck driver walks along a line of slow-moving trucks. The original plan was to track parallel to the driver over a long distance as he approached an office. The trucks would drive by in the background and the driver would be in the foreground. To execute the shot in this way the trucks would have to drive on the shoulder of the road. But let's say that this became impossible on the day of the shoot because heavy rain had rendered the shoulder of the road impassable. The director could devise an alternative shot in which the trucks are in the foreground and the driver is in the background, reversing the staging originally planned. In the new version the trucks obscure the man much of the time as they drive by. A second obstacle (the building) is introduced when the driver enters the office. The camera tracks to the window and zooms in slowly until the driver is framed through the glass speaking with his boss. Still, it is a perfectly acceptable and graphically interesting solution to permit an obstacle to block the primary subject.

Changing Subjects Within a Shot

The previous tracking examples dealt with a single subject. One value of the long tracking shot is its ability to link separate story elements together, moving from subject to subject within the shot. Figure 20.17 is an example of a basic strategy to move from one element to another. Actually, the technique is a cross pan performed as the camera is tracking. The shot

begins by framing the car as it enters the shot (white dolly). It then follows the car on a parallel course. As the car begins to turn away, a boy on a bicycle arrives and the camera picks him up at the cross point, panning with him until the camera is pointed in a new direction. The camera changes direction (black dolly) and follows the boy on a parallel course until he exits the shot. If a new subject entered where the boy exited, the process could be reversed until the camera returned to the position and framing of the opening frames of the shot.

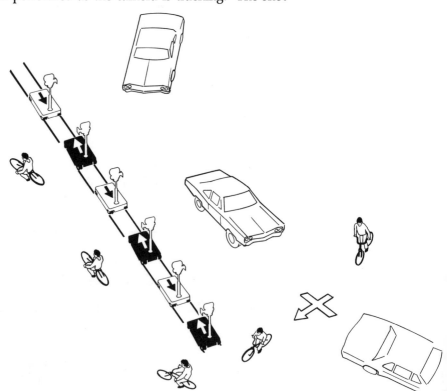

Figure 20.17

Tracking and Staging to Connect Multiple Story Elements

We can carry the previous idea even further by combining lateral tracking, cross pans, mobile blocking and in-depth framing. The following five storyboard panels describe action that could easily be shot as individual frames.

Diagrams A-C, beginning on this page, show how the individual events can be tied together into a single, uninterrupted shot. The separate elements are positioned in depth and move in opposing directions that intersect in front of the camera. The first element is a car that enters the shot in the *foreground* traveling to the background. The camera follows the car in a long tracking shot that moves left to right until the car exits the frame. The second element is three boys who enter the frame in the *middleground*. The camera changes direction moving back over the space just covered and tracking with the boys as they carry on a conversation. The third element is a girl who enters the shot in the *background*. She moves past the boys toward the camera and the camera picks her up, following her to the *foreground*. At this point one of the boys runs over to speak to her.

Diagram A

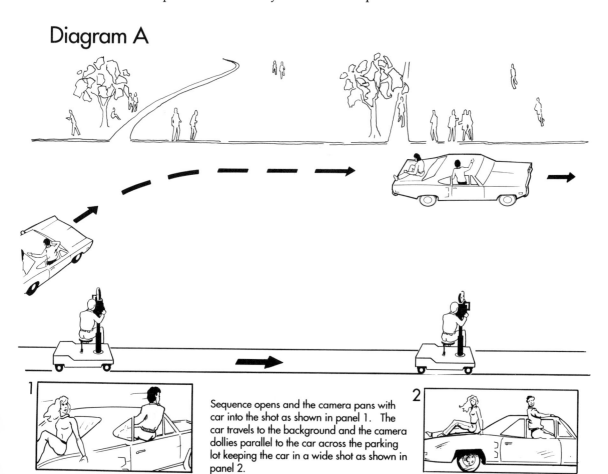

1

2

Sequence opens and the camera pans with car into the shot as shown in panel 1. The car travels to the background and the camera dollies parallel to the car across the parking lot keeping the car in a wide shot as shown in panel 2.

Diagram B

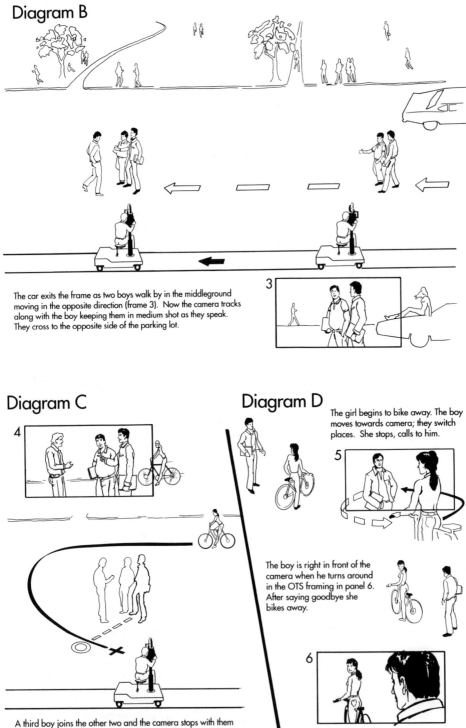

The car exits the frame as two boys walk by in the middleground moving in the opposite direction (frame 3). Now the camera tracks along with the boy keeping them in medium shot as they speak. They cross to the opposite side of the parking lot.

3

Diagram C

4

A third boy joins the other two and the camera stops with them as they speak. A girl on a bike enters the background and coasts to the foreground as shown in panel 4. Now the camera shifts attention to her. One of the boys runs up behind the girl and they speak for a moment (panel 5).

Diagram D

The girl begins to bike away. The boy moves towards camera; they switch places. She stops, calls to him.

5

The boy is right in front of the camera when he turns around in the OTS framing in panel 6. After saying goodbye she bikes away.

6

End of sequence.

Subjective and Modified Subjective Tracking Shots

So far the tracking shots we've looked at frame the subject as seen by a neutral observer. A tracking shot can also be motivated subjectively as either a full POV shot or a modified subjective shot that includes the subject in the frame. For example, a man goes to the edge of a grassy ledge to find his wife and his sister who are seated below on the beach. In the following examples the separate frames represent a continuous tracking shot.

The first version depicts a full subjective tracking shot in which the camera moves towards the two women seated on the beach. The tracking shot would normally be set up in a previous shot of the man looking at the women as he walks towards them.

This next version is a variation on the subjective tracking shot in which the camera moves towards the subject and the man watching them. This is a situation where the man's "look" is implied. Even though we do not see his eyes he is clearly watching the women. As the camera moves towards the man it goes from an objective to a subjective mode. By the time the camera uses the man's arm as a framing device our close proximity to him encourages identification.

In this last version we find an interesting situation in which the man enters his own subjective shot. The camera tracks alongside the man as he approaches the women on the beach. Again, the camera's closeness to the man elicits our identification with him. As the man continues past the edge of the beach the camera stops moving. Now the man climbs down the slope and joins the women and the shot returns to the objective mode.

21 TRANSITIONS

The connections between shots are as important as the shots themselves and usually signify changes in time and place in narrative films. Today, segues of almost every type are used, with the greatest type of experimentation going on in commercials and music videos. In all, there are only seven ways of putting two pieces of film together. They are:

- The cut
- The dissolve
- The wipe
- The fade out
- The fade in
- The white-in
- The white-out
  (or any colored version of this)

The Cut

Habit and convention have established that the dissolve indicates a passage of time, while the cut is a present-tense segue. While this was an acceptable generalization for most of the films in the '30s and '40s, today there are many more exceptions. The cut has undergone the greatest change and is used in much wider application in connecting different periods of time. Television has popularized techniques that speed up the plot, and the cut has become the connection of choice. One use that has become a favored technique in television (now in features, too) is the montage sequence, connected by cuts. Typically the montage sequence covers hours rather than days or weeks. Take, for example, the scene in Steven Spielberg's *Jaws* in which Officer Brody, Captain Quint and Hooper assemble the shark cage on board the fishing vessel, the *Orca*. The scene is made up of six shots each lasting 3 seconds for a total of about 18 seconds, compressing what would probably take half an hour. In this case, the compositions are composed angularly and record strong graphic contrasts in medium and close shots, alerting us to the fact that normal, real-time continuity is being interrupted. The result is a rhythmically compelling sequence that is vigorous yet smooth. Another use of this technique, using a single camera angle and composition, might show the construction of a house or the growth of a family, with weeks and years foreshortened into a few seconds. This type of scene usually maintains frame registration, and the result is a crude form of stop-motion, frequently used for comic effect.

The Dissolve

The dissolve, once approaching the status of a cliché, has begun to look fresh again having been replaced by the cut for many of its uses in recent years. Regardless, it's best if the filmmaker disregards fashion and employs whatever technique does the best job in a given situation.

Because the dissolve can form a bridge between disparate times and places, however shaky the logic of the connection, it has always been thought of as a kind of Band-Aid for badly structured films.

While the practice in the continuity style is to hide the cut, the dissolve is intended to be seen or at least experienced. Dissolves can be any length but usually last anywhere from approximately 1/2 second (10-12 frames) to extremely expressive lengths of over a minute. The shortest dissolve possible, and one rarely seen today, is the so-called soft-cut, a dissolve lasting only 1 to 10 frames. The soft-cut was used in situations where a transition required smoothing, such as nature footage in a documentary. For example, the only available shots of a lion chasing a zebra might force the editor to combine jarring, fast-moving shots to convey the basic action. A dissolve could smooth the transitions but would be confusing and work against the speed of the action. A straight cut would produce jumpy results. In this case, the single-frame dissolve would be employed as a compromise. It would soften the cut but not slow down the action. Usually the soft-cut is undetectable and even most filmmakers cannot tell the difference. Its effect is subliminal.

Focus-In/Out

In a focus-in/out, the tail of one shot loses focus until the image is completely blurred and is dissolved to the next shot, which begins with a new blurred image that is then focused in. Technically, it's a dissolve, but one that is concealed by another effect. Properly executed, the dissolve is invisible because the two unfocused shots are joined at a point where the images are too blurred to be identified. The loss of focus is usually gradual, and the dissolve blends the two shots together as if they were one. Of course, the viewer knows a bit of movie magic is taking place. The effect has often been used as a POV shot, indicating loss of consciousness. One version you've probably seen many times is the patient-in-an-operating-room shot. We share the patient's viewpoint as he is anesthetized and the operating room becomes a blur. Slowly the picture returns to sharpness, and we are in a recovery room hours later.

The Match Shot

Match shots are two adjacent shots that share a graphic element that is registered identically in each. Though described in many screenplays as a match cut, most often a dissolve links the shots. The dissolve helps to smooth out any imperfections in registration and lets the viewer enjoy the change more thoroughly. But this is not always the case. In *A bout de Souffle* (*Breathless*), Jean-Luc Godard makes a match cut on Jean Seberg as she drives in a convertible with the top down. Suddenly the background changes from day to night though the car and driver remain in the same position—a very radical cut in its day. Interestingly, it combines two very different qualities: the disruptive time shift of the jump cut and the graphic smoothness of the match cut.

Wipes

A traditional wipe is rarely seen today unless the filmmaker wants to deliberately recall the Hollywood style of the '30s and '40s. In its most familiar form the wipe is the cross-frame movement of a new shot over an old one and resembles a curtain being drawn. George Lucas used angular wipes in *Star Wars*—homage to the serials made by B studios like Monogram and Republic, which inspired the movie.

Wipes can move in any direction, vertically, horizontally or diagonally across the frame. Circles, squares, and spirals—any conceivable shape—can be used to remove one shot and introduce a new one. A wipe can be shaped to resemble a desired design element like a police badge or a keyhole expanding or contracting until one shot has replaced the other. *Flying Down to Rio* (1933), the movie that introduced the team of Fred Astaire and Ginger Rogers, contains dozens of different wipes used throughout the course of the movie to combine scenes.

Another variation of the wipe, the push-off or push-over, has the incoming shot "pushing" the outgoing shot from the frame so that it appears to be moving intact across the frame. This differs from the traditional wipe in which the new shot appears to move *over* the one it is replacing.

A wipe can also be combined with an element in the shot moving in the same direction and at the same rate—for example, a telephone pole or a tree. In this case, the leading edge of the wipe is matched to the movement of the pole or tree trunk. Cars or joggers or an elevator door, anything moving across the frame, can motivate a wipe of this kind. A version of this type of wipe used in cartoons has an animated character pulling the new shot into place. A recent car commercial shows an outgoing shot of a car "torn" from the screen in strips as if it were paper, revealing a perfectly registered car of a different color underneath.

The Action Wipe

The action wipe lies somewhere between an optical wipe and a match cut and is made in the camera or, to be more specific, in the editing room. The action wipe connects two shots in a scene rather than linking two scenes in different locations. In almost every case, this effect is used to move from a wide shot to a medium or close shot, making the cut smoother by what amounts to an "invisible" cut on action. What distinguishes this cut from a normal cut on action is that the action is not of the principal subject. Instead, some design element within the frame that moves between the camera and the principal subject provides the action. The element can be any object positioned close enough to the camera to completely block the lens while moving through the shot. Typically, the action would be shot twice with the movement the same in each shot and the angle of view identical, but with a change in frame size. Later the two shots would be connected at the point where the subject is blocked from our view. In recent years the action wipes have also been used to connect shots taken from different viewing angles and even different periods of time (Figure 21.1).

As with the match shot, which is similar to the action wipe, a cut or dissolve can connect the shots in an action wipe. Usually a dissolve is used to make the effect as seamless as possible.

Transformations

In special cases the transformation of the principal subject in a shot can be considered a transition. Strictly speaking, the transformation is not the joining of two separate shots—the definition of a transition—but there is a complete change of subject. Figure 21.2 is a series of transformations by the pioneer animator, Emile Cohl, from 1909.

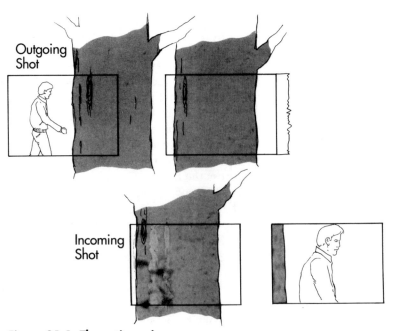

Figure 21.1: The action wipe.

Up until recently, this type of effect was so unusual that there was no reason to consider it anything but a novelty. Computer graphics, however, are now able to execute far more complex transformations between photographic images relatively easily. Portions of the frame, or the entire picture, can be broken down and reconstructed into a new photographic image smoothly with great textural and dynamic variation. So far, these effects have been used almost entirely for graphics in titles for television commercials and a few science fiction films. As computer graphics (and video) make further inroads into film, these transitions will no doubt be used in narrative films. At the moment, these effects are designed for maximum impact to hold viewer attention. This is very nearly the opposite goal of transitions in the continuity style, but computer graphics are capable of any sort of image configuration if the time and energy is spent to execute it. We can expect much more of this in the future.

Fades

The fade to black and the fade up from black has the effect of setting episodes off from one another like

Figure 21.2

chapter headings. In this respect, the purpose of the fade is fundamentally different from the dissolve or cut. The fade separates scenes, while the dissolve and cut connect scenes. Going to black and then coming out of black to picture is a complete departure from the narrative, though if it is done rapidly the pause is minimal.

A fade can employ pictorial elements in the scene. A typical use of this idea would be a scene in a room that ends with the lights being turned off. While still in black, the cut is made to the next scene, which could begin with a train coming out of the darkness of a tunnel.

White-In/White-Out/Color

Fades can be made to and from any color or made to white, an effect that John Huston used for the closing shot of *Prizzi's Honor*. The movie ends at a bright sunny window that slowly becomes blindingly white until the frame is completely bleached out. This is the end of the film, so we don't return to another scene, but obviously all that would be needed to do so is a white-in. This can be motivated by any bright element in the new shot like a bright sky or lamp. The white-out has a particularly ethereal quality, though there is no real convention attached to the mood it produces, unlike the dissolve, which tends toward the lyrical and elegiac.

The Freeze Frame

This effect differs from the other types of visual punctuation we've looked at in that it is usually employed as a period rather than a transition between scenes. The best known use of the freeze frame is in Truffaut's *Les Quartre Cents Coups* (*The 400 Blows*) in the memorable final shot of Antoine Doinel alone on the beach. The elegiac quality of the shot, the sense of finality and inescapable fate became a favorite effect in the '60s and was so overused that it has almost completely disappeared. More recently, the freeze frame has served a more practical use as a species of POV when used to show the viewpoint of a photographer taking a picture. Usually we are watching some action when a burst of white and the sound of a shutter closing indicate a strobe flash and the moment of exposure. The action freezes momentarily showing us the photo that the photographer desires. The effect was used well in Robert Altman's *M.A.S.H.* when Hawkeye and Pierce break in on an officer who is shacked up with a Japanese girl in order to take compromising pictures. We see the pictures as a series of freeze frames as the officer madly scrambles to pull on his trousers.

Montage

Montage is a problematic term. To the Europeans all editing is montage; to the early Soviet filmmakers, Kuleshov, Pudovkin, and Eisenstein, it meant their special brand of associative editing. In the United States and Great Britain, montage has its own special meaning: a brief sequence of linking devices, usually dissolves, used to convey the passage of time or a series of locations. It is this transitional use that is of interest to us here.

Actually, montage of this type is not so much a linking device as a condensed narrative, a form of visual shorthand that uses actual transitions (dissolves, cuts, fade-ins/outs) in rapid succession to link ideas. Montage frequently uses symbolic images to represent change—for instance, piles of coins and dollars that grow larger dissolved against images of the stock exchange and industry to show the financial rise of a character. Slavko Vorkapich, an immigrant from Yugoslavia, became known as a montage specialist in the United States during the late silent and early sound periods creating these types of sequences. Vorkapich was a gifted filmmaker with an interest in experimental films and the avant-garde film movement in Europe. Like other filmmakers experimenting with new techniques, he found work in Hollywood creating new versions of standard narrative sequences depicting dreams, drunkenness, after-death experiences and other altered states and fantastic realms.

The montage is not used much today. When a long period of time is condensed to a short sequence, cuts are preferred to dissolves. Montage that conveys an idea or concept, as in the pile of money example, is rarer still, leaving an opportunity to experiment with old techniques in new ways.

Split-Screen Effects

Actually the split-screen is not exactly a transitional effect, though it is used to join images that would otherwise be seen in separate shots. In 1927 the French director Abel Gance used the technique in several sequences in his epic biography, *Napoleon*, turning the screen into a tryptych. He called this early wide-screen process Polyvision. Three projectors were used to obtain the necessary width for panoramic shots, but they could be used in any combination, each showing a different image or a center image flanked by two identical shots. Occasional use of the split-screen was used in the silent era to show two sides of a telephone conversation simultaneously, and a related technique, created with a multi-image lens, multiplied a single image in a revolving circular pattern. This became a standard representation for hallucinations and nightmares. Later, Busby Berkeley would use this device for purely graphic design.

Split-screen effects were never widely used and all but disappeared by the '40s. The technique was resurrected in the '60s in John Frankenheimer's *Grand Prix* with the screen split into varying patterns of mortices. Anyone familiar with multi-image slide shows would recognize the technique, and though this type of multimedia presentation has continued to develop and thrive in corporate and advertising communication, there has been no cross-over to narrative film.

The only director who has continually experimented with the split-screen is Brian DePalma who has made a genuine effort to use the effect to discover new ways of telling a story. The effect is usually done as an optical at a lab after the film has been shot, but for compositional reasons it is probably best to compose the frame with the split-screen in mind. Simple split-screen effects can also be created in any camera that can be accurately backwound and is therefore well within the means of independent film-makers.

FORMAT

The Frame

Painters, graphic artists and photographers are able to vary the size of their work surface to suit the subject, from life-size murals to locket-size portraits, even though the viewpoint is fixed. The filmmaker finds himself in the opposite situation. He can vary his viewpoint within a film but not the shape or size of the frame that encloses it. He does have a choice, however, in the format he uses for a given film.

The proportions of the film frame are called the aspect ratio, a description of the relationship between the horizontal and vertical dimensions of the picture. The aspect ratio basically determines how wide the picture is, which is about the extent of most moviegoers' awareness of the picture they see in the theater. For most audiences a special viewing experience like 70mm is associated with big-action movies and whether or not the film is being shown in the largest theater at the cineplex—if the theater is untwinned it must be a blockbuster. Sadly, audiences today have come to accept a disappointing viewing experience as routine.

This is due to the offhanded way in which the movie studios—which are really distribution entities now—treat theatrical releases. Not so long ago movies were an event and studios hyped the size of their productions, especially as a way of setting themselves apart from television. That would be counterproductive in today's market since the studios count heavily on video releases for revenue. Their indifference to the format of a picture and the audience that views it overlooks the great differences between the types of formats we see in the movie theater. Far from being unimportant, movie formats have been of great interest to filmmakers from the earliest days of motion pictures.

A Brief History of Formats

George Eastman first made strip film available in the 1890s, and since then there have been over one hundred different systems for photographing and projecting motion pictures. In the silent era, while the studios were just beginning to monopolize the making and distribution of motion pictures, there were a variety of formats, though the predominant aspect ratio was 1.33:1. The confines of this rectangle were not flexible enough for filmmakers like Griffith, who occasionally masked a portion of the frame horizontally or vertically to compose specific scenes. More common temporary maskings of the frame included iris effects that turned the screen into a small soft-edged circle or oval, an effect similar to a close-up for directing our attention to a point on the screen. The most impressive format experiment in the silent period was the Polyvision process used for Abel Gance's *Napoleon*. This was mentioned in the previous chapter because of its use of split-screen effects, but these compositional devices were not the purpose for using three projectors or widening the screen. Gance's main interest was in providing a monumental viewing experience that overwhelmed the audience. While the screen could be stretched to include Napoleon's armies, German director F.W. Murnau preferred to condense the screen width to a square for a smaller film like the lyrical *Sunrise* (1927). Despite these and other experiments, the 1.33:1 proportions remained the all-purpose format throughout the silent period based on a film gauge of 35mm. In 1932 the Academy of Motion Picture Arts and Sciences made this the standard aspect ratio, and, because they now had sound to consider, took some of the available width of the frame for the optical track. To maintain the 1.33:1 ratio the height of the frame was lowered, and the final result was the Academy aperture, with an actual ratio of 1.37:1. This lasted as the accepted standard for nearly 20 years.

In the 1950s the motion picture industry responded to the economic threat of television with a whole array of wide-screen systems designed to entice people out of their living rooms and back into the theaters. This was a repeat of a similar trend way back in the late '20s and early '30s when the sound era began. In fact, many of the wide-screen formats adopted in the '50s were developed or suggested two decades earlier. Among these were several film gauges that were briefly in use, including the Paramount process (56mm), Spoor Natural Vision (63mm) and Fox Grandeur (70mm). These and other innovations—stereophonic sound for one—might have become standardized in the '30s had it not been for the Depression, which caused the studios, who originally backed the changes, to rethink their plans. Motivated by more conservative financial expectations, the studios abandoned the costly replacement of existing equipment.

Twenty years later, when television threw down the gauntlet, most of the technical preparation for wide-screen motion pictures had already been worked out. Not that the technological problems were particularly difficult; motion picture cameras and projectors represent nineteenth century technology (essentially mechanical), and while there have been refinements, no major breakthoughs have been made in the basic design of the camera or projector, with the exception of the IMAX rolling loop system. Some of the wide-screen systems developed over the last four decades are: Cinerama, originally a three-camera, three-projector system similar to Abel Gance's Polyvision; Todd A-O; CinemaScope; VistaVision; Techniscope; Super Panavision 70 and Ultra Panavision 70. Only a few of these systems are in use today, and a mere list of trademarks does not begin to cover the complex subject of available film and camera systems. The systems vary in the size of the negative, the aspect ratio, availability of equipment, and the type of distribution the production will receive. Filmmakers and cameramen must decide which system is best for them based on creative, economic and technical considerations.

Today there are three formats in general use: 1.85:1, 1.66:1 and 1.75:1. In the United States, 1.85:1 is the unofficial standard, while 1.66:1 is popular in Europe. Of the smaller formats, 16mm, Super 16, and Super 8 are widely used, utilizing aspect ratios hovering around the 1.33:1 ratio. 16mm can be used in the Academy and wide-screen formats, which was the original reason for the introduction of Super16 in the early 1970s. Super 16 uses more of the available negative and, therefore, produces a sharper, less grainy image.

The Super Formats

In the last several years new large-format systems have been introduced that represent the cutting edge of film and exhibition technology. In most cases these new presentation formats are intended as specialty attractions in museums, science and cultural centers and theme parks throughout the world, and so far no dramatic features have been shot in any of the major systems. But as high-definition television (HDTV) becomes a reality and home viewing is substantially improved, the exhibition pioneers may be pointing the way to the future of theatrical releases. The general audience expects a minimum of quality for their six dollar admission and will sit ankle-deep in popcorn watching an unfocused picture for just so long. Movie revenues may be up (partially boosted by videocassette sales), but the size of the movie audience has remained flat since the '60s.

The new super systems are serious attempts to create a total sight and sound experience. All use large negatives and multiple track stereo with 360-degree speaker placement and are presented in specially designed theaters. Recently, the "total sensory involvement" concept of these theaters has moved in a new direction. Theme parks are now presenting "movie rides" in which the motion on the screen is synchronized with the movement of the audience's seats.

At the moment drama does not seem to enter into the picture, but hopefully the care and attention paid to giving the audience its money's worth in the theater will filter down to smaller films. The amusement park possibilities of special-venue theaters will probably attract new players, but at the moment there are three super-format companies providing complete creative and technical services, from movie making to theater and equipment design: Showscan, IMAX and Iwerks.

Showscan. Director and special effects designer Douglas Trumbull, frustrated that his meticulously designed images reached the audience seriously degraded by an indifferent exhibition system, decided to do something about the problem. In 1975 he developed the Showscan process. The system photographs pictures on 65mm film at a rate of 60 fps and is projected using 70mm film at a rate of 60 fps. The faster frame rate has three advantages: It permits higher illumination levels on the screen, it eliminates the flicker present at 24 fps and because the sound track is moving faster too, the dynamic range of the sound is increased. Sound is recorded in six-track stereo and played back through multiple speakers in custom-designed theaters. Like all the specialty formats, Showscan is a proprietary system, which can be licensed for the production and distribution of theatrical exhibitions.

IMAX. The IMAX system was developed in Canada and is the only format that has seriously altered camera and projector technology. IMAX uses an entirely different kind of intermittent movement—the patented rolling loop system. Rather than using the pull-down claws of traditional motion picture intermittent movement to advance and register the film, the rolling loop is a "wave" of film that travels around a large horizontal drum and falls gently into place at the aperture. A vacuum system pulls the film into precise registration. The IMAX picture is recorded on 65mm film running sideways with a 15 perf pull-down, utilizing a frame size approximately $2 \times 2^{3}/_{4}$ in. Presently the IMAX system is in limited use throughout the world.

OMNIMAX, a planetarium-type dome-screen version of IMAX, has recently been introduced. This system surrounds the viewer with a 180-degree screen projected from the center of the theater.

Iwerks. Co-founded by Don Iwerks and Stan Kinsey in 1985, Iwerks Entertainment offers several innovative theater systems. Don Iwerks is the son of Ubbe Iwerks, Walt Disney's first business partner and the creator of Mickey Mouse who was also responsible for the 360-degree camera and projector systems used at theme parks. Iwerks' special-venue designs include: Iwerks 870 (a 70mm 8 perf system), Iwerksphere 870 (for domed theaters), High Resolution 70mm and Iwerks 3-D. Other systems are in development. Iwerks films can be projected at either 24 or 30 fps. The image is synchronized with a six-track "surround stereo system" and projected on a giant screen in fully computerized theaters.

Television

The aspect ratio of television is theoretically 1.33:1 and film formats conforming to this ratio should be easily viewed on television. Unfortunately, the broadcast process chops off the edges of the picture during several stages of reproduction before it reaches your television set so that as much as 40% of the picture can be lost. But things get worse still because your television is set by the manufacturer to underscan the broadcast image, eliminating even more of the picture.

Wide-screen pictures suffer the most, which has resulted in the practice of reframing theatrical movies for television. Known as panning and scanning, the process consists of rephotographing the film to include the most important story elements. For instance, two characters positioned at the edges of a wide-screen movie in a master shot cannot be seen simultaneously in the television format. The solution is to pan or cut from player to player as they speak when the film is transferred to video. It's no news to observant viewers that the filmmaker's careful framing of shots is trashed when theatrical features appear on television. Fortunately, this may be a temporary situation—high-definition television with a wider aspect ratio will probably eliminate the worst of these problems within the next decade.

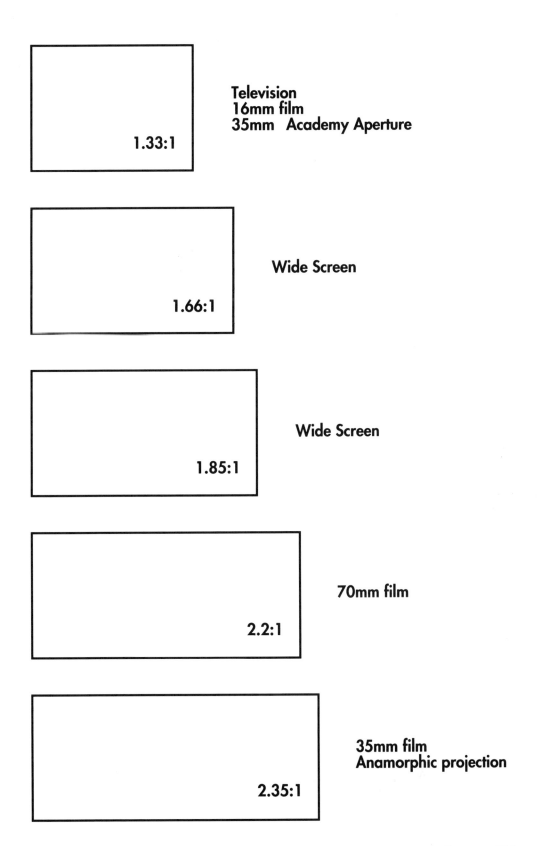

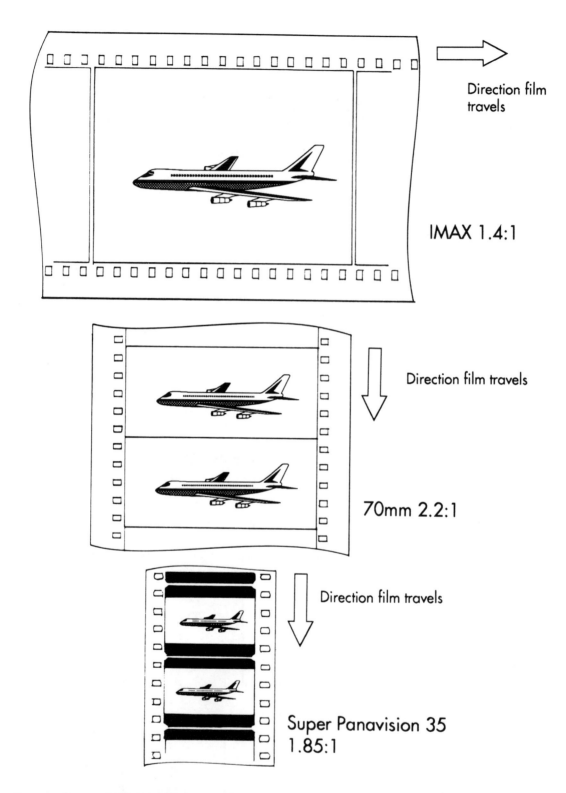

Direction film travels

IMAX 1.4:1

Direction film travels

70mm 2.2:1

Direction film travels

Super Panavision 35
1.85:1

Comparison of IMAX, 70mm and 35mm aspect ratio and negative sizes.

# 23 PARTING SHOTS

The film business is in for some big changes over the next several years. The reason for these changes is the computer and electronic production. This is where the future of mass media lies, and since this is of vital interest to up-and-coming filmmakers, I would like to close the book with my thoughts on the direction of visualization, filmmaking and computers over the next few years.

As a tool and as a system, the computer presents artists with an entirely new approach to the creative process. As might be expected of a device that is modeled on the brain, software designed for artists creates a working environment that simulates the imagination. Of course, by itself, the computer is not imaginative and is limited to the information that an artist loads into memory. But once this is done, sound and images can be manipulated with a speed and fluidity that can be compared only to our own imaginations.

The computer is able to manage images and sounds quickly by converting them to a digital system of zeroes and ones. In a sense, this system is like a universal solvent—the zeroes and ones are essentially particles of image or sound. A film or a painting is ultimately composed of the same particles displayed as pixels. If there is a sufficient number of zeroes and ones, the quality of reproduction for a sound or picture can go beyond our ability to detect reproduction.

While digital storage is a near perfect method of recording information, its greatest virtue is that it is an extraordinarily pliant medium. For instance, the computer can be used to alter the form of an image in a manner that is different from photography, painting or any other known technique or medium. Anything that is created can be instantly altered, and versions of previous designs can be imported into the new version. Artists will find that this allows them to design and create sounds and images in new ways.

To a great extent, this is already possible with musical synthesizers and samplers. Once a sound is digitized, the numerical information can be varied to reshape any aspect of a tone. This can be done intuitively by using the synthesizer as a musical instrument using controls to shape the sound. A computer can also be used to analyze the sine wave or any other objective description of the sound. Using graphic or musical notation the composer can then write a modified description which the computer plays back. With both methods, traditional musical instruments can be precisely recreated in the computer and extended beyond their normal range. Clarinet riffs can be played on a synthesized guitar or both instruments can be combined to create a musical sound that has never existed before.

This same kind of creative freedom is ultimately possible with images, and right now 3-D computer animation is the fullest expression of this idea. While limitations in memory and processing speed still need to be overcome, the technology is progressing at a fantastic rate.

One of the most interesting things about computer graphics is how they can be used to interpret a picture. If a computer is programmed to follow the laws of gravity and other natural effects, animation of a moving car will include the correct ballistics, wind factors and frictional influences found on the road. The parameters can also be creatively altered to produce an animation that obeys the physics and gravitational effects of a fantasy world. While this may sound like a very formulaic approach to invention, there are no limits to the way the computer can be programmed. As 3-D animation becomes more sophisticated so will the art of programming as a means of personal expression. And there will always be artists who use the computer in conjunction with handcrafted works.

While the ultimate control of imagery and the artistic freedom this entails is an exciting prospect, the most provocative development is that this incredible power to create will be in the hands of individuals with personal computers. Filmmakers will find that for the first time crucial parts of the filmmaking production process will be in the hands of just about anyone. Production for an animated film, normally requiring labs, sound studios, expensive photographic equipment and duplication services will be done in a digital format on a desk at home.

The promise is that once plain folk have the technology to make and distribute images, the individual filmmaker or mediamaker will be able to reach an audience without the interference of mass market considerations. If this comes to pass, this new type of populism may be the most important long-term development to come out of Silicon Valley.

A serious alternative to highly restricted distribution channels is still a ways off, but there are more immediate opportunities currently emerging. In the future, filmmakers can expect new job categories to appear in computer-aided film design. Filmmakers, frustrated by the business of film, may find that the most fertile area for creating a challenging position is in computer visualization, computer graphics or editing. This may be a way to stay active (and solvent) while you continue with personal work.

One area that is on the verge of rapid growth is electronic production design. At this point CAD is not in general use by motion picture or television production designers, though it is an affordable and mature technology for set design. When art directors and production designers begin to catch on to what they've been missing, they will need qualified assistants familiar with the computer. A related area worth looking into is electronic storyboarding using the presentation tools now available for personal computers. This is another service that is not currently available (though it could be) only because the motion picture industry is lagging behind the technology. However, when change comes, it could be precipitous. For example, when videotape editing began to replace film editing in the 1970s, most of the industry switched to tape in just two or three years.

These kinds of predictions worry many filmmakers. This is understandable, since new technology has never guaranteed better craftsmanship or content. All too often the goal of technical advances has been faster and cheaper results.

As a filmmaker who has a great love for the silver image and the tactile pleasure of shooting and cutting strips of film, it is difficult to look ahead to a time when some of my hard-earned skills will become outdated. Still, the computer provides some new pleasures, which are becoming as affordable as a video camera, lights and a tripod. As a computer graphics friend of mine recently pointed out to me, he can create a realistic animated sequence with sound on the computer in a couple of afternoons. He has the computer anyway, so his only production expense is the one-time cost of software. Without the computer he could not make similarly complex productions.

Filmmakers who can't imagine sitting indoors to manipulate images on a monitor do not have to worry that the computer represents competition to traditional filmmaking. For all the creative freedom it represents, imagemaking on the computer is not a substitute for the rewards of documenting and interacting with the real world. This requires a camera and the curiosity that inspires the best filmmaking.

APPENDIX: CAMERA ANGLE PROJECTION

A rt director Harold Michelson devised the following method for camera angle projection, which was shown to me by production illustrator Camille Abbott. Once mastered it is a useful technique for previewing set plans and camera placement.

In essence, camera angle projection is a way of taking the information on a plan and elevation and using it to plot a single perspective drawing according to the rules of linear perspective. In linear perspective *all parallel lines and edges of surfaces receding at the same angle are drawn on the picture plane in such a way that they converge toward a single vanishing point*

The angle at which parallel lines and surface edges recede determines the degree of convergence in a perspective drawing in exactly the same way as the focal length of a lens determines the degree of convergence in a photograph. Figure 1 shows a box as it would appear through a long focal length lens (a) and a wide-angle lens (b). Notice that the angle formed near the vanishing point on the horizon line is smaller for a long focal length lens than for a wide-angle lens.

If you consult the *American Cinematographer Manual* you will see that there are lens tables showing the angles of view (height and width) for prime lenses with common focal lengths. The point to remember is that the angle of view for any lens can be used to determine the degree of convergence for a perspective drawing. In this way a perspective drawing can be made to present what any given camera lens would see. If we process the dimensions on the plan and elevation according to the camera angles for a given lens and aspect ratio (which determines the degree of convergence) then we can make a perspective drawing. This is camera angle projection.

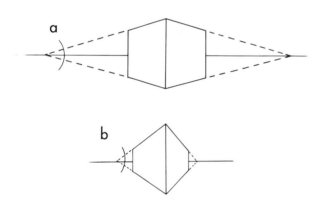

Figure 1

To make a projection drawing for any camera angle and lens we need a blueprint plan and elevation of a set or the dimensions of key points measured at a real location. A projection can be either two-point or three-point perspective. When the camera is tilted up or down less than 25-30 degrees from the ground plane, two-point perspective is sufficiently accurate for the projection. Relatively low- or high-angle shots, however, must be drawn in three-point perspective, which is a considerably more difficult procedure. For most visualization needs, two-point projection is adequate and that is the system we will illustrate here. At the moment there is no text or course that teaches three-point projection, and it can only be learned from an industry professional such as an art director or production illustrator.

Tools for Projection

Projection employs drafting techniques familiar to architects, so you will need a few basic drafting tools: a 90-degree triangle, a protractor, tracing paper, pushpins, a ruler (preferably an architect's scale), a pencil and a divider for transferring measurements. You will also need the table of lens angles printed at the back of this section.

Preparation

Before making the projection, you will need to draw the camera angle on tracing paper. There are two camera angles for any lens, one for the height of the frame and the other for the width, both measured in degrees.

We decide what angle to use based on the general idea we have for the size of the shot. Since the location we will be projecting is a small interior and we would like to see a good portion of the room, a wide-angle lens is appropriate. For our drawing a 25mm lens is a good choice. We will be projecting the drawing using the 1.85:1 aspect ratio shown in Figure 2.

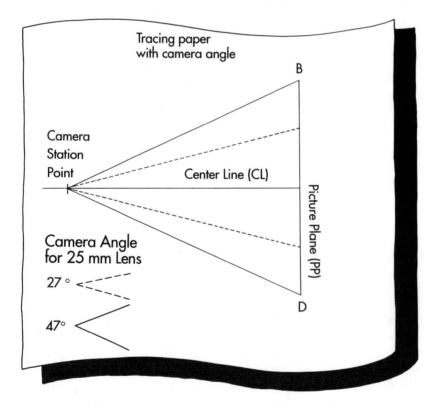

Figure 2

Because our projection camera angles will eventually be transferred to the plan you should draw the angle large enough to cover a good portion of the plan drawing.

The angular outer lines represent the width of the space the camera sees, an angle of 47 degrees. The inner dotted lines represent the height of the space the camera sees, an angle of 27 degrees. The camera is positioned at the point where the four angle lines converge. This is called the *camera station point* (SP) and represents the location of the camera. An additional line is placed down the center of the angles. This is called the *center line* (CL). The center line represents two things: the center line of the width of the frame and the horizon line of the height of the picture plane.

Line BD is perpendicular to the center line and is called the *picture plane*. The picture plane represents the view we are drawing.

Since the relationship between these dimensions is the aspect ratio, the angles vary with the format. Figure 3 shows the relationship between the camera angles and the aspect ratio. The *projection plane* is the frame in which the perspective drawing will be made.

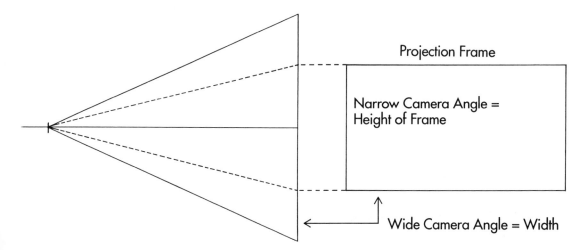

Projection Frame

Narrow Camera Angle = Height of Frame

Wide Camera Angle = Width

Figure 3

Now we can add the horizon line FG to the projection frame in Figure 4. As with any linear perspective drawing, our horizon line represents the eye-level of the viewer, which in our case is the camera. Since the camera is 4 ft. off the ground, our horizon line is also set at 4 ft. in the picture. In other words, any object in our picture will be 4 ft. off the ground where it touches the horizon line.

We will also add a vertical line HI that vertically bisects the horizon line in the center of the frame. The *vertical line HI represents the center line of the width of the aspect ratio. The horizontal line FG represents the horizon line.*

Next, we place the plan and elevation (Figure 5) on a thick piece of drawing board. This is done so that we can put a pushpin where the camera is placed.

Now we're ready to frame the shot using the lens angle on the tracing paper. Place the angle over the plan as shown in Figure 6 and position the angle so that the width of the angle includes the portion of the set you would like to see in the final drawing. Transfer the camera position, or station points (SP), and place the pushpin at this point. This will come in handy when you line up a ruler along the camera station point in later steps.

The width angle on the plan is used to measure the width of all objects in the shot. However, we still need a way to determine the height of the camera and the height of the objects (tables, doors and windows, etc.) in the shot. We'll do this by placing a horizon line on the elevation, as shown at the top of Figure 6. This horizon line is placed at the camera height, which

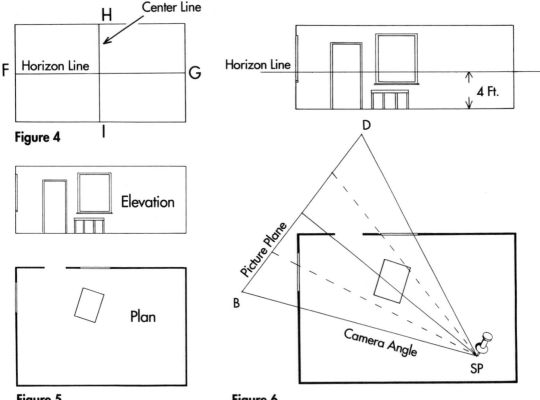

Figure 4

Figure 5

Figure 6

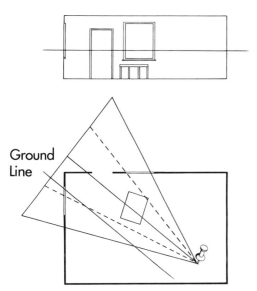

Ground Line

Figure 7

we will set at 4 ft., just below eye-level. Most plans you will encounter are in $1/4$-in. scale, but for reasons of space the scale of the following diagrams will vary.

In Figure 7 we add a ground line, which is drawn parallel to the center line. The purpose of the ground line is to determine where objects—a door, table, person or anything else in the room—touch the floor or ground.

The ground line is always placed at a distance from the center line equal to the camera height on the elevation.

Beginning the Projection

Now we are ready to transfer points from the plan to the projection frame. We begin by establishing the location of the floor for one of the elements on the plan. This is a two-step process and will be repeated over and over for every object on the plan and elevation.

STEP ONE: (determining width) We will begin by choosing the first area of the plan to be transferred to the projection frame. It is a matter of standard practice in camera angle projection to project a wall within the set, because this helps give you your bearings for all the other objects you will be locating.

It makes the most sense to locate the walls at the corner of the room since this will establish the basic layout of the room. The corner we'll be working with is circled on the plan in Figure 8. Step one consists of finding out where this corner will fall left and right on the projection drawing. To do this take a ruler or straight edge and line it up so that it intersects the camera station point (SP), the corner of the room and the picture plane. (This is where the pushpin is helpful since the ruler is merely pushed up against it and pivoted over to the circled corner as shown in Figure 8.)

What we're interested in is the distance on the picture plane from the center line to the point at which the straight edge crosses

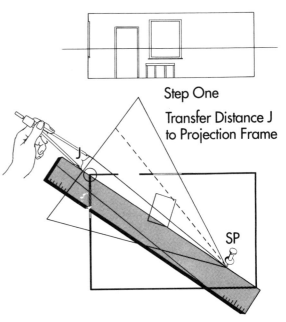

Step One

Transfer Distance J to Projection Frame

SP

Figure 8

the picture plane, indicated as distance J in Figure 8. Dividers can be used to transfer this distance to the projection plane.

Moving to the projection plane in Figure 9, we transfer distance J to the drawing, measuring from the center line to the left. Mark this point lightly in pencil. Actually you can draw a vertical line lightly through this point since this is where the corner of the room will line up. What we need to find now are the tops and bottoms of the walls.

Note: We can pause for a moment here to consider the process. Since the camera angle picture plane on the plan is the same as the projection frame (both are derived from the camera angle), any point to the left or right of the center line on the plan will fall in the same place on the projection drawing.

STEP TWO: (determining height) Our next step is to find the point at which the wall touches the floor. To do this, line up a 90-degree triangle perpendicular to the center line so that the triangle intersects the circled corner of the room. Mark the point where the triangle intersects the ground line. This point is surrounded by two circles as shown in Figure 10.

Moving to Figure 11, we take the straight edge again and line it up so that it intersects the camera station point (the pushpin) and the new point we just found on the ground line. Mark

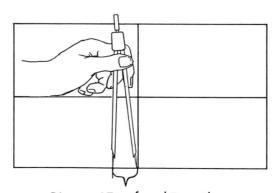

Distance J Transferred From Plan

Figure 9

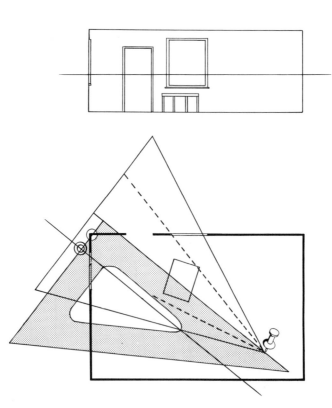

Figure 10

with a pencil where this touches the picture plane and measure the distance from the mark to the center line (distance K). Transfer this distance to the projection frame.

Taking this latest measurement (distance K) we measure down from the horizon line on the projection frame as shown in figure 12. Since we've already found the point left and right where the two walls meet using Step One, the point at which this line intersects distance K is where the two walls touch the floor. This point is circled in figure 12.

Our next job is to find a second point where the wall touches the floor. This will enable us to locate the vanishing point for the wall using Step One. An easy point to plot is a location where the wall intersects the camera angle width line (the edge of the shot). This point is circled in Figure 13. As you can see the point lies on the camera angle line. Since this line carries the point out to the picture plane as though it were a ruler or a straight edge, it duplicates the function of Step One. Therefore, we save a step. In fact, anytime a point lies on the edge of the picture plane we do not need to transfer the distance because either camera angle line for width represents the side of the projection frame. We can jump directly to Step Two in this case.

Using the triangle method from Step Two we find where the circled point crosses the

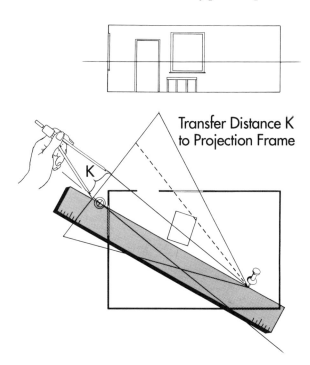

Transfer Distance K
to Projection Frame

K

Figure 11

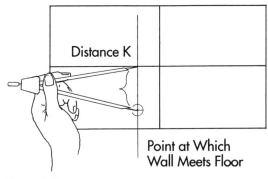

Distance K

Point at Which
Wall Meets Floor

Figure 12

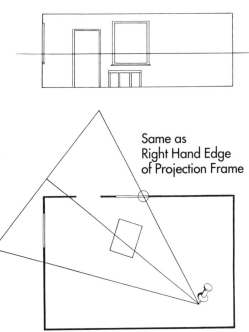

Same as
Right Hand Edge
of Projection Frame

Figure 13

ground line using a ruler, as shown in Figure 14. You'll need the ruler to reach across the center line so you can mark the point on the ground line (circled twice).

Finish Step Two in Figure 15 by lining up the straight edge with the point you just marked on the ground line. As before, measure the height distance (L) to the center line with the dividers.

Transfer height distance L to the projection frame as shown in Figure 16, measuring down from the horizon line along the side of the projection frame. (Remember that we skipped Step One because our point on the plan was on the camera angle width line.)

We now have located two points where the right hand touches the wall. By connecting them and carrying the point to the horizon line, we find the vanishing point for that wall.

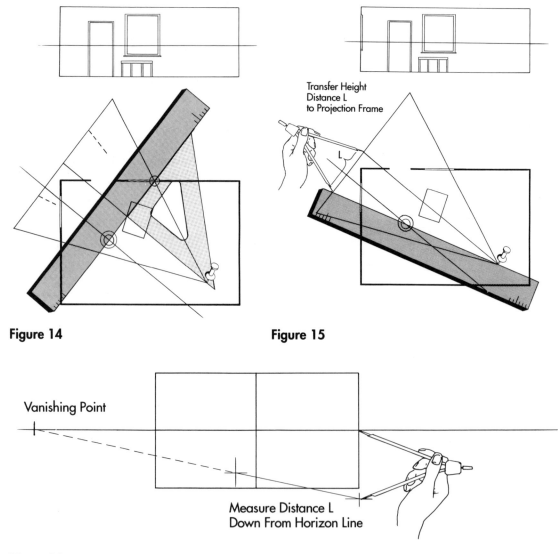

Figure 14   **Figure 15**

Figure 16

We can repeat this procedure for the left-hand wall by first finding the point where it touches the camera angle for width. As before, this is equivalent to the edge of the frame on the projection frame (the circled point in Figure 17).

We repeat Step Two for the circled point in Figure 17, transferring it to the projection frame with dividers. (Since we have just done this for a point on the opposite side of the frame the entire process will not be shown. Just repeat the steps shown in Figures 13, 14, 15 and 16 for the new point.)

The new point is shown in place in Figure 18 circled on the left-hand side of the projection frame. Connecting the two wall points we find the vanishing point for the left-hand wall.

Before moving to the next step we can look at one shortcut for finding the vanishing point of walls or tables or any other object that has right-angle construction. Here's how it's done: First draw two lines beginning at the station point but parallel to the walls of the room (Figure 19). Now find the point at which these lines touch the picture plane by extending the line for the picture plane. The points at which each broken line intersects the picture plane are the vanishing points for the walls of the room.

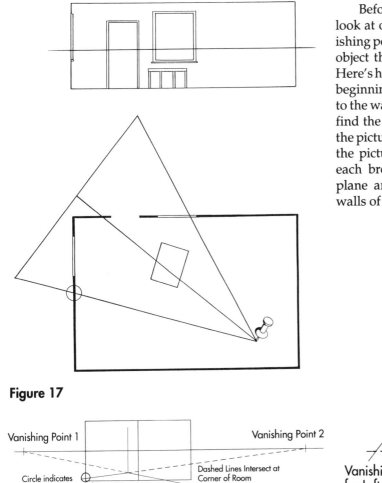

Figure 17

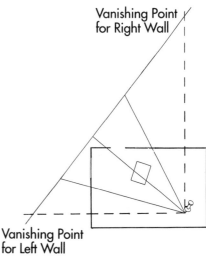

Vanishing Point for Right Wall

Vanishing Point for Left Wall

Figure 19

Vanishing Point 1

Vanishing Point 2

Circle indicates width of camera angle

Dashed Lines Intersect at Corner of Room

Figure 18

Next we need to locate the height of each of the walls. To do this we will use a new technique.

STEP THREE: If we want to plot the height of the wall we can return to the first point we plotted at the corner where the walls meet. Remember, the ground line is set at 4 ft. above the floor. Therefore the distance from any point on the floor *to the horizon line on the projection frame* is 4 ft. This is shown in Figure 20.

If we were to divide the distance from the bottom of the wall to the horizon point into four equal parts, each part would equal 1 ft. This is very useful because we can use these 1-ft. increments to measure straight up or down any distance we choose above or below the horizon line, even beyond the perimeter of the projection frame. This will work for any of the points we have located. In Figure 20 the vertical line where the walls meet has been divided into 1-ft. increments.

To make use of this fact, we consult the elevation where we can measure any object in the room for height since the drawing is in scale (Figure 21). Using an architect's scale, we quickly determine that the table is 2 ft. high; the door is 8 ft. high, and the top of the wall is set at 9 ft. Using these measurements we can locate these objects on the projection drawing.

It is important to remember that in the perspective drawing each

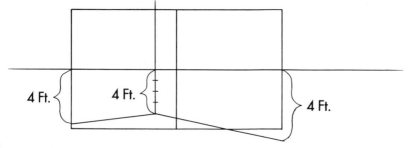

4 Ft.   4 Ft.   4 Ft.

Figure 20

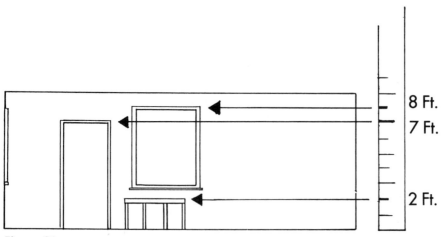

8 Ft.

7 Ft.

2 Ft.

Figure 21

distance on the wall will divide into 1-ft. increments differently. Objects closer to us will be in larger increments than those farther away. Ordinarily it would be very time-consuming to divide the varying distances into equal parts, but there is a trick we can use to simplify this job.

Take the architect's ruler and find any scale with a division of four units slightly larger than the distance from any of the floor points for the wall to the horizon line. Now angle the ruler so that the four-increment distance on the ruler is exactly the same distance as the space you're measuring, as shown in Figure 22. You can continue to mark 1-ft. increments above the horizon line as far as necessary or below the bottom of the frame. This method will work for any line perpendicular to the floor, such as walls, tables or other furniture with right angles. As you can see, the top of the wall is outside the projection frame at the 9 ft. mark.

We can find the top of the adjacent wall by the same method and then connect these points with the vanishing points on the horizon line, as shown in Figure 23. The circled point is the top of the wall we just located with the architect's scale.

Notice that by connecting either vanishing point with the top of either outside wall (broken lines) we automatically find the ceiling point where

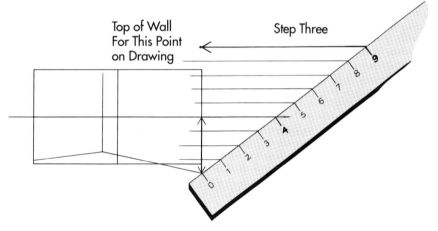

Figure 22

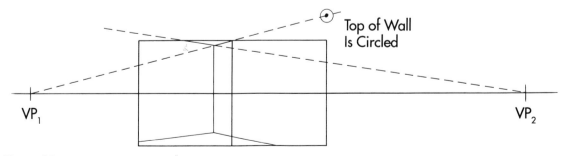

Figure 23

the walls meet at the corner. Now we can get a fairly good idea of how the room is going to lay out and we can project the doors and windows. This will go more quickly because we have established vanishing points that apply to the doors and windows along the same plane as the walls.

When locating doors and windows we will still need to transfer points from the plan to place them at the proper width distance along the wall using Step One. However, we do not need Step Two to establish where they touch the floor now that we have located the floor line along the wall. Obviously, the bottom of the door (which lies along the same plane as the wall) is the same as the floor line. The floor line for the wall is useful for helping us locate doors, windows, picture frames or cabinets that touch or are in the wall. We can see how this works for the window on the right-hand wall.

By now, the Step One method of transferring points from the plan should be clear. (If you need to review the process look at Figures 8 and 9.) Therefore we will skip the preliminary transferring steps and go directly to the projection frame with the left-hand and right-hand sides of the window already placed on the drawing. They are indicated by the vertical dotted lines in Figure 24 and represent the width of the window and its placement on the wall. Now continuing on the same diagram we have to find the height of the window above the floor. To do this we consult the elevation and find that the bottom of the window is 3 ft. above the floor and has a top height of 8 ft.

Returning to the perspective drawing we'll use Step Three (ruler method) to find the top and bottom of the window for one side of the window. We only need to locate the height on one side of the window because when we connect the vanishing points to the circled height points

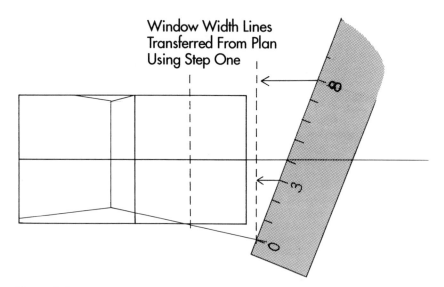

Window Width Lines
Transferred From Plan
Using Step One

Figure 24

in Figure 25 we automatically find the top and bottom of the opposite side of the window. As you can see, once you have established the floor point and the vanishing points you require fewer steps to project the rest of the plan and elevation.

Repeating this last set of procedures, we project the remaining window and door. The results are shown in Figure 26.

We have now seen all the techniques required for the Michelson method of camera angle projection. While it may seem confusing at first, once the three steps become familiar you will be able to project any two-point drawing easily.

But we're not quite finished. We still must project the table in the middle of the set. This has been left for last as a review of the three steps. I have simplified the drawings and placed the plan adjacent to the projection frame so the connection between them is clear. If you forget one of the steps

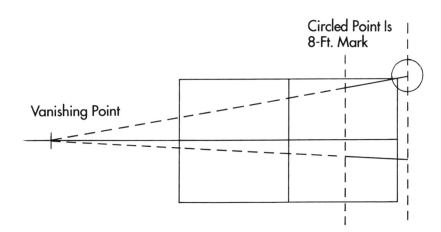

Figure 25

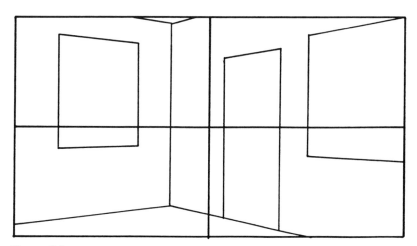

Figure 26

the page number for the full explanation is included on the diagram. To avoid confusion, the review diagrams are lettered A-E.

We begin by locating the distance from the center line for each of the table legs by using the Step One method (explained in full on page 341). This is shown in diagram A (Figure 27).

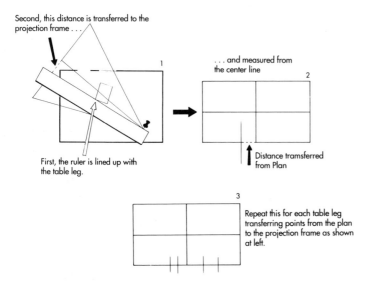

Second, this distance is transferred to the projection frame . . .

. . . and measured from the center line

Distance tramsferred from Plan

First, the ruler is lined up with the table leg.

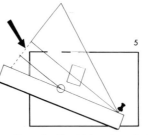

Repeat this for each table leg transferring points from the plan to the projection frame as shown at left.

Figure 27: Review diagram A.

In diagram B (Figure 28) we use the Step Two method to locate the distance from the horizon line to the point at which each table leg touches the floor. (Step Two is explained in full on page 342.)

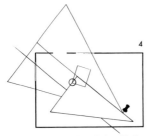

Line up the triangle with the table leg. Mark the point where the triangle crosses the ground line.

Line up the ruler with the point marked on ground line. Transfer the distance on the picture plane (broken line).

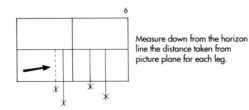

Measure down from the horizon line the distance taken from picture plane for each leg.

Figure 28: Review diagram B.

In diagram C (Figure 29) we find the vanishing point on the horizon line for the table legs. We will use this in a moment to complete the table top.

We're almost done. Now we can locate the height of the table top. In diagram D (Figure 30) we first consult the elevation and find that the table is 2 ft. high.

Using Step Three (shown in full on page 346) on the projection frame, we angle the ruler to divide the vertical distance for one of the table legs into 1-ft. increments. We mark the 2 ft. point, which is the top of the table for that leg.

Moving to the next projection frame we connect this new 2 ft. point to the vanishing point, and this locates the table leg behind the one just established.

We also do this on the opposite side of the

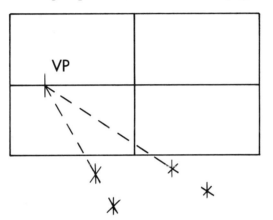

Connect the table leg points (where each leg touches floor) to locate the vanishing point.

Figure 29: Review diagram C.

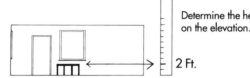

Determine the height of the table on the elevation.

2 Ft.

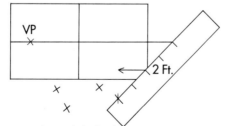

Using the angled ruler determine the 2-ft. table height above the point where the table leg touches the floor.

Figure 30: Review diagram D.

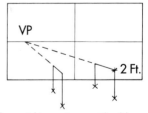

Line the vanishing point up with table top point we just found. This establishes the rear table top point. Do this for the left side of the table. Now connect all the lines on the table top to complete the basic outline.

table. (It is important to remember that the table is not parallel to the walls and therefore has a different vanishing point.) To finish the table just connect all the top points.

That's it! The outline of the table is complete. By adding details to the table and the other elements in the room we end up with the finished drawing in figure 31 below. In an actual plan and elevation all the details can be obtained and transferred in scale without resorting to the three step method. Once the basic geometry and outline of the room is established, door and window frames can be estimated and drawn in. Usually, this is accurate enough for projecting a viewpoint for the director, though it is possible to painstakingly transfer every point for greater accuracy.

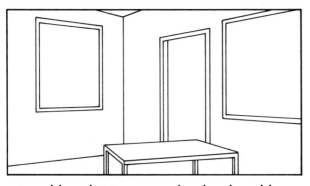

By adding the necessary detail to the table, windows and doors, we have a finished projected drawing for the 25 mm lens.

Figure 31: Review diagram E.

Back Projection

It is also possible to reverse the projection process so that a photograph of a location can be "back projected" so that a plan is created. This process relies on the method for locating vanishing points shown in Figure 20 for front projection, which appears on page 346. You might want to review the process before beginning the back projection.

Step One

For the sake of clarity the line drawing in Figure 32 will be substituted for a photograph. We begin by placing a piece of tracing paper over the photograph. The tracing paper

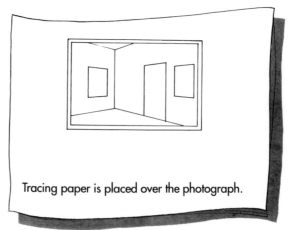

Tracing paper is placed over the photograph.

Figure 32

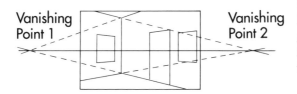

Vanishing Point 2

should be several times larger than the photograph so that there is sufficient room to draw in the plan.

Figure 33

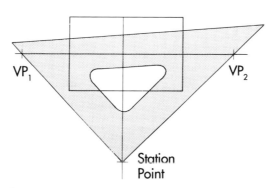

VP₁

VP₂

Station Point

Figure 34

Next find the vanishing points where the line of the ceiling and floor meet (the dotted lines) as shown in Figure 33. Draw a horizontal line between the vanishing points. This is the horizon line. This is also the picture plane.

In Figure 34 draw a vertical line down the center of the photo crossing the horizon line and extending below the photograph. This is the center of the camera angle. Now take a large 90-degree triangle and position it so that the edges touch both vanishing points and the center of the camera angle simultaneously. *The point where the triangle meets the center of the camera angle is the station point.* The station point is where the camera is located. Place a push pin here.

Now we can begin plotting points. This is just a reverse of the procedure for front projection. First we will find how far the corner of the room is from the center line. We do this by lining up the ruler so that it touches the station point (the pushpin) at the lower end. At the top end the ruler is lined up so that it touches the vertical wall line at the corner of the room *where it crosses the horizon line* (Figure 35).

Next, add the ground line (Figure 36). Remember that the ground line is placed at a distance from the vertical center line equal to the distance of the camera above the ground. Unless you took the photograph and know

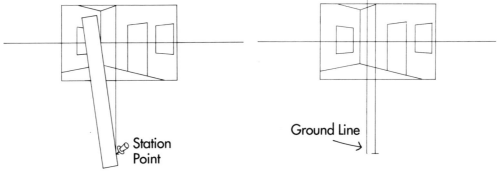

Station Point

Ground Line

Figure 35

Figure 36

the camera height this will have to be estimated. Judging from the photograph the camera height appears to be below eye-level, or about 4 ft. We can set the scale of the drawing at any ratio we like. If, for example, we can establish $1/16$ in. = 1 ft. The ground line would be placed $1/4$ in. from the center line.

Now we are ready to find where the corner of the room is located in the plan (Figure 37). We begin by using dividers to measure the distance from the horizon line down to the floor at the corner of the room.

In Figure 38 the vertical distance measured with the dividers is transferred to the horizon

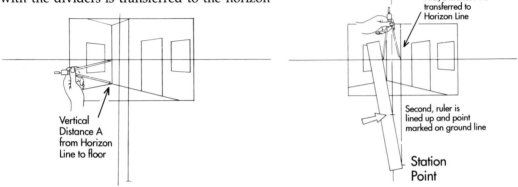

First, Distance A is transferred to Horizon Line

Vertical Distance A from Horizon Line to floor

Second, ruler is lined up and point marked on ground line

Station Point

Figure 37   **Figure 38**

line. Use a straight edge to line up this new point and the station point. Mark where the straight edge crosses the ground line as indicated by the arrow.

In Figure 39 we see both points we have located. The black dot is the height point we located in Figure 38. The dotted line represents the ruler line located earlier in Figure 35. To make the next step clearer a detail drawing shows an enlarged view. As you can see a 90-degree triangle is lined up so that it crosses the ground line at the height point (black dot). The intersection of the triangle's horizontal edge and the dotted width line (circled point) is the location of the corner of the room on the plan.

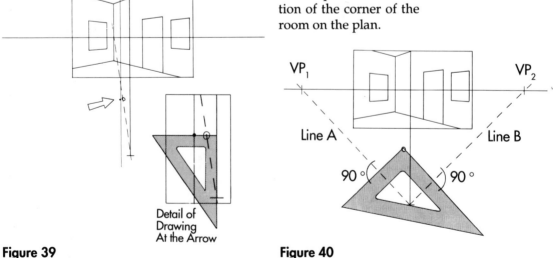

Detail of Drawing At the Arrow

Figure 39

VP$_1$ VP$_2$

Line A   Line B

90°   90°

Figure 40

We can use the vanishing point shortcut to locate the walls of the room (Figure 40). The shortcut is based on the fact that the lines connecting the station point to the vanishing points (broken lines A and B) are parallel to

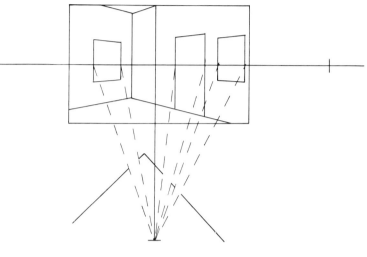

the walls of the room. Therefore, by placing a 90-degree triangle on the corner point we just plotted and positioning it until the edges of the triangle are parallel to lines A and B, the walls of the room are properly oriented in the plan.

Next we can locate the doors and windows in the plan, as shown in Figure 41. Using a straight edge draw lines from the station point to the sides of the windows and doors where they intersect the horizon line.

Figure 41

The point where these broken lines cross the walls of the room on the projected plan locates them in correct proportion. Because certain architectural features such as doors have predictable dimensions, we can begin to estimate the size and placement of objects in the room. Most doors are approximately 30 in. wide, so by using a scale ruler and measuring a doorway we can find out the scale of the plan. With that information it is easy to determine the width of windows, the size of furniture or any other width and depth dimensions.

That's all there is to it. The finished plan is a relatively accurate

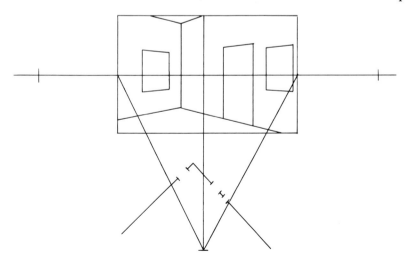

orthographic plan of the photographed space. In Figure 42 we can add lines from the station point to the edge of the photograph at the horizon line. This is our camera angle for width. Using a protractor we find that it is 40 degrees. If we divide the width dimension of the photograph by the height dimension we have an aspect ratio of 1.444. This is not equivalent to any motion picture format, but if we crop the height of the shot

Figure 42

to conform to the 1:1.85 aspect ratio then we can use the camera angle of 40
degrees to determine what focal length camera lens is needed to cover this
space with the same perspective. If we consult the table for camera angles
in the 1:1.85 ratio we find that a 30mm lens has a width angle of 39.5 degrees.
That's close enough. We now know that this photo could be duplicated in
this space using a 30mm lens.

Camera Angles

While it is possible to project a perspective drawing using any camera angle,
a few basic lens choices are used most of the time. The five most commonly
used focal lengths are listed below for three aspect ratios. Using a protractor, you can draw these angles on white paper and have them turned into
$8^{1}/_{2}$ x 11 transparencies at almost any duplication shop.

1: 1.33 Full-Screen Aperture (television and 16mm motion picture)

		Width	Height
25mm	—	Width angle = 52.9°	Height angle = 41°
30mm	—	Width angle = 45°	Height angle = 35°
35mm	—	Width angle = 34.6°	Height angle = 26.2°
50mm	—	Width angle = 27.9°	Height angle = 21.1°
75mm	—	Width angle = 18.8°	Height angle = 14.2°

1: 1.85 Flat "Unsqueezed" Wide-Screen

		Width	Height
25mm	—	Width angle = 48°	Height angle = 26°
30mm	—	Width angle = 39.5°	Height angle = 21°
35mm	—	Width angle = 34°	Height angle = 18°
50mm	—	Width angle = 24°	Height angle = 13°
75mm	—	Width angle = 16°	Height angle = 8.6°

1: 2.35 Anamorphic Wide-Screen (35mm Panavision)

		Width	Height
25mm	—	Width angle = 82.8°	Height angle = 41°
30mm	—	Width angle = 72.6°	Height angle = 34.6°
35mm	—	Width angle = 64.5°	Height angle = 29.8°
50mm	—	Width angle = 47.6°	Height angle = 21.1°
75mm	—	Width angle = 32.8°	Height angle = 14.2°

GLOSSARY

T his partial list of terms includes the basic technical vocabulary used in this book. A more complete collection of film terms can be found in *How to Read a Film*, by James Monaco; *Focal Encyclopedia of Film and Television Techniques*, by Raymond Spottiswoode; and the current standard comprehensive dictionary of film, *The Complete Film Dictionary*, by Ira Konigsberg.

A

AERIAL SHOT   An extremely high-angle view of a subject, usually taken from a plane, helicopter, crane or stationary elevated camera position.

AMERICAN SOCIETY OF CINEMATOGRAPHERS (ASC)   A non-profit craft organization of cinematographers with headquarters in Hollywood, California. This organization publishes both the *American Cinematographer Manual* and *The American Cinematographer*, a monthly magazine.

ANGLE OF VIEW   The size of the field covered by a lens measured in degrees. A wide-angle lens has a wide angle of view while a telephoto lens has a narrow angle of view. Because a rectangular aperture masks the film, the angle of view for any given lens is described according to the height and width of the lens.

ASPECT RATIO   The relationship between the height and width of a motion picture or television frame expressed numerically. There are several aspect ratios now in use: The Academy Aperture is 1.33:1; standard wide-screen in Europe is 1.66:1; standard wide-screen in America is 1.85:1; the anamorphic is 2.35:1; and a 70mm frame is 2.2:1.

B

BLOCKING THE SCENE   The arrangement and choreographed movement of actors and major props (e.g., automobiles, horses) for the camera. Since the camera can also move, blocking the scene may include the movement of the camera.

BOOM   1. Camera boom. A mechanical arm counterweighted to support a camera and attached to a dolly. Operated manually or by remote control, it permits a technician to move the camera over or through spaces that would otherwise be inaccessible. 2. Microphone boom. A telescoping arm that supports a microphone. The sound man positions the microphone just outside the camera frame while recording sound within the scene.

C

CAMERA ANGLE   The viewpoint chosen by the director or cinematographer to photograph a subject.

CAMERA ANGLE PROJECTION   A method of turning the architectural plan and elevation for a set into a perspective drawing for the purpose of previewing how the finished set will appear to the camera when using a particular lens, camera position and aspect ratio.

CANTED FRAME   Sometimes called Chinese or Dutch angles.   The angling of the camera so that the horizontal frame line is not parallel to the horizon. A slightly canted frame dynamically charges the composition, while extreme angling has become a conventional way of conveying disorder and mayhem.   The canted frame was used extensively in Carol Reed's *The Third Man*.

CONTINUITY STYLE   The photographic and editorial style that creates the illusion of a spatial/temporal continuum so that a sequence of shots appears to present events as they happened.   The continuity style is the predominant style of narrative films, sometimes called the Hollywood classical style or in France, découpage classique.

COUNTERING   Camera movement that is in the opposite direction of a moving subject.

COVER SHOT   See *MASTER SHOT*.

CROSS-CUTTING   The alternating of shots from two or more scenes to indicate parallel action.

CUTAWAY   A single shot inserted into a sequence that momentarily interrupts the general flow of action.   The inserted shot may introduce a pertinent detail or a new location related to the action.

D

DEEP FOCUS   A style of cinematography and staging that uses wide-angle lenses and small lens apertures to emphasize depth by keeping objects in the extreme foreground and background in focus simultaneously.

DEPTH OF FIELD   The amount of space in front of and in back of the focus plane that appears acceptably sharp through a lens.

DETAIL SHOT   A tighter, more highly magnified version of the close-up used to show a fragment of a whole subject or a small object in its entirety.

DOLLY SHOT   Any shot made from a moving dolly.   Also called a tracking or traveling shot.

E

ESTABLISHING SHOT   Typically a long shot at the beginning of a scene designed to inform viewers of a change in location and to orient them to the general mood and relative placement of subjects in the scene.

F

FLASH CUT   An extremely brief shot, as short as one frame, which is nearly subliminal in effect. Also, a series of short staccato shots that create a rhythmic effect.

FOCUS IN, OUT   A transition effect by which an incoming shot comes into focus or an outgoing shot goes out of focus.

FOCUS PULL/FOLLOW FOCUS   The refocusing of the lens during a shot to keep a moving subject within the depth of field.

FOLLOW SHOT   A tracking shot, pan or zoom move that follows a moving subject.

FORMS, OPEN AND CLOSED   Styles of graphic composition. *OPEN FORMS* tend to emphasize looser, less controlled positioning of elements in the frame as if they were unplanned, extending beyond the boundaries of the frame as though the camera just discovered them. Open form compositions are characteristic of documentary films, accounting for their reputation as being more realistic. *CLOSED FORMS* tend toward self-contained compositions carefully arranged to include everything of importance within the frame.

FRONTALITY   A style of figure placement in composition, popular in Western art, in which the subject of a painting or drawing faces the general direction of the viewer.

I

INSERT, INSERT SHOT   Usually a close-up showing an important detail of a scene.

INTERCUT   See *CROSS-CUTTING*.

J

JIB ARM   A mechanical arm supported on a dolly and counterweighted to hold the camera for an increased range of motion, usually vertical.

JUMP CUT   A linkage of shots in a scene in which the appearance of real continuous time has been interrupted by omission. In certain situations jump cuts are an accepted convention for compressing time. They can also be used as a deliberately disruptive device to make the viewer aware of film technique as in the work of Godard. Recent trends have seen the use of the staccato jump cut in music videos and commercials for purely rhythmic effect.

L

LOCKED-OFF CAMERA   When the camera is on a tripod or other stable support, the mechanism that controls the movement of the camera, such as a fluid or geared head, can be locked in position for a static shot.

LOOSE   Refers to the composition of a shot. Loose framing includes a great deal of space around a subject.

M

MASTER/MASTER SHOT   The viewpoint of a scene in which the relationships between subjects are clear and the entire dramatic action could be understood if no other shots were used (as opposed to the wider establishing shot).

MATCH CUT   A transition effect between shots in a scene, or as a transition. 1. Two shots of the same action joined so that continuous motion is preserved. 2. Two or more shots of the same subject joined to preserve continuous placement and motion in each shot to indicate the passage of time. 3. Two shots of different subjects that share graphic elements or motion with precisely registered contours.   For example, an image of the moon in a first shot lines up exactly with a circular mirror in a second shot. In Bob Fosse's *All That Jazz*, several dancers in a rehearsal hall are seen from one angle executing the same steps. Match cuts connect the actions as if they were performed by one dancer in an unbroken movement.

MISE-EN-SCÈNE   In French, "putting in the scene." Originally the term described the physical production of a play: the sets, props and staging of a scene. Over the years the term has been adapted to the description of filmic space—that is, the manipulation of staging and action within a shot during filming as opposed to the manipulation of space afterwards in the editorial process.

MONTAGE   From the French term "to assemble."   In European film montage is a description of the editorial process.   In Soviet film, under the influence of the early Soviet directors, particularly Sergei Eisenstein, montage represented the very essence of film art.   In the United States, montage has a special meaning, referring to a concentrated narrative device, usually lasting only a minute, in which a portion of the story is expressed without dialogue using a series of dissolves to connect short, expressive, often symbolic shots.

MOVING SHOT   A shot in which the camera is moved to follow a moving subject.

O

OFF CAMERA (OC)   Same as offscreen.

OFFSCREEN (OS)   Direction in a screenplay when a subject or sound is outside of the camera frame.

ON CAMERA   Term indicating that a player or object can be seen by the camera.

OVER THE SHOULDER (OTS)   A shot in which a subject who is facing us is composed using the back of the head and the shoulder of another subject in the extreme foreground as a framing device.

P

PERSPECTIVE   In the graphic arts and film, the illusion of depth on a two-dimensional surface.

POINT OF VIEW (POV) SHOT   A subjective viewpoint, one that is understood to represent an individual's vision.

PRESENCE   1. In audio recording, the ambient sound characteristic of a room or location. 2. The term used by André Bazin to identify the illusion of real third-dimensional space that the viewer experiences when watching a film. Bazin regarded this as a further development of Renaissance linear perspective.

PRINCIPAL PHOTOGRAPHY   The main photography of a film and the period of time during which it takes place.

PULL-BACK SHOT   A dolly shot or zoom effect that begins in close-up on an object and slowly widens to include more of the area surrounding the object.

R

REACTION SHOT   In a dialogue scene the shot of a player listening while another player's voice continues on the sound track. Most reaction shots are close-ups.

RETRACKING   The backward movement of the camera on a dolly (on or off track) along a path that it has already covered in the same shot or in a previous shot in the same scene.

REVERSE ANGLE   A shot that is turned approximately 180 degrees in relation to the preceding shot.

S

SEQUENCE SHOT   A traveling camera shot in which choreographed action and camera movement replace the need for individual shots to describe complex action.

SETUP   The choice of camera angle, shot size and staging. It is frequently described by the number of players in a shot: A two-shot, over-the-shoulder shot, and close-up are all typical setups.

SHALLOW FOCUS   A shallow depth of field. Shallow focus is sometimes used to isolate a subject in focus from the indistinct background and foreground.

SIGHT LINE   An imaginary line that is drawn between a subject and the object he or she is looking at.   When individual CUs of two subjects in conversation are joined together in a sequence their sight lines must match in order that they appear to be looking at each other.

SINGLE   A shot with only one subject in the frame.

STATIC CAMERA   Any shot in which the camera does not move.

SUBJECTIVE CAMERA   A camera technique that presents the viewpoint of a character in the scene. See *POINT OF VIEW (POV) SHOT*.

SWISH PAN   A rapid panning movement that blurs the frame. It is often used as a transition. Also called a *FLASH PAN*.

T

TAKE   One version of a shot. The director has the cast and crew repeat the action of the shot in successive takes until he or she is satisfied it is correct.

TIGHT   Describes the size of a shot relative to its subject. A tight frame encloses a subject with very little space surrounding it.

TRACKING SHOT   A shot taken from a camera mounted on a dolly or some other moving vehicle.

TRAVELING SHOT   Any shot in which the camera moves through space. A crane shot and a tracking shot are both traveling shots. A pan shot, however, is not a traveling shot since the camera remains at one location pivoting a stationary point.

TWO-SHOT   A shot that frames two people.

V

VOICE-OVER (VO)   The voice of an unseen narrator. Voice-over may also be used to indicate the thoughts of a character in a scene when the character is not speaking.

W

WIPE   A transition between shots.

Z

ZIP PAN   See *SWISH PAN*.

ZOOM   The movement of a zoom lens or the lens itself.

RECOMMENDED READING

Cinematography and Photographic Practice

Campbell, Russell. *Photographic Theory for the Motion Picture Cameraman.* New York: A.S. Barnes, 1974.

Campbell, Russell. *Practical Motion Picture Photography.* New York: A.S. Barnes, 1970.

Detmers, Fred, ed. *American Cinematographer Manual.* 6th ed. Hollywood, Calif.: American Society of Cinematographers, 1986.

Fielding, Raymond. *The Focal Encyclopedia of Film and T.V. Techniques.* New York: Hastings House, 1969.

Fielding, Raymond. *The Technique of Special Effects Cinematography.* 4th ed. Boston: Focal Press, 1985.

Lipton, Lenny. *Independent Filmmaking.* rev. ed. New York: Simon & Schuster, 1983.

Malkiewicz, Kris. *Cinematography.* 2d ed. New York: Prentice Hall Press, 1989.

Neblette, C. B. *Photography, Its Principles and Practice.* New York: D. Van Nostrand Company, Inc., 1942.

Ray, Sidney F. *The Lens in Action.* Boston: Focal Press, 1976.

Samuelson, David W. *Motion Picture Camera & Lighting Equipment.* 2d ed. Boston: Focal Press, 1986.

Samuelson, David W. *Motion Picture Camera Techniques.* Boston: Focal Press, 1984.

Wilson, Anton. *Cinema Workshop.* Hollywood, Calif.: A.S.C. Holding Corp., 1983.

Computer Design

Wells, Michael. *Desktop Video.* White Plains, N.Y.: Knowledge Industry Publications Inc., 1990.

The use of the computer in film design is so new that there are very few books available on the subject. However, a number of publications on personal computing and multimedia include articles on film design and related arts, and right now this is the best source of information.

Publications on Computer Design:

Cadence Magazine
Using AutoCAD in the professional environment
Ariel Communications, Inc.
P.O. Box 203550
Austin, TX 78720-3550

Computer Graphics World
One Technology Park Drive
P.O. Box 987
Wesford, MA 01886

Computer Pictures
Montage Publishing, Inc.
701 Westchester Ave.
White Plains, NY 10604

Macintosh-Aided Design. Edited by Joseph Greco. Auerback Publishers, 1 Penn Plaza, New York, NY 10119

MacUser. Edited by Paul Somerson. Ziff-Davis Publishing Co., 800 Boylston St., 11th fl., Boston, MA 02199

MCN
Computer Automated Solutions for Design and Engineering
Ariel Communications, Inc.
P.O. Box 203550
Austin, TX 78720-3550

NewMedia Age. Edited by Ben Calica. Hypermedia Communications Inc. (HCI), 323 N. Mathilda Ave., Sunnyvale, CA 94086

Continuity and Production Planning

Chamness, Danford. *The Hollywood Guide to Film Budgeting and Script Breakdown.* rev. ed. Los Angeles: S.J. Brooks Co., 1986.

Miller, Pat P. *Script Supervising and Film Continuity.* 2d ed. Boston: Focal Press, 1990.

Directing and General Film Technique

Arijon, Daniel. *Grammar of the Film Language*. Boston: Focal Press, 1976.

Bernstein, Steven. *The Technique of Film Production*. Boston: Focal Press, 1988.

Dmytryk, Edward. *Cinema Concept and Practice*. Boston: Focal Press, 1988.

Eisenstein, Sergei. *Film Form*. New York: Harcourt, Brace & World, Inc., 1949.

Eisenstein, Sergei. *Film Sense*. New York: Harcourt Brace Jovanovich Publishers, 1942.

Marner, Terrence St. John, ed. *Directing Motion Pictures*. New York: A. S. Barnes and Co., 1972.

Nilsen, Vladimir. *The Cinema as a Graphic Art*. New York: Hill and Wang, 1973.

Nizhny, Vladimir. *Lessons With Eisenstein*. New York: Da Capo Press, Inc., 1979.

Pudovkin, V.I. *Film Technique and Film Acting*. 1929, 1937; reprint, New York: Grove, 1970.

Film Theory and Criticism

Arnheim, Rudolf. *Film as Art*. Berkeley, University of California Press, 1957.

Bazin, Andre. *What is Cinema?* 2 vols. Selected and translated by Hugh Gray. Berkeley: University of California Press, 1967, 1971.

Giannetti, Louis. *Understanding Movies*. 2d ed. Englewood Cliffs, N.J.: Prentice-Hall, 1976.

Godard, Jean-Luc. *Godard on Godard*. Translated by Tom Milne. New York: Viking, 1972.

Kracauer, Siegfried. *Theory of Film: The Redemption of Physical Reality*. New York: Oxford University Press, 1960.

Mast, Gerald, and Marshall Cohen, eds. *Film Theory and Criticism*. New York: Oxford University Press, 1974.

Monaco, James. *How to Read a Film*. New York: Oxford University Press, 1977.

Editing and Postproduction

Dmytryk, Edward. *On Film Editing*. Boston: Focal Press, 1988.

Reisz, Karel, and Gavin Millar. *The Technique of Film Editing,*. 2d ed. Boston: Focal Press, 1982.

Production Design

Albrecht, Donald. *Designing Dreams. Modern Architecture in the Movies*. New York: Harper & Row in collaboration with The Museum of Modern Art, 1987.

Barsacq, Léon. *Caligari's Cabinet and Other Grand Illusions*. Boston: New York Graphic Society, 1976.

Carrick, Edward. *Designing for Films*. New York: The Studios Publications Inc., 1949.

Marner, Terrence St. John, ed. *Film Design*. New York: A. S. Barnes and Co., 1974.

THE INDEPENDENT FILM & VIDEOMAKER'S GUIDE
–2ND EDITION
Michael Wiese

Wiese has packed 25 years experience in film and video into the most comprehensive and most useful book ever for filmmakers seeking both independence and success in the marketplace. Loaded with insider's tips to help filmmakers avoid the pitfalls of show business, this book is the equivalent of a "street smart degree" in filmmaking.

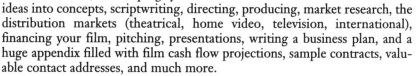

This new, completely expanded and revised edition has all the information you need from raising the cash through distribution that caused the original edition to sell more than 35,000 copies.

Contents include writing mission statements, developing your ideas into concepts, scriptwriting, directing, producing, market research, the distribution markets (theatrical, home video, television, international), financing your film, pitching, presentations, writing a business plan, and a huge appendix filled with film cash flow projections, sample contracts, valuable contact addresses, and much more.

> *"A straightforward and clear overview on the business of making films or videos. Wiese covers the most important (and least taught) part of the job: creative deal-making. The book is full of practical tips on how to get a film or video project financed, produced, and distributed without sacrificing artistic integrity. A must for any aspiring independent producer."*
> **Co-Evolution Quarterly** (about the first edition)

$29.95, Approx. 500 pages, over 30 illustrations, 6 x 8 1/4, ISBN 0-941188-57-4, Order # 37RLS

On Sale
September 1998

To order this book for classroom use, please call Focal Press at 1-800-366-2665.

DIRECTING ACTORS
CREATING MEMORABLE PERFORMANCES FOR FILM & TELEVISION
Judith Weston

DIRECTING ACTORS reveals a method for establishing great collaborative relationships with actors, getting the most out of rehearsals, fixing poor performances, and bringing forth your actors' creativity.

Internationally-renowned directing coach Weston demonstrates what constitutes a good performance, what actors want from a director, what directors do wrong, script analysis and preparation, how actors work, and shares insights into the director/actor relationship.

This book, based on the author's twenty years of professional acting and eight years of teaching Acting for Directors, is the first book to directly address film and television directors about working with actors. Her seminars are taught in Los Angeles, New York, and Europe.

"After living on movie sets for over fifteen years, Judith's class opened a door for me to an aspect of that creative process about which I had never really been aware - acting"
Ron Judkins, Production Sound Mixer
Jurassic Park, Schindler's List

"Filled with constructive information that would serve not only the neophyte but also the skilled professional director seeking to improve his or her communication skills with actors. A mustread for any director working with actors."
DGA Magazine July-August 1997

A Doubleday Stage & Screen Book Club Selection

$26.95, 300 pages, 6 x 8 1/2
ISBN 0-941118-24-8
Order # 4RLS

THE DIRECTOR'S JOURNEY

THE CREATIVE COLLABORATION
BETWEEN DIRECTORS, WRITERS AND ACTORS
Mark W. Travis

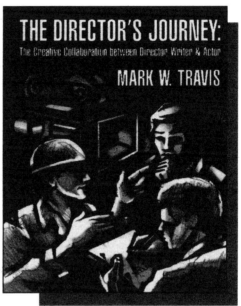

What if you could be instructed, one-on-one with a top-notch directing coach who would help you develop your own directorial style?

Mark W. Travis takes the mystery out of directing. His refreshing approach will enhance and broaden your directing skills and help you deliver powerful performances and well-conceived cohesive films.

Contents include material on the script, script breakdown, assembling the team, casting, rehearsing, production and postproduction.

This long-awaited book is based on the methods Travis has developed in his popular directing seminars, which have been attended by hundreds of film directors in Los Angeles, New York, and Japan.

MARK W. TRAVIS has directed over 50 plays, many hours of episodic television, and the Warner Brothers' feature film, *Going Under*.

"A comprehensive and inspired exmaination of craft. A must-read for any serious professional."
Mark Rydell, Director,
On Golden Pond, The Rose

"With an astonishing clarity Mark Travis articulates the techniques and skills of film directing."
John Badham, Director,
Saturday Night Fever, War Games, Blue Thunder

The #1 Best Selling Non-Fiction Paperback, Los Angeles Times,
September 1997
A Doubleday Stage & Screen Book Club Selection

$26.95
350 pages, 6 x 8-1/2
ISBN 0-941188-59-0
Order # 29RLS

CALL 24 Hours A Day
1-800-833-5738

FILM DIRECTING
CINEMATIC MOTION
Steven Katz

Learn how to stage and block those tricky
scenes. This idea-packed book includes
discussions of scheduling, staging without
dialogue, staging in confined spaces, actor
and camera choreography in both large and
small spaces, sequence shots, and much
more. Learn the production requirements
from a well-known cinematographer, director, production manager, continuity person,
and actor as they discuss approaches to camera space and movement. This book will
clear up anxieties on your very next shoot.

$24.95, ISBN 0-941188-14-0, 200 pages,
7 x 10, over 400 illustrations
Order # 6RLS

PRODUCER TO PRODUCER
INSIDER TIPS FOR ENTERTAINMENT MEDIA
- 2ND EDITION
Michael Wiese

Here's a wide range of insightful advice on
creative techniques that will save and earn
you thousands of dollars when producing,
financing, or marketing.

Twenty-one new chapters on independent
producing, home studios, starting out,
directing, network specials, direct-to-video
movies, legal issues, creating hit videos and
much more are here for you to use today.

MICHAEL WIESE is a producer and director
with more than 25 years experience in film, television, pay TV, and home
video. He has presented independent film seminars in Europe, Australia,
Indonesia, and throughout the United States.

$24.95, 350 pages, 6 x 8-1/4
ISBN 0-941188-61-2
Order # 28RLS

THE WRITER'S JOURNEY
MYTHIC STRUCTURE FOR WRITERS - 2ND EDITION
Christopher Vogler

This new edition provides fresh insights and observations from Vogler's ongoing work on mythology's influence on stories, movies, and man himself.

Learn why thousands of professional writers have made THE WRITER'S JOURNEY a best-seller which is considered "required reading" by many of Hollywood's top studios! Learn how master storytellers have used mythic structure to create powerful stories which tap into the mythological core which exists in us all.

Writers of both fiction and nonfiction will discover a set of useful myth-inspired storytelling paradigms (i.e., *The Hero's Journey*) and step-by-step guidelines to plot and character development. Based on the work of Joseph Campbell, THE WRITER'S JOURNEY is a must for writers of all kinds.

First released in 1993, THE WRITER'S JOURNEY quickly became one of the most popular books on writing from an independent publisher in the past 50 years. With international editions in French, German, and Portuguese, THE WRITER'S JOURNEY also made its mark on the global writing community.

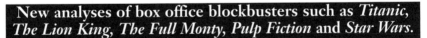

New analyses of box office blockbusters such as *Titanic, The Lion King, The Full Monty, Pulp Fiction* and *Star Wars*.

PLUS OTHER NEW MATERIAL INCLUDING:

- A foreword describing the worldwide reaction to the first edition and the continued influence of The Hero's Journey Model.
- Vogler's new observations on the adaptability of The Writer's Journey for international markets, the changing profile of the audience.
- The latest observations and techniques for using the mythic model to enhance modern storytelling.
- New subject index and Filmography.
- How to apply THE WRITER'S JOURNEY paradigm to your own life.

$22.95
ISBN 0-941188-70-1

ORDER FORM

To order these products please call 1-800-833-5738 or fax (818) 986-3408 or mail this order form to:

MICHAEL WIESE PRODUCTIONS
11288 Ventura Blvd., Suite 821
Studio City, CA 91604
1-818-379-8799

BOOKS:

_____
_____
_____
_____

Subtotal $ _____
Shipping $ _____
8.25% Sales Tax (Ca Only) $ _____

TOTAL ENCLOSED _____

Please make check or money order payable to
Michael Wiese Productions

(Check one) ____ Master Card ____ Visa ____ Amex

Company PO# _____

Credit Card Number _____
Expiration Date _____
Cardholder's Name _____
Cardholder's Signature _____

SHIP TO:

Name _____
Address _____
City _____ State _____ Zip _____
Country _____ Telephone _____

Ask about our free catalog

VISIT OUR HOME PAGE www.mwp.com

Please allow 2–3 weeks for delivery.
All prices subject to change without notice.

CREDIT CARD ORDERS

CALL
1-800-833-5738

or FAX
818-986-3408

OR E-MAIL
mwpsales@earthlink.net

SHIPPING

ALL ORDERS MUST BE PREPAID

UPS GROUND SERVICE
One Item - $7.00
For each additional item, add $2.00.

Special Reports-$2 ea.

EXPRESS DELIVERY
3 Business Days
Add an additional
$12.00 per order.

OVERSEAS
Surface - $15.00 ea. item
Airmail - $30.00 ea. item